THE LIFE OF
FRANCIS MARION

Battle of Fort Moultrie

THE LIFE OF
FRANCIS MARION

THE TRUE STORY OF SOUTH CAROLINA'S SWAMP FOX

WILLIAM GILMORE SIMMS

THE ORIGINAL 1844 TEXT WITH A NEW
INTRODUCTION BY
SEAN BUSICK

Charleston   London

THE
History
PRESS

Published by The History Press
Charleston, SC 29403
www.historypress.net

Cover image: Marion and His Men in the Swamp, oil painting by William D. Washington, c. 1865. Courtesy of South Caroliniana Library, University of South Carolina, Columbia.

First published 1844
The History Press edition 2007
Second printing 2013

Manufactured in the United States

ISBN 978.1.59629.263.5

Library of Congress Cataloging-in-Publication Data

Simms, William Gilmore, 1806-1870.
The life of Francis Marion / William Gilmore Simms; introduction by Sean R. Busick.
p. cm.
"This new edition contains the full text and illustrations from the 1844 text of The life of Francis Marion, published by Henry G. Langley"--T.p. verso.
Includes bibliographical references.
ISBN 978-1-59629-263-5 (alk. paper)
1. Marion, Francis, 1732-1795. 2. Generals--United States--Biography. 3. South Carolina--Militia--Biography. 4. United States--History--Revolution, 1775-1783--Biography. 5. South Carolina--History--Revolution, 1775-1783--Campaigns. 6. Georgia--History--Revolution, 1775-1783--Campaigns. 7. United States--History--Revolution, 1775-1783--Campaigns.
I. Title.
E207.M3S5 2007
973.3'3092--dc22
[B]
2007010540

From the publisher: This new edition contains the full text and illustrations from the 1844 publication of The Life of Francis Marion, published by Henry G. Langley, New York. All efforts have been made to maintain the integrity of the original text, including spelling and punctuation. Footnotes within the original text have been set as endnotes in this edition and the table of contents has been corrected.
Notice: The information in this book is true and complete to the best of our knowledge. It is offered without guarantee on the part of the author or The History Press. The author and The History Press disclaim all liability in connection with the use of this book.

CONTENTS

INTRODUCTION

South Carolina's "Swamp Fox," Francis Marion, has always been one of the most popular heroes of the American Revolution. More places have been named in honor of Marion than for any other soldier of the Revolution, excepting George Washington. Marion had no male heir to carry on his family name, but he has given his name to counties in seventeen states, a university, a national forest and many cities. Numerous Confederate military units, such as the Marion Rangers, the Marion Artillery and the Marion Rifles also took his name.[1] Marion has also inspired several biographies, novels, children's books, songs, poems, films, a comic book and a 1950s television series starring Leslie Nielsen. The most recent and best-known film based on Marion's exploits is *The Patriot*, released in 2000, starring Mel Gibson.

How did Marion earn such renown? He kept alive the hope of patriots in the Southern states when victory and independence were most in doubt—after the fall of Charleston and the rout of the Continental Army at Camden. In the darkest hours of the Revolution, when the Continental Army had been run out of South Carolina, Marion and his small band of citizen soldiers took the field against the British Regulars. By keeping up a constant harassment, they made sure the British were never able to rest after their victories in South Carolina, and eventually helped to drive them from the state and toward their final defeat at Yorktown.

Despite all the attention that Marion has received over the years, Simms's biography, first published in 1844, remains the best. *The Life of Francis Marion* was the most commercially successful work of nonfiction by William Gilmore Simms (1806–1870), perhaps South Carolina's greatest author. It was one of the best-selling history books the year it was published. The first edition sold out in less than a week—with no advertising. It continued to sell briskly, went through three editions in its first three months off the press and had been through ten editions by January 1847.[2] *The Life of Francis Marion* also contains some of the best history that Simms wrote.[3] It was widely praised by reviewers in such periodicals as the New York *Morning News*, the *Knickerbocker*, the *American Review* and the *United States Democratic Review*. "The probability is that it will be one of the most successful publications of the day," Simms boasted. "But enough of egotism for one sitting."[4]

Simms began planning his biography of Marion in 1840 and, after more than three and a half years of research, wrote the book in early 1844. His goal was to make known the facts of Marion's life "and to justify, by the array of authentic particulars, the high position which has been assigned him" in the pantheon of America's Revolutionary heroes. Simms recognized that arraying authentic particulars presented special challenges to the biographer of Marion. "The story of the Revolution in the Southern colonies has been badly kept," he wrote. "Documentary proofs are few, bald and uninteresting." Lacking abundant hard evidence, the facts of Marion's life had "escaped the ordinary bounds of history" and become inseparably interwoven with myth and legend. This process of mythmaking transformed the story of an individual into what Simms called a "people's history" written in the hearts of Marion's countrymen instead of in their books. As a "people's history," Marion's story possessed value that it would lose if confined to the page in a lifeless recording of dry facts. Simms thus saw both a challenge and an opportunity before him. The challenge was to fashion a biography from the scanty evidence that was true to both reliable oral traditions and the meager documentary sources available. The opportunity was the possibility of exercising his imaginative and narrative skills in truthfully filling in the gaps in the evidentiary record.

Because Simms, in his own informal style, employed footnotes and provided the book with a selective bibliography, we have a pretty good idea what most of his sources were. Among the most important sources were "five volumes of MS. Letters from distinguished officers of the Revolution in the South. From the Collection of Gen. Peter Horry." Also valuable was "a MS. Memoir of the Life of Brig. Gen. P[eter] Horry. By Himself." Unfortunately, the valuable memoir of Peter Horry, who served under Marion during the Revolution, has been partially lost. All that remains of some of the missing sections are the passages quoted by Simms, thus increasing the significance of this biography.[5] These manuscript sources were supplemented by his extensive familiarity with local oral history. Simms's generation of American historians was the last that could interview eyewitnesses of the Revolution. Evidence scattered throughout his writings indicates that he actively sought local history and traditions from still-living witnesses of and participants in the war, including surviving members of Marion's brigade.[6] Ever the careful historian, Simms weighed his sources and indicated when they could not be trusted. He also pointed out when the record was silent instead of simply filling in the gaps with his artistic imagination without telling readers what he was up to.

The book begins with an extended description of the Huguenot settlements in South Carolina. A good Romantic and historical materialist, Simms believed national spirit, as well as personal circumstances and condition, played a role in helping to shape history. However, he recognized that the most powerful force in shaping history was personal character. Marion came from Huguenot stock, and Simms sought insight into his character in the peculiar spirit and circumstances of this people. "The Huguenots were a better sort of people" than the typical Europeans who settled in America, wrote Simms. As French Protestants who were persecuted and then expelled from France, they were better prepared for the hardships of life in a new country and were more appreciative of the liberties they gained. "They were a people of principle," and "pure habits." Their devotion to their principles was evidenced by their endurance of the persecution they suffered for their religious faith. The Huguenot refugees arrived in Carolina poor and were distrusted by the English who had been their traditional enemies. Yet in time the Huguenots would thrive in Carolina and be fully accepted by the English colonists. Their eventual success was the result of perseverance and tireless industry. These virtues, part of the Huguenot spirit, were inherited by Marion.

Throughout the biography, Marion is portrayed as a man of extraordinary character. Without resorting to the blatant historical sins of Mason Locke Weems's biography of Marion, which was as much fiction as history, Simms sought to give expression to the almost mythic status his hero had already achieved in the hearts of his countrymen. One way of showing this was by comparing Marion to George Washington, the father of his country. So consistent is the comparison between Marion and Washington that it can be viewed as one of the central theses around which the biography is organized. The first reference to a similarity between Marion and Washington appears early in the second chapter. Here, after noting that the two Revolutionary heroes were both born in 1732, Simms goes on to explain:

> *This coincidence, which otherwise it might seem impertinent to notice here, derives some importance from the fact that it does not stand alone, but is rendered impressive by others, to be shown as we proceed; not to speak of the*

striking moral resemblances, which it will be no disparagement to the fame of the great Virginian to trace between the two.

As boys, both Washington and Marion dreamed of careers in the Royal Navy. Washington's mother convinced her son otherwise; Marion's plans were altered by a shipwreck. After returning from sea, Marion took up farming and his further education. Here again, Simms draws a parallel between the lives of the two men. Neither man received a proper formal education. "Equally denied the advantages of education, they equally drew from the great mother-sources of nature," wrote Simms. "Thrown upon their own thoughts, taught by observation and experience—the same results of character,—firmness, temperance, good sense, sagacious foresight, and deliberate prudence—became conspicuous in the conduct and career of both." Later, Simms remarks on how both men had similar even-keeled temperaments. Marion's expression was "never darkened by gloom, it was seldom usurped by mere merriment" either, he wrote. Marion maintained a Spartan control over his emotions whether in triumph or defeat, never allowing himself to be carried away to excess. "The equable tone of his mind reminds us again of Washington," wrote Simms. As a young farmer, Marion, the Carolina Cincinnatus, displayed "quiet and persevering industry" but had not quite outgrown his restlessness. In 1759, his pastoral tranquility was disturbed by war with the Cherokee. Marion left the farm to fulfill his civic duty by volunteering to serve in South Carolina's defense. As soon as the threat had passed Marion again took up the bucolic life of the farmer. In 1775 his peace was disturbed yet again when, facing war with England, Marion's neighbors called upon him to lead them. Like Washington, he was no orator, but he nevertheless served ably in the Provincial Congress. Both were preeminently men of action who best served their countrymen on the battlefield rather than in legislative chambers.

We learn from Simms that British officers condescended to both Marion and Washington, preferring to call them "Mr." rather than use their official military titles. "The very attempt here made to sneer away the official, adds to the personal importance of the individual," wrote Simms. The republican simplicity and virtue of "plain Mr. Marion" and "his ragged followers, who, untitled, could give such annoyance to His Majesty's officers," warrants "a degree of respect which his title might not otherwise have commanded." After the war, when his country's hour of danger had passed, Marion, like Washington, retired to the peace and quiet of his farm only to have his retirement interrupted by the call to political service. Late in life Marion took a wife but, like Washington, his marriage produced no heirs.

In the course of his biography Simms also compares Marion to Napoleon as well as the stock Romantic figures of Robin Hood and a feudal baron. Simms writes that Marion and Napoleon held similar notions about the punishment of soldiers. Marion preferred not to mete out "brutal" punishments on his soldiers. Instead he, like Napoleon, "endeavored by his punishments, to elevate the sense of character in the spectators."

Encamped at his swamp retreat on Snow's Island, Marion reminds Simms of the most picturesque scenes of romance. "In this snug and impenetrable fortress, he reminds us very much of the ancient feudal baron of France and Germany…perched on castle eminence," wrote Simms. With the swamp for a moat and tall pine and cypress trees for towers, Marion was as secure in his swamp encampment as any baron in his castle upon the Rhine. The Carolina swamps and forests protected Marion and his brigade not unlike Sherwood Forest sheltered Robin Hood and his merry men. Marion is described as being chivalrous; Simms calls one of his men a knight-errant and the moss-draped trees around the partisan encampment bring images of Gothic architecture to the author's mind.

Simms paints a far more balanced picture of the Revolution than many historians before or since. His sympathies clearly lie with the Whigs, but he never hesitates to condemn those patriots who behaved barbarously or to praise those Tories and Englishmen who acted chivalrously. Both Whigs and Tories were guilty of atrocities. "The sanguinary warfare," he wrote, "was perpetuated by mutual excesses." Simms even quotes Peter Horry's description of some of Marion's recruits as "volunteers assuredly, not to fight, but plunder." While not all of Simms's patriots are hailed as pillars of virtue, not all of their adversaries are denounced as knaves. For example, Colonel Watson, a British officer, is singled out for his chivalry. According to Simms, "he took no pleasure in burning houses, the hospitality of which he had enjoyed; he destroyed no cattle wantonly, and hung no unhappy prisoner."

Not even prisoners of war were safe from cruel reprisals. Although, according to Simms, Marion personally gave no countenance to such outrages, quarter was seldom given or expected on either side once men got in the habit of murdering prisoners and the cycle of revenge began. "Safety lay in victory alone, and the vanquished, if they could not find refuge in the swamps, found no mercy from the conqueror," Simms wrote. "There were a few infuriated men, who defied subordination, by whom, on both sides, the unhappy captives were sure to be sacrificed." Such "ferocities" Marion rebuked when committed by his subordinates. And others were dismissed from his brigade and had their "outlawry" proclaimed throughout the country for committing "numerous offences against humanity." Doubtless,

INTRODUCTION

on these occasions Marion was painfully reminded of the 1761 campaign against the Cherokee and the atrocities committed against them by the Carolinians that he found so personally disturbing.

Yet Simms admits that even Marion saw the necessity, in certain circumstances, of retaliating in kind for the execution of prisoners. He notes that "Weems represents Marion as being greatly averse to this measure of retaliation, and as having censured those officers of the regular army who demanded of Greene the adoption of this remedy" after the execution of Isaac Hayne by the British in Charleston. But Weems "wrote rather from his own benevolent nature than from the record." Marion, Simms asserts, clearly saw "the necessity for such a measure in particular cases;...however much he might wish to avoid its execution." Fortunately, in this particular case, retaliation by Marion proved unnecessary.

Such a conflict, fought in a sparsely settled state with insufficient routes of travel and communication, proved an almost ideal theater for the operation of local partisan militia. In South Carolina the militia proved its worth time and again against a numerically superior foe that had driven the Continental Army from the state. In spite of this, Simms felt the militia had been unfairly disparaged by regular army officers for its lack of discipline. Further, its accomplishments had been slighted by historians and a public that preferred to commemorate the victories of the Continental Army—on such fields as Saratoga and Yorktown—instead of backwoods victories won by small, ragged bands. Simms conceded that the poorly equipped militia could never have expelled the British from the state without assistance from the Continental Army. Nevertheless, "but for this militia, and the great spirit and conduct manifested by the partisan leaders in Carolina, no regular force which Congress would or could have sent into the field, would have sufficed for the recovery of the two almost isolated States of South Carolina and Georgia," wrote Simms. The local partisan militia kept up the conflict while the Continental Army was too weak to take the field. It maintained a constant harassment of British and Loyalist forces; cut off their detachments, endangered their supplies and forced the British to divide their forces, while inspiring local patriots. Simms assured readers he meant none of this to detract from credit owed the Continental Army. "It is only intended to insist upon those claims of the partisans, which...have been a little too irreverently dismissed by others," he wrote.

Simms believed the militia had been unjustly charged with displaying high rates of desertion as well as cowardice in battle when compared to regular troops. Sometimes what has been mistakenly called desertion, he wrote, was actually better explained by the unavoidable comings and goings of nonprofessional citizen soldiers during planting and harvest seasons to attend to their crops and families. The charge that militiamen were more prone to cowardice than regular troops was equally faulty. When properly employed by commanders who were familiar with their strengths and weaknesses the militia behaved admirably in battle. Simms argued here, as elsewhere in his writings about the Revolution, that the problem was that they were frequently misused by ignorant or incompetent commanders. For example, poorly trained, ill-equipped militia could not be expected to unflinchingly withstand a bayonet charge by British Regulars when they themselves lacked bayonets for their own defense. Yet, when exposed to precisely that situation, the militia was criticized by regular officers for taking flight. "The history of American warfare shows conclusively that, under the right leaders, the American militia are as cool in moments of danger as the best drilled soldiery in the universe," wrote Simms. Some of the success of leaders like Marion, Pickens and Sumter was due to their familiarity with their men and the land in which they fought, as well as their understanding of how best to employ the militia under their command.

Under the command of good leaders familiar with the "native spirit" of their men, the Carolina partisan militia proved a formidable military force despite its meagerness in men, material and training. At such battles as Quinby Bridge and Eutaw Springs, Simms noted, Marion's and Pickens's troops exhibited courage and steadiness under fire that, in the words of General Greene, "would have graced the veterans of the great king of Prussia [Frederick the Great]." With able leadership the militia seldom faltered, and it and its officers are due much credit for the eventual American victory in the Deep South. "But for these leaders, Marion, Sumter, Pickens, [William Richardson] Davie, [Wade] Hampton and some fifty more well endowed and gallant spirits," Simms wrote, "the Continental forces sent to Carolina would have vainly flung themselves upon the impenetrable masses of the British."

The Life of Francis Marion is as engagingly written as any of Simms's histories, shows a close attention to truthfulness and, even though it is a biography of a military hero, focuses its attention not solely on a great man. Simms was very much aware that the success of South Carolina's patriots was due more to the sacrifices of the humble than to the decisions of the famous. He even makes a point of praising "those great dames of the Revolution, to whom the nation is so largely indebted for the glory of that event." This is, undoubtedly, why he considered the moral education of South Carolinians through the preservation and publication of stories like Marion's so vitally important. Future generations could then recall in hours of trial the selfless patriotism of Marion and all those who fought alongside him. And Simms's own generation could be reminded of the virtue and self-sacrifice of their fathers.

Sean R. Busick
Assistant Professor of History
Athens State University

I would like to dedicate my efforts on this printing to Jennifer, Ashley Rose and Cora, my grandparents, and Mamaw and Papaw.

1. At the beginning of the Civil War, Samuel Clemens briefly joined together with some of his friends from Hannibal, Missouri, in forming a military unit they chose to call the Marion Rangers, before embarking on a campaign that failed.

2. Simms to James Lawson, 2 January 1847, in *The Letters of William Gilmore Simms*, eds. Mary C. Simms Oliphant, Alfred Taylor Odell, and T.C. Duncan Eaves (Columbia: University of South Carolina Press, 1953), 2:250.

3. For more on Simms's work and reputation as a historian, see: Sean R. Busick, *A Sober Desire for History: William Gilmore Simms as Historian* (Columbia: University of South Carolina Press, 2005).

4. New York, *Morning News*, 10 and 19 October 1844; [Lewis Gaylord Clark,] *Knickerbocker*, December 1844, 570-571 *American Review*, January 1845, 104-108; *United States Democratic Review*, January 1845, 103-104; Simms to George Frederick Holmes, 6 November 1844, *Letters*, 434-435.

5. Peter LeRoy Shillingsburg, "The Use of Sources in Simms's Biography of Francis Marion," (master's thesis, University of South Carolina, 1967).

6. For Simms's use of oral history, see: "Ellet's Women of the Revolution," *Southern Quarterly Review*, July 1850, 351–52; *Katharine Walton*, 521–22, n.469.20; and William Peterfield Trent, *William Gilmore Simms* (Boston: Houghton, Mifflin and Company, 1892), 106.

THE LIFE OF FRANCIS MARION

In preparing this biography, the following works have been consulted:

1. A Sketch of the Life of Brig. Gen. Francis Marion, and a History of his Brigade, &c. By Wm. Dobein James, A. M. Charleston, S.C. 1821.
2. The Life of Gen. Francis Marion, &c. By Brig. Gen. P. Horry, and M.L. Weems. Philadelphia. 1833.
3. A MS. Memoir of the Life of Brig. Gen. P. Horry. By Himself.
4. Sketches of the Life and Correspondence of Nathanael Greene, &c. By William Johnson. Charleston. 1822.
5. Memoirs of the American Revolution, &c. By William Moultrie. New York. 1802.
6. Anecdotes of the Revolutionary War in America (1st and 2d series). By Alex. Garden. 1822 and 1828.
7. Memoirs of the War in the Southern Department of the United States. By Henry Lee, &c. Philadelphia. 1812.
8. Memoirs of the American Revolution, &c., as relating to the State of South Carolina, &c. By John Drayton, LL.D. Charleston, 1821.
9. The History of South Carolina, &c. By David Ramsay. Charleston. 1809.
10. The History of Georgia, &c. By Capt. Hugh M'Call. Savannah. 1811.
11. A History of the Campaigns of 1780 and 1781, in the Southern Provinces of North America. By Lieut. Col. Tarleton, Commandant of the late British Legion. London. 1797.
12. Strictures on Lieut. Col. Tarleton's History, &c. By Roderick Mackenzie, late Lieutenant in the 71st Regiment, &c. London. 1787.
13. History of the Revolution of South Carolina from a British Province to an Independent State. By David Ramsay, M.D. Trenton. 1785.
14. An Historical Account of the Rise and Progress of the Colonies of South Carolina and Georgia. (Hewatt.) London. 1779.
15. A New Voyage to Carolina, &c. By John Lawson, Gent., Surveyor-General of North Carolina. London. 1709.
16. The History of the Rise, Progress, and Establishment of the Independence of the United States of America, &c. By William Gordon, D.D. New York. 1789.
17. Five volumes of MS. Letters from distinguished officers of the Revolution in the South. From the Collection of Gen. Peter Horry.

PREFACE

The facts, in the life of Francis Marion, are far less generally extended in our country than his fame. The present is an attempt to supply this deficiency, and to justify, by the array of authentic particulars, the high position which has been assigned him among the master-workers in our revolutionary history. The task has been a difficult, but I trust not entirely an unsuccessful one. Our southern chronicles are meagre and unsatisfactory. South Carolina was too long in the occupation of the British—too long subject to the ravages of civil and foreign war, to have preserved many of those minor records which concern only the renown of individuals, and are unnecessary to the comprehension of great events; and the vague tributes of unquestioning tradition are not adequate authorities for the biographer, whose laws are perhaps even more strict than those which govern the historian. Numerous volumes, some private manuscripts, and much unpublished correspondence, to which reference has been more particularly made in the appendix, have been consulted in the preparation of this narrative. The various histories of Carolina and Georgia have also been made use of. Minor facts have been gathered from the lips of living witnesses. Of the two works devoted especially to our subject, that by the Rev. Mr. Weems is most generally known—a delightful book for the young. The author seems not to have contemplated any less credulous readers, and its general character is such as naturally to inspire us with frequent doubts of its statements. Mr. Weems had rather loose notions of the privileges of the biographer; though, in reality, he has transgressed much less in his Life of Marion than is generally supposed. But the untamed, and sometimes extravagant exuberance of his style might well subject his narrative to suspicion. Of the " Sketch" by the Hon. Judge James, we are more secure, though, as a literary performance, it is quite as devoid of merit as pretension. Besides, the narrative is not thorough. It dwells somewhat too minutely upon one class of facts, to the neglect or the exclusion of others. I have made both of these works tributary to my own whenever this was possible.

Woodland, S.C., May 25. 1844.

CHAPTER I

INTRODUCTION † THE HUGUENOTS IN SOUTH CAROLINA

The name of FRANCIS MARION is identified, in the history of South Carolina, his parent state, with all that is pleasing and exciting in romance. He is, *par excellence*, the famous partisan of that region. While Sumter stands conspicuous for bold daring, fearless intrepidity and always resolute behavior; while Lee takes eminent rank as a gallant Captain of Cavalry, the eye and the wing of the southern liberating army under Greene; Marion is proverbially the great master of strategy—the wily fox of the swamps—never to be caught, never to be followed,—yet always at hand, with unconjectured promptness, at the moment when he is least feared and is least to be expected. His pre-eminence in this peculiar and most difficult of all kinds of warfare, is not to be disputed. In his native region he has no competitor, and it is scarcely possible to compute the vast influence which he possessed and exercised over the minds and feelings of the people of Carolina, simply through his own resources, at a period most adverse to their fortunes, and when the cause of their liberties, everywhere endangered, was almost everywhere considered hopeless. His name was the great rallying cry of the yeoman in battle—the word that promised hope—that cheered the desponding patriot—that startled, and made to pause in his career of recklessness and blood, the cruel and sanguinary tory. Unprovided with the means of warfare, no less than of comfort—wanting equally in food and weapons—we find him supplying the one deficiency with a cheerful courage that never failed; the other with the resources of a genius that seemed to wish for nothing from without. With a force constantly fluctuating and feeble in consequence of the most ordinary necessities—half-naked men, feeding upon unsalted pottage,—forced to fight the enemy by day, and look after their little families, concealed in swamp or thicket, by night—he still contrived,—one knows not well how,—to keep alive and bright the sacred fire of his country's liberties, at moments when they seemed to have no other champion. In this toil and watch, taken cheerfully and with spirits that never appeared to lose their tone and elasticity, tradition ascribes to him a series of achievements, which, if they were small in comparison with the great performances of European war, were scarcely less important; and which, if they sometimes transcend belief, must yet always delight the imagination. His adventures have given a rich coloring to fable, and have stimulated its performances. The language of song and story has been employed to do them honor, and our children are taught, in lessons that they love, to lisp the deeds and the patriotism of his band. "Marion"—"Marion's Brigade" and "Marion's men," have passed into household words, which the young utter with an enthusiasm much more confiding than that which they yield to the wondrous performances of Greece and Ilium. They recall, when spoken, a long and delightful series of brilliant exploits, wild adventures, by day and night, in swamp and thicket, sudden and strange manœuvres, and a generous, unwavering ardor, that never found any peril too hazardous, or any suffering too unendurable. The theme, thus invested, seems to have escaped the ordinary bounds of history. It is no longer within the province of the historian. It has passed into the hands of the poet, and seems to scorn the appeal to authentic chronicles. When we look for the record we find but little authority for a faith so confiding, and seemingly so exaggerated. The story of the Revolution in the southern colonies has been badly kept. Documentary proofs are few, bald and uninteresting. A simple paragraph in the newspapers,—those newspapers issued not unfrequently in cities where the enemy had power, and in the control of Editors, unlike the present, who were seldom able to expatiate upon the achievement which they recorded;—or the brief dispatches of the Captain himself, whose modesty would naturally recoil from stating more than the simple result of his performances;—these are usually the sum total of our authorities. The country, sparsely settled, and frequently overrun by the barbarous enemy, was incapable of that patient industry and persevering care, which could chronicle the passing event, give place and date to the brilliant sortie, the gallant struggle, the individual deed of audacity, which, by a stroke, and at a moment, secures an undying remembrance in the bosoms of a people. The fame of Marion rests very much upon tradition. There is little in the books to justify the strong and exciting relish with which the name is spoken and remembered through out the country. He was not a bloody warrior. His battlefields were never sanguinary. His ardor was never of a kind to make him imprudent. He was not distinguished for great strength of arm, or great skill in his weapon. We have no proofs that he was ever engaged in single combat: yet the concurrent testimony of all who have written, declare, in general terms, his great services: and the very exaggeration of the popular estimate is a partial proof of the renown for which it speaks. In this respect, his reputation is like that of all other heroes of romantic history. It is a people's history, written in their hearts, rather than in their books; which their books could not write—which would lose all its golden glow, if subjected to the cold details of the phlegmatic chronicles. The tradition, however swelling, still testifies to that large merit which must have been its basis, by reason of which the name of the hero was selected from all others for such peculiar honors; and though these exaggerations suggest a thousand difficulties in the way of sober history, they yet serve to increase the desire, as well as the necessity, for some such performance.

The family of Marion came from France. They immigrated to South Carolina somewhere about the year 1685, within twenty years after the first British settlement of the province. They belonged, in the parent country, to that sect of religious dissenters which bore the name of Huguenots; and were among those who fled from the cruel persecutions which, in the beginning of the reign of Louis XIV., followed close upon the re-admission of the Jesuits into France. The edict of Nantz, which had been issued under the auspices of Henri IV., and by which the Huguenots had been guaranteed, with some slight qualifications, the securities of the citizen, almost in the same degree with the Catholic inhabitants, had, under the weak and tyrannous sway of the former monarch, proved totally inadequate to their protection. Long before its formal revocation, the unmeasured and inhuman persecutions to which they were subjected, drove thousands of them into voluntary banishment. The subsequent decree of Louis, by which even the nominal securities of the Huguenots were withdrawn, increased the number of the exiles, and completed the sentence of separation from all those ties which bind the son to the soil. The neighboring Protestant countries received the fugitives, the number and condition of whom may be estimated by the simple fact, not commonly known, that England alone possessed "eleven regiments composed entirely of these unhappy refugees, besides others enrolled among the troops of the line. There were in London twenty French churches supported by Government; about three thousand refugees were maintained by public subscription; many received grants from the crown; and a great number lived by their own industry.[1] Some of the nobility were naturalized and obtained high rank; among others, Ruvigny, son of the Marquis, was made Earl of Galway, and Schomberg received the dignity of Duke."[2]

America, the new world, was naturally a land of refuge, and soon received her share of these unhappy fugitives. The transition was easy from England to her colonies. Every facility was afforded them for transportation, and the wise policy which encouraged their settlement in the new countries was amply rewarded by the results. Altogether, the Huguenots were a much better sort of people than those who usually constituted the mass of European emigrants. The very desperation of their circumstances was a proof of their virtues. They were a people of principle, for they had suffered everything for conscience sake. They were a people of pure habits, for it was because of their religion that they suffered banishment. In little patriarchal groups of sixty, seventy, or eighty families, they made their way to different parts of America; and with the conscious poverty of their own members, were generally received with open arms by those whom they found in possession of the soil. The English, as they beheld the dependent and destitute condition of the fugitives, forgot, for a season, their usual national animosities; and assigning ample tracts of land for their occupation, beheld them, without displeasure, settling down in exclusive colonies, in which they sought to maintain, as far as possible, the pious habits and customs of the mother country. One of these communities, comprising from seventy to eighty families, found their way to the banks of the Santee in South Carolina.[3] From this point they gradually spread themselves out so as to embrace, in partial settlements, the spacious tract of country stretching to the Winyah, on the one hand, and the sources of Cooper River on the other; extending upward into the interior, following the course of the Santee nearly to the point where it loses its identity in receiving the descending streams of the Wateree and Congaree. These settlers were generally poor. They had been despoiled of all their goods by the persecutions which had driven them into exile. This, indeed, had bean one of the favorite modes by which this result had been effected. Doubtless, also, it had been, among the subordinates of the crown, one of the chief motives of the persecution. It was a frequent promise of his Jesuit advisers, to the vain and bigoted Louis, that the heretics should be brought into the fold of the Church without a drop of bloodshed; and, until the formal revocation of the edict of Nantz, by which the Huguenots were put without the pale and protection of the laws, spoliation was one of the means, with others, by which to avoid this necessity. These alternatives, however, were of a kind not greatly to lessen the cruelties of the persecutor or the sufferings of the victim. It does not fall within our province to detail them. It is enough that one of the first and most obvious measures by which to keep their promise to the king, was to dispossess the proscribed subjects of their worldly goods and chattels. By this measure a two-fold object was secured. While the heretic was made to suffer, the faithful were sure of their reward. It was a principle faithfully kept in view; and the refugees brought with them into exile, little beyond the liberties and the virtues for which they had endured so much. But these were possessions, as their subsequent history has shown, beyond all price.

Our humble community along the Santee had suffered the worst privations of their times and people. But, beyond the necessity of hard labor, they had little to deplore, at the outset, in their new condition. They had been schooled sufficiently by misfortune to have acquired humility. They observed, accordingly, in their new relations, a policy equally prudent and sagacious. More flexible in their habits than the English, they conciliated the latter by deference; and, soothing the unruly passions of the Indians—the Santee and Sewee tribes, who were still in considerable numbers in their immediate neighborhood—they won them to alliance by kindness and forbearance. From the latter, indeed, they learned their best lessons for the cultivation of the soil. That, upon which they found themselves, lay in the unbroken forest. The high lands which they first undertook to clear, as less stubborn, were most sterile; and, by a very natural mistake, our Frenchmen adopted the modes and objects of European culture; the grains, the fruits and the vegetables, as well as the implements, to which they had been accustomed. The Indians came to their succor, taught them the cultivation of maize, and assisted them in the preparation of their lands; in return for lessons thought equally valuable by the savages, to whom they taught, along with gentler habits and morals, a better taste for music and the dance! To subdue the forest, of itself, to European hands, implied labors not unlike those of Hercules. But the refugees, though a gentle race, were men of soul and strength, capable of great sacrifices, and protracted self-denial. Accommodating themselves with a patient courage to the necessities before them, they cheerfully undertook and accomplished their tasks. We have more than one lively picture among the early chroniclers of the distress and hardship which they were compelled to encounter at the first. But, in this particular, there was nothing peculiar in their situation. It differed in no respect from that which fell to the lot of all the early colonists in America. The toil of felling trees, over whose heavy boughs and knotty arms the winters of centuries had passed; the constant danger from noxious reptiles and beasts of prey, which, coiled in the bush or crouching in the brake, lurked day and night, in waiting for the in cautious victim; and, most insidious and fatal enemy of all, the malaria of the swamp, of the rank and affluent soil, for the first time laid open to the sun; these are all only the ordinary evils which encountered in America, at the very threshold, the advances of European civilisation. That the Huguenots should meet these toils and dangers with the sinews and the hearts of men, was to be expected from their past experience and history. They had endured too many and too superior evils in the old world, to be discouraged by, or to shrink from, any of those which hung upon their progress in the new. Like the hardy Briton, whom, under the circumstances, we may readily suppose them to have emulated, they addressed themselves, with little murmuring, to the tasks before them. We have, at the hands of one of their number,—a lady born and raised in affluence at home,—a lively and touching picture of the sufferings and duties, which, in Carolina, at that period, neither sex nor age was permitted to escape. "After our arrival," she writes, "we suffered every kind of evil. In about eighteen months our elder brother, unaccustomed to the hard labor we were obliged to undergo, died of a fever. Since leaving France, we had experienced every kind of affliction, disease, pestilence, famine, poverty and hard labor! I have been for six months together without tasting bread, working the ground like a slave; and I have even passed three or four years without always having it when I wanted it. I should never have done were I to attempt to detail to you all our adventures."[4]

We may safely conclude that there was no exaggeration in this picture. The lot of all the refugees seems to have been very equally severe. Men and women, old and young, strove together in the most menial and laborious occupations. But, as courage and virtue usually go hand in hand with industry, the three are apt to triumph together. Such was the history in the case of the Carolina Huguenots. If the labor and the suffering were great, the fruits were prosperity. They were more. Honors, distinction, a goodly name, and the love of those around them, have blessed their posterity, many of whom rank with the noblest citizens that were ever reared in America. In a few years after their first settlement, their forest homes were crowned with a degree of comfort, which is described as very far superior to that in the usual enjoyment of the British colonists. They were a more docile and tractable race; not so restless, nor—though this may seem difficult to understand to those who consider their past history—so impatient of foreign control. Of their condition in Carolina, we have a brief but pleasing picture from the hands of John Lawson, then surveyor-general of the province of North Carolina.[5] This gentleman, in 1701, just fifteen years after its settlement, made a progress through that portion of the Huguenot colony which lay immediately along the Santee. The passages which describe his approach to the country which they occupied, the hospitable reception which they gave him, the comforts they enjoyed, the gentleness of their habits, the simplicity of their lives, and their solicitude in behalf of strangers, are necessary to furnish the moral of those fortunes, the beginning of which was so severe and perilous. "There are," says he, "about seventy families seated on this river, *who live as decently and happily as any planters in these southward parts of America. The French being a temperate, industrious people*, some of them bringing very little of effects, *yet, by their endeavors and mutual assistance among themselves* (which is highly to be commended), *have outstript our English, who brought with them larger fortunes*, though (as it seems) less endeavor to manage their talent to the best advantage. 'Tis admirable to see what time and industry will (with God's blessing) effect," &c...."We lay all that night at Mons. *Eugee's* (Huger), and the next morning set out farther, to go the remainder of our voyage by land. At ten o'clock we passed over a narrow, deep swamp, having left the three Indian men and one woman, that had piloted the canoe from Ashley river, having hired a Sewee Indian, a tall, lusty fellow, who carried a pack of our clothes, of great weight. Notwithstanding his burden, we had much ado to keep pace with him. At noon we came up with several French plantations. Meeting with several creeks by the way, *the French were very officious in assisting us with their small dories to pass over these waters:* whom we met coming from their church, *being all of them very clean and decent in their apparel*; their houses and plantations suitable in neatness and contrivance. They are all of the same opinion with the church of Geneva,[6] there being no difference among them concerning the punctilios of their Christian faith; *which union hath propagated a happy and delightful concord in all other matters throughout the whole neighborhood; living amongst themselves as one tribe or kindred, everyone making it his business to be assistant to the wants of his countrymen, preserving his estate and reputation with the same exactness and concern as he does his own: all seeming to share in the misfortunes, and rejoice at the advance and rise of their brethren.* Lawson fitly concludes his account of the settlers upon the Santee, by describing them as "a very kind, loving, and affable people"—a character which it has been the happy solicitude of their descendants to maintain to the present day.[7]

A more delightful picture than this of Mr. Lawson, could not well be drawn by the social perfectionist. The rational beauty of the voluntary system could not find a happier illustration; and, duly impressed with its loveliness, we shall cease to wonder at the instances of excellence, equally frequent and admirable, which rose up among this little group of exiles, to the good fortune of the country which gave them shelter, and in attestation of their own virtues. But this happy result was due entirely to their training. It would be wonderful, indeed, if such an education, toil and watch, patient endurance of sickness and suffering, sustained only by sympathy with one another and a humble reliance upon divine mercy, should not produce many perfect characters—men like Francis Marion, the beautiful symmetry of whose moral structure leaves us nothing to regret in the analysis of his life. Uncompromising in the cause of truth, stern in the prosecution of his duties, hardy and fearless as the soldier, he was yet, in peace, equally gentle and compassionate, pleased to be merciful, glad and ready to forgive, sweetly patient of mood, and distinguished throughout by such prominent virtues, that, while always sure of the affections of followers and comrades, he was not less secure in the unforced confidence of his enemies, among whom his integrity and mercy were proverbial. By their fruits, indeed, shall we know this community, the history of which furnishes as fine a commentary upon the benefit of good social training for the young—example and precept happily keeping concert with the ordinary necessities and performances of life, the one supported by the manliest courage, the other guided by the noblest principle—as any upon record.[8]

When our traveller turned his back upon this "kind, loving, and affable people," to pursue his journey into North Carolina, his first forward step was into a howling wilderness. The Santee settlement, though but forty miles distant from Charleston, was a frontier—all beyond was waste, thicket and forest, filled with unknown and fearful animals, and

> *"sliding reptiles of the ground,*
> *Startlingly beautiful,"*—

which the footstep of man dreaded to disturb. Of the wild beasts by which it was tenanted, a single further extract from the journal of Mr. Lawson will give us a sufficient and striking idea. He has left the Santee settlements but a single day—probably not more than fifteen miles. His Indian companion has made for his supper a bountiful provision, having killed three fat turkeys in the space of half an hour. "When we were all asleep," says our traveller, "in the beginning of the night, we were awakened with the most dismal and most hideous noise that ever pierced my ears. This sudden surprise incapacitated us of guessing what this threatening noise might proceed from; but our Indian pilot (who knew these parts very well) acquainted us that it was customary to hear such music along that swampside, there being endless numbers of panthers, tygers, wolves, and other beasts of prey, which take this swamp for their abode in the day, coming in whole droves to hunt the deer in the night, making this frightful ditty till day appears, then all is still as in other places."—*Page 26.*

Less noisy, except in battle, but even more fearful, were the half-human possessors of the same regions, the savages, who, at that period, in almost countless tribes or families, hovered around the habitations of the European Always restless, commonly treacherous, warring or preparing for war, the red men required of the white borderer the vigilance of an instinct which was never to be allowed repose. This furnished an additional school for the moral and physical training of our young Huguenots. In this school, without question, the swamp and forest partisans of a future day took some of their first and most valuable lessons in war. Here they learned to be watchful and circumspect, cool in danger, steady in advance, heedful of every movement of the foe, and—which is of the very last importance in such a country and in such a warfare as it indicates—happily dextrous in emergencies to seize upon the momentary casualty, the sudden chance— to convert the most trivial circumstance, the most ordinary agent, into a means of extrication or offence. It was in this last respect particularly, in being quick to see, and prompt to avail themselves of the happy chance or instrument, that the partisans of the revolution in the southern colonies, under Marion and others, asserted their vast superiority over the invader, and maintained their ground, and obtained their final triumph, in spite of every inequality of arms and numbers.

CHAPTER II

THE MARION FAMILY † BIRTH OF FRANCIS
MARION † HIS YOUTH † SHIPWRECK

We have dwelt upon the Huguenot Settlement in Carolina, somewhat more largely than our immediate subject would seem to require. Our apology must be found in the obvious importance and beauty of the fact, could this be shown, that the character of Francis Marion was in truth a remarkable illustration, in all its parts, of the moral nature which prevailed in this little colony of exiles: that, from the harmony existing among them, their purity of conduct, propriety of sentiment, the modesty of their deportment and the firmness of their virtues, he most naturally drew all the components of his own. His hardihood, elasticity, great courage and admirable dexterity in war, were also the natural results of their frontier position. We do not pretend that his acquisitions were at all peculiar to himself. On the contrary, we take for granted, that every distinguished person will, in some considerable degree, betray in his own mind and conduct, the most striking of those characteristics, which mark the community in which he has had his early training; that his actions will, in great measure, declare what sort of moral qualities have been set before his eyes, not so much by his immediate family, as by the society at large in which he lives; that he will represent that society rather than his immediate family, as it is the nature of superior minds to rush out of the narrow circles of domestic life; and that his whole after-performances, even where he may appear in the garb and guise of the reformer, will indicate in numerous vital respects, the tastes and temper of the very people whose alteration and improvement he seeks. The memoir upon which we are about to enter, will, we apprehend, justify the preliminary chapter which has been given to the history of the Huguenots upon the Santee. Gabriel Marion, the grandfather of our subject, was one of those who left France in 1685. His son, named after himself, married Charlotte Cordes, by whom he had seven children, five of whom were sons and two daughters.[9] Francis Marion was the last. He was born at Winyah, near Georgetown, South

Carolina, in 1732; a remarkable year, as, in a sister colony (we are not able to say how nearly at the same time), it gave birth to GEORGE WASHINGTON. This coincidence, which otherwise it might seem impertinent to notice here, derives some importance from the fact that it does not stand alone, but is rendered impressive by others, to be shown as we proceed; not to speak of the striking moral resemblances, which it will be no disparagement to the fame of the great Virginian to trace between the two.

The infancy of Marion was unpromising. At birth he was puny and diminutive in a remarkable degree. Weems, in his peculiar fashion, writes, "I have it from good authority, that this great soldier, at his birth, was not larger than a New England lobster, and might easily enough have been put into a quart pot." It was certainly as little supposed that he should ever live to manhood, as that he should then become a hero. But, by the time that he had reached his twelfth year, his constitution underwent a change. His health became good. The bracing exercises and hardy employments of country life invigorated his frame, and with this improvement brought with it a rare increase of energy. He grew restless and impatient. The tendency of his mind, which was so largely developed in the partisan exercises of after years, now began to exhibit itself. Under this impulse he conceived a dislike to the staid and monotonous habits of rural life, and resolved upon seafaring as a vocation. Such, it may be remarked, was also the early passion of Washington; a passion rather uncommon in the history of a southern boy. In the case of Washington the desire was only overcome at the solicitations of his mother. The mother of Marion, in like manner, strove to dissuade her son from this early inclination. She did not succeed, however, and when scarcely sixteen, he embarked in a small vessel for the West Indies. The particulars of this voyage, with the exception of the mode in which it terminated, have eluded our inquiry. We have looked for the details in vain. The name of the vessel, the captain, the port she sailed from, have equally escaped our search. To the wanton destruction of private and public records by the British, together with the heedless improvidence of heads of families in the South, we owe this poverty of historical resource. The voyage must have been taken somewhere about the year 1747–48. At that period there were perils of the sea to which the mariner is not often exposed at the present day. The waters of the Gulf of Mexico, in particular, were covered with pirates. The rich produce of New Spain, the West Indies, and the Southern Colonies of the English, were rare temptations. The privateers of Spain and France, a sort of legalized pirates, hung about the ports of Carolina, frequently subjecting them to a condition of blockade, and sometimes to forced contributions. In the occasional absence of the British armed vessels appointed for the protection of these ports, the more enterprising and spirited among their citizens frequently fitted out their own cruisers, drawing them, for this purpose, from the merchant service; manning in person, and requiting themselves for their losses of merchandize by the occasional capture of some richly laden galleon from New Spain. No doubt the imagination of young Marion was fired by hearing of these exploits. The sensation produced in the community, by the injuries done to its commerce, in all probability gave the direction to his already excited and restless disposition. It does not appear, however, that Marion's first and only voyage was made in an armed vessel. Such, we may well suppose, would have been his desire; but the period when he set forth to procure service upon the seas, may not have been auspicious. He may have reached the seaport a moment too soon or too late, and the opportunities of this kind were necessarily infrequent in a small and frontier city, whose commerce lay mostly in the hands of strangers. His small size and puny appearance must have operated very much against his hopes of obtaining employment in a service which particularly calls for manhood and muscle. In what capacity, or in what sort of vessel he obtained a berth, we are left wholly to conjecture. Choosing the sea as a vocation, and laudably resolved on acquiring a proper knowledge of his business (as from what we know of his character, we may suppose was the case), he most probably went before the mast. His first and only voyage was unfortunate. The ship in which he sailed was no doubt equally frail and small. She foundered at sea, whether going or returning is not said; in consequence, we are told, of injuries received from the stroke of a whale, of the thorn-back species. So suddenly did she sink, that her crew, only six in number, had barely time to save themselves. They escaped to the jolly boat, saving nothing but their lives. They took with them neither water nor provisions and for six days, hopeless of succor, they lay tossing to and fro, upon the bald and cheerless ocean. A dog, which swam to them from the sinking vessel, was sacrificed to their hunger. His raw flesh was their only food, his blood their only drink, during this distressing period. Two of their number perished miserably.[10] The survivors, on the seventh day, were found and taken up by a passing vessel, nourished carefully and finally restored to their homes.

Francis Marion was one of these survivors. The puny boy lived through the terrors and sufferings under which the strong men perished. So intense were their sufferings, so terrible the trial, that it will not greatly task the imagination to recognize in the preservation of the youth,— looking to his future usefulness—the agency of a special providence. The boy was preserved for other times and fortunes; and, in returning to his mother, was perhaps better prepared to heed her entreaties that he should abandon all idea of an element, from which his escape had been so hazardous and narrow. It was well for himself and country that he did so. It can scarcely be conjectured that his achievements on the sea would have been half so fortunate, or half so honorable to himself and country, as those which are now coupled with his name.

Returning to his home and parents, young Marion sunk once more into the humble condition of the farmer. His health and strength had continued to improve. His adventures by sea had served, seemingly, to complete that change for the better, in his physical man, which had been so happily begun on land; and, subduing his roving inclinations, we hear of him only, in a period of ten years, as a tiller of the earth. In this vocation he betrayed that diligent attention to his duties, that patient hardihood, and calm, equable temper, which distinguished his deportment in every part of his career. He is represented as equally industrious and successful as a farmer. The resources of his family seem to have been very moderate. There were several children, and before Francis was yet twenty-five years of age, he lost his father. In 1758 he was planting with his mother and brother Gabriel, near Friersons Lock on the Santee Canal. In 1759 they separated. Gabriel removed to Belle Isle—the place where the mortal remains of Francis Marion now repose—while the latter settled at a place called Pond Bluff in the Parish of St. John. This place he continued to hold during life. It is still pointed out to the traveller as Marion's plantation, and is the more remarkable, as it lies within cannon shot of the battle ground of Eutaw, which his valor and conduct contributed to render so justly famous in the history of his native state. During this long period of repose—the interval between his shipwreck, and removal to Pond Bluff—we are only left to conjecture his employments. Beyond his agricultural labors, we may suppose that his chief tasks were the cultivation of his mind, by close application to those studies which, in the condition of the country, sparsely settled, and without teachers, were usually very inadequately urged. It does not appear that his acquisitions in this respect were more valuable than could be afforded at the present day by the simplest grammar-school of the country. Here again we may trace the resemblance between his career and that of Washington. Equally denied the advantages of education, they equally drew from the great mother-sources of nature. Thrown upon their own thoughts, taught by observation and experience—the same results of character,—firmness, temperance, good sense, sagacious foresight, and deliberate prudence—became conspicuous in the conduct and career of both. In the fortunes of neither—in the several tasks allotted to them,—in their various situations,—did their deficiencies of education appear to qualify their successes, or diminish the respect and admiration of those around them,—a singular fact, as indicative equally of the modesty, the good sense, and the superior intrinsic worth of both of these distinguished persons. In the case of Marion, his want of education neither lessened his energies, his confidence in himself, nor baffled any of his natural endowments. On the contrary, it left his talents free to their natural direction. These, it is probable, were never of a kind to derive, or to need, many advantages from a very superior or scientific education. His mind was rather practical than subtle—his genius prompted him to action, rather than to study,—and the condition and necessities of the country, calling for the former rather than the latter character, readily reconciled him to a deficiency the importance of which he did not feel.

CHAPTER III

MARION A FARMER † VOLUNTEERS IN THE CHEROKEE CAMPAIGN

From the readiness with which young Marion yielded himself to the entreaties of his mother, and resumed the occupations of agriculture, and from the quiet and persevering industry with which he pursued them for about ten years, it might be supposed that the impatience and restlessness of mood, which had formerly led him to revolt at the staid drudgery of rural life, had been entirely extinguished in his bosom. But such was not the case. It was only subdued, and slumbering for a season, ready to awaken at the first opportunity, with all the vigor and freshness of a favorite passion. That opportunity was at hand. Events were in progress which were to bring into the field, and prepare by the very best sort of training, for the most noble trials, the great military genius of the Partisan. At the opening of the year 1759, the colony of South Carolina was on the eve of an Indian war. The whole frontier of the Southern Provinces, from Pennsylvania to Georgia, was threatened by the savages, and the scalping-knife had already begun its bloody work upon the weak and unsuspecting borderers. The French had been conquered upon the Ohio. Forts Frontenac and Duquesne had fallen. British and Provincial valor, aided by strong bodies of Cherokee warriors, had everywhere placed the flag of Britain above the fortresses of France. With its elevation, the Indian allies of the French sent in their adhesion to the conquerors; and, their work at an end, the Cherokee auxiliaries of Britain prepared to return to their homes, covered with their savage trophies, and adequately rewarded for their services. It happened, unfortunately, that, while passing along the frontiers of Virginia, the Cherokees, many of whom had lost their horses during the campaign, supplied themselves rather unscrupulously from the pastures of the colonists. With inconsiderate anger, the Virginians, forgetting the late valuable services of the savages, rose upon their footsteps, slew twelve or fourteen of their warriors, and made prisoners of as many more. This rash and ill-advised severity aroused the nation. The young warriors flew to arms, and pouring their active hordes upon the frontier settlements, proceeded to the work of slaughter, without pausing to discriminate between the offending and the innocent. The emergency was pressing, and Governor Lyttleton, of South Carolina, called out the militia of the province. They were required to rendezvous at the Congarees, about one hundred and forty miles from Charleston. To this rendezvous Francis Marion repaired, in a troop of provincial cavalry commanded by one of his brothers.[11] But he was not yet to flesh his maiden valor upon the enemy. The prompt preparation of the Carolinians had somewhat lessened the appetite of the savages for war. Perhaps their own preparations were not yet sufficiently complete to make them hopeful of its issue. The young warriors were recalled from the frontiers, and a deputation of thirty-two chiefs set out for Charleston, in order to propitiate the anger of the whites, and arrest the threatened invasion of their country. Whether they were sincere in their professions, or simply came for the purpose of deluding and disarming the Carolinians, is a question with the historians. It is certain that Governor Lyttleton doubted their sincerity, refused to listen to their explanations, and, carrying them along with him, rather as hostages than as commissioners in sacred trust, he proceeded to meet the main body of his army, already assembled at the Congarees. The treatment to which they were thus subjected, filled the Cherokee deputies with indignation, which, with the usual artifice of the Indian, they yet contrived to suppress. But another indiscreet proceeding of the Governor added to the passion which they felt, and soon baffled all their powers of concealment. In resuming the march for the nation, he put them into formal custody, placed a captain guard over them, and in this manner hurried them to the frontiers. Whatever may have been the merits of this movement as a mere military precaution, it was of very bad policy in a civil point of view. It not only degraded the Indian chiefs in their own, but in the eyes of their people. His captives deeply and openly resented this indignity and breach of faith; and, brooding in sullen ferocity over the disgrace which they suffered, meditated in silence those schemes of vengeance which they subsequently brought to a fearful maturity. But though thus impetuous and imprudent, and though pressing forward as if with the most determined purposes, Lyttleton was in no mood for war. His policy seems to have contemplated nothing further than the alarm of the Indians. Neither party was exactly ripe for the final issue. The Cherokees needed time for preparation, and the Governor, with an army ill disciplined and imperfectly armed, found it politic, when on the very confines of the enemy's country, to do that which he might very well have done in Charleston—listen to terms of accommodation. Having sent for Attakullakullah, the wise man of the nation, who had always been the staunch friend of the whites, he made his complaints, and declared his readiness for peace;—demanding, however, as the only condition on which it could be granted, that twenty-four men of the nation should be delivered to him, to be disposed of as he should think proper, by death or otherwise, as an atonement of that number of Carolinians, massacred in the late foray of the savages. A treaty was effected, but with some difficulty, on these terms. Compliance with this requisition was not so easy, however, on the part of the Cherokee chiefs. The moment it was understood, the great body of their people fled to the mountains, and the number of hostages could be secured only by the detention of twenty-two of those chiefs already in the Governor's custody. The captives were placed, for safe keeping, at the frontier fort of Prince George.

But the natural sense of the savage is not inferior to that by which the laws of the civilized are prescribed, in their dealings with one another. The treaty thus extorted from their leaders, while in a state of duresse, was disregarded by the great body of the nation. They watched their opportunity, and, scarcely had the Governor disbanded his forces, when the war-whoop resounded from the frontiers.

Fort Prince George was one of the most remote of a chain of military posts by which the intercourse was maintained between the several white settlements of the seaboard and the interior. It stood on the banks of the Isumdiga River, about three hundred miles from Charleston, within gunshot of the Indian town of Keowee. This post, to which the Cherokee hostages were carried, was defended by cannon, and maintained by a small force under Colonel Cotymore. It was in this neighborhood, and, as it were in defiance of this force, that the war was begun. Fourteen whites were massacred at a blow, within a mile of this station. This was followed up by a stratagem, by which Occonostota, one of the principal warriors, aimed to obtain possession of the fort. Pretending to have something of importance to communicate to the commander, he dispatched a woman who had usually obtained access to the station, to solicit an interview with him. This was to take place on the banks of the river. Meanwhile the savage prepared his ambush. Cotymore imprudently assented to the meeting, and, attended by Lieutenants Bell and Foster, walked down towards the river, from the opposite side of which Occonostota addressed him. While they spoke, the Indian was seen to wave a bridle over his head. This was the signal agreed upon with the ambushed warriors. At this signal they rose and poured in their fire. Cotymore was slain on the spot, and his companions wounded. But the savages failed to get possession of the fort. Suspecting a concerted movement among the hostages, by which they would co-operate with the assailing foe without, the officer in command of the fort gave orders to secure them with irons. The attempt to obey these orders ended in a bloody tragedy. The Indians resisted with arms, and, stabbing three of the soldiers, so exasperated the rest, already excited by the murder of their captain, that they fell upon the miserable wretches and butchered them to a man.

This unhappy event, completing what the indiscreet severities of Governor Lyttleton had begun, united the whole nation of Cherokees in war. There had been a strong party favorable to peace, and friendly to the whites. This unfortunate proceeding involved the loss of this party. The hostages were among their chief men, and scarcely a family in the nation but lost a relative or friend in their massacre. They were now unanimous for battle; and, numerous parties rushing simultaneously down upon the frontiers, baffled the courage and prevented the flight of the fugitives. They fell without distinction upon men, women and children. "Such as fled to the woods and escaped the scalping-knife, perished of hunger...Every day brought fresh accounts to the capital of their ravages, murders and desolations. But while the back settlers looked to their governor for relief, the smallpox raged to such a degree in town that few of the militia could be prevailed upon to leave their distressed families to serve the public."[12] Lyttleton, meanwhile, by whom all the mischief was occasioned, was made Governor of Jamaica, and the charge of the colony devolved on William Bull, a native—"a man of great integrity and erudition." In the almost hopeless condition of the province, her sisters, North Carolina and Virginia, raised seven troops of rangers for the frontiers; and Colonel Montgomery, afterwards Earl of Eglintoun, was dispatched from Canada, with a battalion of Highlanders and four companies of Royal Scots. Before the end of April, 1760, the camp of rendezvous for a new invasion of the Cherokee territories was established at Monk's Corner. Meanwhile, the health of Carolina had undergone some improvement, and the gentlemen of the country were not idle. They turned out in force as volunteers, and under the spirited direction of Governor Bull, the whole disposable force of the province was put in requisition. Among these, it is not so sure, but is believed, that Francis Marion once more made his appearance as a volunteer. From what we know of his character, his temperament, and that unsatisfied craving which he seems to have shown from the beginning for such excitements, it is reasonable to infer his presence in the field. But, though asserted by tradition, we confess that the records are silent on the subject. Unsatisfactory as at that period they generally are, on this point they are particularly so; and but that his share in this war, before its final conclusion, was not only unquestionable but conspicuous, we should pass over the campaign of Montgomery, with a simple reference to its results.

The Cherokees, meanwhile, were not unobservant of the preparations and approaches of the Carolinians. They gathered themselves up for defence, and in silence matured their half civilized, half primitive modes of warfare. This people, at the period of which we write, were a people of very superior endowments and resources to any of the neighboring savage nations. If less warlike, in the simple sense of the word, than their rivals the Creeks, they were really more to be feared, as it was in consequence of their superior civilisation that they had lost some of their brute ferocity. If they were less reckless, they were better skilled; if less frantic in their fury, they coupled it with a wary vindictiveness which rendered the blow more fatal when it fell. The advances which they had made in civilisation had naturally increased their numbers; while the novel tastes by which their wandering habits were diminished, had necessarily added to their love of country, in adding to the resources and improvements by which its comforts and delights were increased. Thus, neither degraded by the lowest condition in which we find the human animal, nor enervated by the superior luxuries to which he may attain, the Cherokee was perhaps at this time in possession of his greatest vigor; not very remote, in his moral and physical condition, from the Roman when he overcame his Etrurian and Sabine neighbors. The Cherokees occupied a country equally broad and beautiful. It lay in fertile valleys, green meadows, sunny slopes, and mighty forests, along the sides of lofty summits, that circled their extensive territory with natural fortresses of giant grandeur. Spreading from the Broad, or Cherokee river, beyond the Tennessee and the Savannah, it comprised every variety of soil and surface, and while adapted in a high degree to the hands of the agriculturist, seemed almost as easily made secure against the footsteps of invasion. Its apparent securities had made them insolent. Their mountain recesses had never known the presence of this foe. Their fruits and fields, their villages and towns, with the exception of a district that lay upon the Atlantic slopes, were generally fenced in, and admirably protected, by wild and rugged masses of rocky mountains, natural defences, impenetrable, unless through certain passes which a few determined hearts might easily make good against twenty times their number. But the numerical force of this great aboriginal people, seemed of itself sufficiently strong to promise security to their country. At the time of Montgomery's invasion they had no less than sixty-four towns and villages. In an emergency, they could send six thousand warriors into the field. Many of these were armed with the weapons of European warfare——were accustomed to that warfare, and were thus doubly prepared to encounter the enemy in whose ranks they had received their best military lessons. Such a force very far exceeded that of the Carolinians. Mustering but two thousand men, Col.

Montgomery found it advisable to urge his march upon the nation with equal celerity and caution. Having reached a place called Twelve-mile River, within twenty miles of the Indian town of Estatoee, he advanced by night upon it, secretly, and with a view to its surprise. In his march, surrounding the town of Little Keowee, not a warrior of the Cherokees escaped the sword. His success was less complete at Estatoee. The Indians, apprised of his approach, with few exceptions, succeeded in making their escape; but the town, consisting of more than two hundred houses, and well stored with corn, hogs, poultry and ammunition, perished in the flames. Shugaw Town and every other settlement in the "Lower Nation," shared the same fate. The lightning-like rapidity of the march had taken the savages everywhere, in this part of the country, by surprise. They fled rather than fought, and while they lost everything in the shape of property, but few of them were slain. They sought for shelter among their more numerous and better protected brethren of the mountains; a people neither so easily approached, nor so easily overcome.

Montgomery, having finished this part of his work so successfully, hurried on to the relief of Fort Prince George, which, from the time when their Chiefs were so cruelly butchered within its walls, had been closely invested by a formidable force of Cherokees. The fort was relieved. The Indians fled at his approach; and, thinking that the severe chastisement which he had inflicted upon them, had inclined their hearts to peace, the General of the Carolinians paused in his progress, to give them an opportunity to sue for it, as the former friends and allies of the English. But he had mistaken the stubborn nature of his foe. They were not sufficiently humbled, and it was resolved to march upon the "middle settlements." To this task, that which had been performed was comparatively easy. They were now to enter upon a different country, where the Indians were better prepared for them—nay, where they *had* prepared for them,—in all probability, to the neglect of the lower towns. Toilsome and full of peril was this march. Dismal and dense was the wilderness which they were now to penetrate. Rugged paths, narrow passes, gloomy thickets and dark ravines, encountered them in their hourly progress, calling for constant vigilance and the maintenance of all their courage. Rivers, fordable in unfrequent places and overlooked by precipitous banks on either side, crowned most commonly by dense and intricate masses of forest, through which and without a guide, our little army was compelled to pass,—presented opportunities for frequent ambush and attack, in which, very inferior forces, if properly commanded, might, with little danger to themselves, overwhelm and utterly destroy an advancing enemy. It was in such a region that the Cherokees made their first and formidable stand. Within five miles of Etchoee, the nearest town of the middle settlements, the army of Montgomery approached a low valley, clothed with a thicket so dense that the soldiers could scarcely discern objects three paces ahead. Through this thicket ran a muddy river, enclosed between steep banks of clay. This passage, where but few men could act in unison, was that through which it became necessary that the army should proceed. It was the very spot, which, over all others, a sagacious warrior would choose in which to place an ambush, or meet a superior assailant. Montgomery knew his enemy, and prepared for the encounter. Captain Morrison, commanding a company of rangers, native marksmen and well acquainted with the forest—was sent forward to scour the thicket. His advance was the signal for battle. Scarcely had he entered upon the dismal passage when the savages rose from their hiding-places and poured in a severe fire. Morrison, with several of his men, perished at the first discharge. They were sustained by the light Infantry and Grenadiers, who boldly advanced upon the wood in the face of the invisible foe. A heavy fire followed on both sides, the Cherokees, each with his eye upon his man, the Carolinians aiming at the flash of the enemy guns. The pass was disputed by the savages with a degree of conduct and courage, which left the issue doubtful. The necessity was apparent for extraordinary effort. The Royal Scots, who were in the rear, were now pushed forward to take possession of a rising ground on the right, while the Highlanders were marched forward to the immediate support of the infantry and Grenadiers. This movement had the effect of bringing the enemy into close action. The bayonet stirred and laid bare the thicket. The woods resounded with the shouts and yells of the Cherokees, but they no longer fell with terror upon the ear of the whites. They had grown familiar. The savages yielded slowly as the bayonet advanced. Suffering severely as they fled, they yet displayed the native obstinacy of their race,—turning upon the pursuer when they could, availing themselves of tree or thicket to retard, by shot or stroke, the assailants; and, even in flight, only so far keeping ahead of the bayonet as to avoid its stroke. As he beheld this, Montgomery changed the head of his army, and advanced upon the town of Etchoee, which it had been their purpose to defend, and from which they now strove to divert him. This movement alarmed them for their wives and children. Their retreat became a flight; and, satisfied with having inflicted upon them this measure of punishment, the British General prepared to march back to Fort Prince George.

This decision was the result of his exigencies. The situation of his army was neither a safe nor an agreeable one. The victory was with the Carolinians, yet the affair was very far from decisive in its consequences. The enemy had only retired from one advantageous position to another. They waited his approach only to renew a conflict in which even victory might be without its fruits. To gain a battle, unless a final one, was, with a force so small as his, a matter of very doubtful advantage. He was already encumbered with his wounded, to furnish horses for whom, he was compelled to discard, and to destroy, a large quantity of the provisions necessary for the army. What remained was measured with a nice reference to their absolute wants on the return march to Prince George. Under these suggestions of prudence the retreat was begun. It was conducted with admirable regularity. The Cherokees, meanwhile, hung upon the retiring footsteps of the invaders, annoying them to the utmost of their power. Sixty miles of mountainous country were traversed in this manner, and under various hardships, with a skill and intrepidity which confer the highest credit upon the English captain. A large train of wounded was brought to the frontier without the loss of a man.

We have admitted an uncertainty as to the presence of Marion in this campaign. It would be impertinent and idle, therefore, to speculate upon his performances, or the share which he might have taken in its events. Tradition simply assures us that he distinguished himself. That, if present, he did his duty, we have no question; and, enduring with becoming resolution the worst severities of the march, proved himself possessed of the first great requisite for soldiership in Indian warfare.

CHAPTER IV

CHEROKEE WAR CONTINUED † MARION LEADS THE FORLORN HOPE AT THE BATTLE OF ETCHOEE

The Cherokees were very far from being subdued or satisfied. The snake had been "scotched not killed," and stung, rather than humbled by the chastisement they received, they prepared to assume the offensive with sudden vigor. Concentrating a numerous force upon the distant garrison of Fort Loudon, on the Tennessee river, they succeeded in reducing it by famine. Here they took bloody revenge for the massacre of their chiefs at Prince George. The garrison was butchered, after a formal surrender upon terms which guaranteed them protection. This wholesale and vindictive barbarity, while it betrayed the spirit which filled the savages, had the still farther effect of encouraging them in a warfare which had so far gratified very equally their appetites for blood and booty. In addition to this natural effect, the result of their own wild passions, there were other influences, from without, at work among them. Certain French emissaries had crept into their towns and were busily engaged, with bribes and arguments, in stimulating them to continued warfare. This, in all probability, was the secret influence, which, over all, kept them from listening, as well to their own fears, as to the urgent suggestions of the British authorities, for peace. Hitherto, the Cherokees had given no ear to the temptations of the French, whom they considered a frivolous people, and whose professions of faith they were very likely to have regarded with distrust. But the labors of their emissaries at this juncture, harmonizing with the temper of the nation, were necessarily more than usually successful. One of these emissaries, Louis Latinac, an officer of considerable talent, proved an able instigator to mischief. He persuaded them, against the better reason of their older chiefs, to the rejection of every overture for peace. Their successes at Fort Loudon were, perhaps, sufficient arguments for the continuance of war, but there were others not less potent. The king of France was now to be their ally in place of him of Great Britain. The one "great father" was no less able than the other to minister to their appetites and necessities. His arms and ammunition replaced those which had been withdrawn by the latter; and we may suppose that the liberality of the new allies was such as to admit of very favorable comparison and contrast with that which they had experienced at the hands of the British. Their very excesses in the war were favorable to its continuance; as they might very well doubt the binding force of treaties between parties, the bad faith of whom had been written so terribly in blood. At a great meeting of the nation, at which Louis Latinac was present, he, with something of their own manner, seizing suddenly upon a hatchet, struck it violently into a block of wood, exclaiming, as he did so, "Who is the warrior that will take this up for the king of France?" Salouee, a young chief of Estatoee, instantly tore the weapon from the tree. He declared himself for instant and continued war. "The spirits of our slain brothers," was his cry, "call upon us to avenge their massacre. He is a woman that dares not follow me!"

Such being the spirit of the savages, the Carolinians had no alternative but to resume their arms. Col. Montgomery having gone to England, the command devolved upon Colonel Grant, and the Highlanders were once more ordered to the relief of the province. The Carolinians were now somewhat better prepared to co-operate with their allies. A native regiment of twelve hundred men was raised, and the command given to Col. Middleton, a brave and accomplished provincial officer.

To this regiment Marion was attached, under the immediate command of Moultrie. Many of his associates in this Cherokee war became subsequently, like himself, distinguished in the war with Great Britain. Among these may be mentioned the names of Moultrie,[13] Henry Laurens, Andrew Pickens and Isaac Huger. These were all officers, even in that early day, and Marion himself held a lieutenancy—some proof that, however little we may know of the circumstances by which he secured the confidence of his neighbors, he was already in full possession of it. How much of the future acts and successes of these brave men was due to the exercises and events of this Cherokee war, may reasonably be conjectured by every reader who knows the value of a stern apprenticeship to a hazardous profession. Its successive campaigns against no inferior enemy, and under circumstances of peril and privation of no common order, were such as must have afforded them frequent opportunity of making themselves familiar equally with the exigencies and responsibilities of command.

To the united forces of Colonels Grant and Middleton, were added a certain number of Chickasaw and Catawba Indians; making a total of twenty-six hundred men. This army reached Fort Prince George on the 29th of May, 1761. On the 7th of June following, it took up the line of march for the enemy's country. The advance was conducted with caution, but without molestation, until it reached the place where Montgomery, in the previous campaign, had encountered the Indians, near the town of Etchoee. Here the Cherokees were again prepared to make a stand, and to dispute a pass which, above all others, seemed to be admirably designed by nature for the purposes of defence. Their position was not exactly what it had been on the previous occasion, but its characteristic advantages were the same. Hitherto, the Indians had shown considerable judgment in the selection of their battlegrounds, and in the general employment of their strength. This judgment they probably owed in great part to their present adversaries. Quick in their instinct, and surprisingly observant, they had soon learned the use of European weapons. The various lessons of European tactics, the modes of attack and defence, were, in their united struggles with the French, equally open to their study and acquisition. They had not suffered these lessons to escape them. But they probably owed something of their skill in the present war to the active counsels of the French emissaries. The fact is not recorded by the historian, but there is no reason to suppose that the officers who counselled the war, would withhold themselves when the opportunity offered, from giving directions in the field. The French had frequently distinguished themselves, by leading on forces entirely composed of Indians. The practice was common. Even at the defeat of Braddock, the French troops bore but a small proportion to their Indian allies. There is no reason to suppose that Louis Latinac was not present at one or both of the bloody fields of Etchoee.

The provincial army marched in good order upon the suspected position. The Indian auxiliaries, who were in the van, first discovered signs of an enemy. The Cherokees were in possession of a hill, strongly posted, and in considerable force, upon the right flank of the army. Finding themselves discovered, they opened their fire upon the advanced guard, and followed it up with a gallant charge. But the van being vigorously and promptly supported, they were driven back, and resumed their position upon the hill. Under this hill the line of march lay for a considerable distance. To attempt, therefore, to continue the march before dislodging the enemy in possession of it, would be to expose the troops to a protracted fire, the more murderous, as it would be delivered by a foe in a position of perfect security. The advanced guard was ordered upon this duty, and from this body a forlorn hope of thirty men was chosen, to force the perilous entrance to the foe. The command of this devoted corps was assigned to Francis Marion, still a lieutenant under the command of Moultrie, in the provincial regiment of Middleton. The ascent of the hill was by means of a gloomy defile, through which the little band, headed gallantly by their leader, advanced with due rapidity; a considerable body of the army moving forward at the same time in support of the advance. Scarcely had the detachment penetrated the defile, when the war-whoop gave the signal. The savages, still concealed, poured in a deadly fire, by which no less than twenty-one of this fated band were prostrated.[14] Fortunately their leader was not among them. He seems, like Washington, to have been the special care of Providence. The residue were only saved from destruction by the proximity of the advance, whose hurried approach, while giving them safety, brought on the main action. The battle was fought with great carnage on both sides. The Cherokees were not only well posted, but they were in great numbers. Repeatedly dislodged by the bayonet, they as repeatedly returned to the attack; and, driven from one quarter, rallied upon another, with a tenacious and unshaken valor becoming in men who were defending the passes to the bosom of their country. From eight in the morning until noon, the fight was continued, not only without intermission, but seemingly without any decisive results on either side. But, at length, the patient resolution of the whites prevailed; and, about two o'clock in the day, the field was yielded by the reluctant Cherokees to their superior foes. This victory determined the fate of Etchoee, a town of considerable size, which was reduced to ashes.

The result of this fierce engagement seems to have broken the spirit of the nation. They had chosen the position of greatest strength to make their stand, and brought to the struggle their best spirits and bravest warriors. In the issue, they had shown, by their dogged and determined valor, the great importance which it carried in their eyes. The day once decided against them, they appeared to be equally without heart and hope; they no longer appeared in arms—no longer offered defence—and the army of the Carolinians marched through the heart of the nation, searching its secret settlements, and everywhere inflicting the severest penalties of war. The rest of the campaign was an easy progress, and terrible was the retribution which it brought with it. No less than fourteen of their towns, in the middle settlements, shared the fate of Etchoee. Their granaries were yielded to the flames, their cornfields ravaged, while the miserable fugitives, flying from the unsparing sword, took refuge, with their almost starving families, among the barren mountains, which could yield them little but security. A chastisement so extreme was supposed to be necessary, in order to subdue for ever that lively disposition for war, upon the smallest provocation, which, of late years, the Cherokees had manifested but too frequently; but it may be doubted whether the means which were employed for administering this admonitory lesson, were of the most legitimate character. We must always continue to doubt that humanity required the destruction of towns and

Marion leading the Forlorn Hope, at the Battle of Etchou.

hamlets, whose miserable walls of clay and roofs of thatch could give shelter to none but babes and sucklings—women with their young—those who had never offended, and those who could not well offend—the innocent victims to an authority which they never dared oppose. The reckless destruction of their granaries—fields yet growing with grain—necessarily exposed to the worst privations of famine only those portions of the savage population who were least guilty. The warrior and hunter could readily relieve himself from the gnawing necessities of hunger. He could wander off to remote tribes, and, armed with rifle or bow, could easily secure his game, sufficient for his own wants, from the contiguous forest. But these were resources inaccessible to the weak, the old, the timid, and the imbecile. Surely, it was a cruel measure of war, and if necessary to the safety of the whites, renders still more criminal the wanton excesses of the latter, by which it was originally provoked. It is pleasing to be able to show that Marion felt, in this matter, as became that rare humanity which was one of the most remarkable and lovely traits in his character,—the more remarkable, indeed, as shining out among endowments which, in particular, designated him for a military life—a life which is supposed to need for its stimulus so much that is sanguinary, if not brutal, in one's nature. It is recorded of him, that the severities practised in this campaign filled him, long after, with recollections of sorrow. Writing to a friend,[15] he gives a brief description of the calamities of the war, in terms equally touching and picturesque. "We arrived," he writes, "at the Indian towns in the month of July. As the lands were rich, and the season had been favorable, the corn was bending under the double weight of lusty roasting ears and pods of clustering beans. The furrows seemed to rejoice under their precious loads—the fields stood thick with bread. We encamped the first night in the woods, near the fields, where the whole army feasted on the young corn, which, with fat venison, made a most delicious treat.

"The next morning we proceeded, by order of Colonel Grant, to burn down the Indian cabins. Some of our men seemed to enjoy this cruel work, laughing very heartily at the curling flames as they mounted, loud-crackling, over the tops of the huts. But to me it appeared a shocking sight. "Poor creatures!" thought I, "we surely need not grudge you such miserable habitations." But when we came, *according to orders*, to cut down the fields of corn, I could scarcely refrain from tears. For who could see the stalks that stood so stately, with broad green leaves and gaily-tasselled shocks, filled with sweet milky fluid, and flour, the staff of life—who, I say, without grief, could see these sacred plants sinking under our swords, with all their precious load, to wither and rot untasted, in their mourning fields!

"I saw everywhere around the footsteps of the little Indian children, where they had lately played under the shelter of the rustling corn. No doubt they had often looked up with joy to the swelling shocks, and gladdened when they thought of their abundant cakes for the coming winter. When we are gone, thought I, they will return, and peeping through the weeds with tearful eyes, will mark the ghastly ruin poured over their homes, and the happy fields where they had so often played. "Who did this?" they will ask their mothers. "The white people, the Christians did it!" will be the reply.

"It would be no easy matter," says Hewatt, the earliest regular historian of Carolina, "to describe the hardships which this little army endured, in the wilderness, from heat, thirst, watching, danger, and fatigue. Thirty days did Colonel Grant continue in the heart of the Cherokee territories, and upon his return to Fort Prince George, the feet and legs of many of his army were so mangled, and their strength and spirits so much exhausted, that they were unable to march farther." But the chastisement which the Indians had received, secured the object for the attainment of which it was inflicted. The Cherokees sued for peace, and Marion once more retired to the obscurity of rural life; we may well believe with a human sense of satisfaction, that the painful duty upon which he had been engaged was at length over. Unhappily, the details of the war, beyond those which we have given, do not enable us to ascertain the extent of his services. We are simply told that he behaved well, with skill and spirit. More than this perhaps it would be unreasonable to expect from any degree of talent, in the subordinate situation which he at that time occupied.

CHAPTER V

1775 † MARION IS RETURNED TO THE PROVINCIAL CONGRESS FROM ST. JOHN'S, BERKELEY † MADE CAPTAIN IN THE 2D REGIMENT † FORT JOHNSON TAKEN † BATTLE OF FORT MOULTRIE

E ngaged in rural and domestic occupations we hear no more of Marion, except as a citizen and farmer, until the beginning of the year 1775. In the latter capacity he is reputed to have been successful; and between the labors and sports of the field, the more violent humors of youth seem to have been dissipated in exercises which are seldom followed by reproach. He was very fond of angling and hunting, and with rod or gun, his leisure was employed in a way that would not have displeased the gentle Isaak Walton. These constituted his chief pastimes for the fourteen years that had elapsed since his Cherokee campaigns. His connection with public events had long since ceased; but, from all accounts, he still continued, in some degree, to fill the eyes of his countrymen. His firmness and purity of character, his gentle temper, known bravery, and the conduct which he had already manifested in war, had secured to him the confidence and the affections of his neighbors. He had attained that place in their esteem which naturally brought him conspicuously before their eyes in the moment of emergency. Emergencies were now approaching of a kind well calculated to bring into the field all the energies, with all the patriotism of the country. The great struggle was at hand between the colonies and that mighty empire by which they had been established. Of the part taken by South Carolina in this conflict, history has already sufficiently informed us. Her movements were made without reserve—her resolves taken promptly, and steadily maintained with her best blood and treasure. Her battles were among the boldest and bloodiest, as they were among the first and last of the revolution. Of the political steps by which she committed herself to that event, it does not need that we should enter into details. These belong rather to general history than to biography. It will be enough to exhibit those particulars only, of her progress, in which the subject of our memoir was more immediately interested. That he took an early and deep concern in the contest may be inferred from his character. That he should not have become an active politician may also be inferred from his known modesty, and the general reserve of his deportment in society. He was no orator, and no doubt felt quite as awkward in debate as Washington. But his opinions were well known; he was not the person about whose ways of thinking, in trying times, his neighbors could entertain either doubt or discussion. He formed his opinions as promptly as he fought for them, and his character was above concealment. We find him accordingly, in 1775, returned to the Provincial Congress of South Carolina, as a member from St. John, Berkeley.[16] This Congress distinguished itself by committing the people of South Carolina to the final destinies of the Revolution. It adopted the American Bill of Rights, as declared by the Continental Congress—adopted the famous "act of association," recommended by the same federative body to all the colonies, by which the subscribers bound themselves to refuse and to prevent the importation of goods, wares and merchandize, from the mother country; established committees of safety throughout the province, and, in short, in possession of almost dictatorial powers, did not hesitate to use them for the public welfare. It was at particular pains to infuse a martial spirit among the people; and, influenced by this spirit, and under the immediate suggestion, and by direct participation, of this assembly, certain overt acts of treason were committed. The public armory in Charleston was broken open by night, and eight hundred stand of arms, two hundred cutlasses, besides cartouches, flints, matches and other necessary materials of war, were withdrawn without discovery. One party possessed itself of the public powder at Hobcau; another emptied Cochran's Magazine, while a third, as above stated, relieved the state armory of its contents. In all these proceedings, the members of the Provincial Congress displayed the energies of men, who, having once set their hands to the plough, have resolved not to be turned away from it. Under that bolder policy which, by provoking the danger, compels the timid to a part in it from which they might otherwise shrink in terror, they were personally engaged in these acts of treason. We may reasonably conclude that, however silent as a member, Francis Marion was not the person to forbear taking active part in the more hazardous duties which distinguished the doings of the body to which he belonged. There was a generous impulse in his character, which hurried him into performance, whenever work was to be done, or daring became necessary. He could approach such duties with a degree of cheerfulness, which to the ordinary mind, thoughtful only of the consequences and responsibilities of action, seemed to partake of levity and recklessness. There was, indeed, an element of playfulness, we had almost said fun, in his character; a quiet and unobtrusive humor, which enlivened his utterance, and softened, with a gentle aspect, a countenance that might otherwise have been esteemed severe. We have no doubt that the native courage, and the elastic spirit of his temperament made him an active participant in all those deeds of decision, which the deliberations of the body to which he belonged, deemed it necessary should be done. We can very well imagine him conspicuous among those masked and midnight bands, commissioned to do mischief for the public good, by which the arsenals were stripped of their contents, and the tea-chests tumbled into Cooper river.[17]

The Provincial Congress having thus committed the country, without doubt, to the destinies of war, and having, to some extent, provided against its consequences, adjourned to re-assemble on the 20th June, 1775. But this interval was shortened by the occurrence of events equally unexpected and important. The battle of Lexington, in the meantime, had taken place, and any hopes which might have been entertained, of a final reconciliation between the two countries, without a trial of strength, was fairly dismissed from every reflecting, if not every loyal mind. Instead of the 20th of June, the Provincial Congress was brought together on the first day of that month.[18]

The members of this body, assembling according to summons, proceeded, with the utmost vigor, to the consideration of the subjects before them. They approached their tasks with equal speed and solemnity. Their labors were commenced with Divine Service, and an act of association was then passed, though not without considerable opposition. This act ran as follows:—

"The actual commencement of hostilities against this Continent by the British troops, in the bloody scene of the 19th of April last, near Boston—the increase of arbitrary imposition from a wicked and despotic ministry—and the dread of insurrections in the Colonies—are causes sufficient to drive an oppressed people to the use of arms. We, therefore, the subscribers, inhabitants of South Carolina, holding ourselves bound by that most sacred of all obligations, the duty of good citizens to an injured country, and thoroughly convinced, that, under our present distressed circumstances, we shall be justified before God and man, in resisting force by force—do unite ourselves, under every tie of religion and honor, and associate as a band in her defence, against every foe— hereby solemnly engaging, that, whenever our Continental and Provincial Councils shall deem it necessary, we will go forth, and be ready to sacrifice our lives and fortunes to secure her freedom and safety. This obligation to continue in force, until a reconciliation shall take place between Great Britain and America, upon Constitutional principles—an event which we most ardently desire. And, we will hold all those persons inimical to the liberty of the Colonies, who shall refuse to subscribe to this association."[19]

This open declaration was followed up with measures equally fearless and decisive. On the fourth day of the session, the Provincial Congress resolved to raise fifteen hundred infantry, rank and file, in two regiments; and four hundred and fifty horse, constituting another regiment. The troops so to be raised, were to be subjected to military discipline, and to the articles of war, in like manner with the British. On the fourteenth day of their session, a million of money was voted, and a council of safety was elected, vested with the executive power of the colony. Among other acts of this body, non-subscribers to the association were made amenable to the General Committee, and punishable *according to sound policy*. Absentees having estates, were, with certain exceptions, required to return; and it was further resolved that no persons ought to withdraw from the service of the Colony, without giving good and sufficient reasons to the Provincial Congress. Military duty was performed day and night, as in a state of actual warfare, by the militia companies in rotation; and thus, having placed the province in a state of preparation, with arms in the hands of the people, and given to the newly arrived Governor, Lord William Campbell, a reception which boded small repose to his authority, the Provincial Congress adjourned itself on the 22nd day of June, leaving their authority, in great part, to the Council of Safety and General Committee.

It has been seen that the only share which Marion had in the proceedings of this body, was that of an assenting member. He was not endowed with those talents which could have rendered him conspicuous in a deliberative assembly. But he is not the less entitled to his share in the merit of those proceedings, which so admirably declared and illustrated the patriotism and the spirit of the province; and one of the last, decisive measures of the Provincial Congress, happily enabled him to appear in the character upon which he was more likely to confer distinction, than that of the orator. He was elected a captain in the Second Regiment, of which William Moultrie, formerly his captain in the Cherokee campaign, was made Colonel. The duties of this appointment were immediately begun, with a promptness at once due to the necessities of the case, and his own character. As a proof of the zeal by which the newly made officers were distinguished, we find them seeking recruits so early as the 20th of June, and while the body to which they belonged were still engaged in the most laborious duties of the session.[20]

Marion's commission was made out on the 21st June. Weems, in his life of our author, gives us some pictures, equally lively and ludicrous, of his progress in the business of recruiting, upon which, in connection with his friend, Captain Horry, he at once begun. This gentleman received his appoint as captain at the same time, and in the same regiment, with Marion. The Provincial Congress had voted a million of money, by which to carry out their measures, but this was yet to be procured, and, as it appears, rather more upon the credit of individuals than that of the colony. But money, in times of danger, seems to have an instinct of its own, by which it hides itself readily from sight and touch. It was no easy matter for our captains to obtain the requisite sums. But faith and zeal did more for them, and for the cause, than gold and silver; and with very inadequate supplies, but in fresh and showy uniforms, our young officers set forth on the recruiting service. Their route lay in the several neighborhoods of Georgetown, Black River, and the Great Pedee. In these parts both of them were known. Here, indeed, Marion was already a favorite. Accordingly, they succeeded beyond their expectations, and were soon enabled to complete the full number for their two companies, of fifty men each. Another circumstance, apart from their personal popularity, probably facilitated their objects. Some of the settlements into which they penetrated were originally founded by the Irish. The bitter heritage of hate to the English, which they brought with them to America, was transmitted with undiminished fervor to their descendants. It was easy to show that the power which had trampled upon the affections of their fathers, and tyrannized over their rights in the old world, was aiming at the same objects in the case of their children in the new. At one remove only from the exiled and suffering generation, the sons had as lively a recollection of the tyrannies of Britain as if the experience had been immediately their own. To this cause our recruiting officers owed some of their success in the present expedition. Some of the bravest fellows of the second regiment were picked up on this occasion. It was the spirit which they brought, and to which the genius of Marion gave lively exercise, that imparted a peculiar vitality at all times to his little brigade. Among these gallant young men there were two in particular, of whom tradition in Carolina will long retain a grateful recollection; these were Jasper and Macdonald. Of these two, both of whom sealed their patriotism with their blood, we shall yet have something further to deliver.

While the friends of liberty were thus active, the adherents of the crown, in the colony, were not less so. These, in many parts of the country, were equally numerous and influential. They possessed, indeed, certain advantages in the discussion, which, in some degree, served to counterbalance the impelling and stimulating influences which always belong to a *mouvement* party. They carried with them the *prestige* of authority, of the venerable power which time and custom seemed to hallow; they appealed to the loyalty of the subject; they dwelt upon the dangers which came with innovation; they denounced the ambition of the patriot leaders; they reminded the people of the power of Great Britain—a power to save or to destroy—which had so frequently and so successfully been exerted in their behalf in their numerous and bloody conflicts with the Indians, and which might be brought, with such fearful emphasis, upon their own heads. They reminded the people that the Indians were not exterminated, that they still hung in numerous hordes about the frontiers, and that it needed but a single word from the Crown, to bring them, once more, with tomahawk and scalping-knife, upon their defenceless homes. Already, indeed, had the emissaries of Great Britain taken measures to this end. The savage was already shaking off his apathy, scenting the carnage from afar, and making ready for the onset. The assurance, that such was the case, was doing the work of numerous arguments among the timid and the exposed. Such were the suggestions, appealing equally to their fears and gratitude, which the leading loyalists addressed to the people. They were supported by other suggestions, scarcely less potent, which naturally flowed from their own thoughts. Why should they dare the conflict with Great Britain? There was no such reason for it as in the case of the northern colonies. They had known her chiefly by benefactions; they did not conflict with her in shipping or in manufactures; and the arguments for discontent and resistance, as urged by the patriot leaders, did not reach them with sufficient force. What was the tax on tea, of which they drank little, and the duty on stamps, when they had but little need for legal papers? And why should not taxes follow protection, which Great Britain had not often withheld in the need of a favorite colony, as South Carolina had unquestionably been? Let us do justice to this people. The loyalists—or, as they were more commonly called, and as we shall hereafter be compelled to call them, the Tories—were, probably, in the majority of cases, governed by principle, by a firm and settled conviction, after deliberate examination of the case. That they might have thought otherwise, nay, would gradually have adopted the opinions of the patriots, is not improbable, had more time been allowed them, and had the course of the latter been more indulgent and considerate. Unfortunately, this was not the case; and the desire to coerce where they could not easily convince, had the effect of making a determined and deadly, out of a doubtful foe. This was terribly proved by the after history. To this cause we may ascribe, in some degree, the terrors of that sanguinary strife, in which, to use the language of a distinguished officer, they "pursued each other rather like wild beasts than men."[21] We shall see something of this history as we proceed in ours.

There was yet another circumstance which tended, in some degree, to give courage to the Tories. It was the somewhat temporizing policy of the patriots. There was still a feeling of doubt, a hesitancy, on the part of the latter, as the prospects grew stronger of a final breach with Great Britain. There were many who still clung to the hope that the differences of the two nations might yet be reconciled; and though the means of such reconciliation did not make themselves obvious, they yet fondly cherished the conviction that something might turn up, at the last moment, to prevent the absolute necessity of bloodshed. This portion of the patriots necessarily influenced the rest; those who, looking beyond the moment, saw the true issue, and properly regarded the declared objects of difference as pretexts which must suffice when the better reasons might not be expressed. They dared not openly broach the idea of national independence, which, there is very little question that the noblest of the American patriots everywhere, though secretly, entertained from the beginning. The people were not prepared for such a revelation—such a condition; and appearances were still to be maintained. Their proceedings, accordingly, still wore, however loosely, a pacific aspect. Though actively preparing for war, the professions of the patriots declared their measures to be precautionary only—a refuge, an alternative, in the event of greater oppression. They still spoke the language of loyalty, still dealt in vague assurances of devotion to the crown. But such professions deceived nobody, and least of all the loyalists. They derived courage from the reluctance of the patriots to embark in a struggle, for the fruits of which, if successful, they evidently longed. They were not less active—nay, in the interior, they were even more active—than their opponents; had already taken arms, and gained advantages, which nothing but decisive movements on the part of the people along the seaboard could possibly induce them to forego. This necessity was apparent for other reasons. In consequence of the temporizing policy already mentioned, the crown was still in possession of most of the shows of power in and about Charleston. The royal governor was still in the city, and in some degree exerting his authority. Fort Johnson, on James' Island, was suffered to remain in the hands of the king's troops for more than three months after the Provincial Congress had ordered a levy of troops, and had resolved on taking up arms. Two British armed vessels, the Tamar and Cherokee, lay in Rebellion Roads, opposite Sullivan's Island. This force was quite sufficient, under existing circumstances, to have destroyed the town. But the royal leaders were not prepared for this issue; they shared the reluctance of the patriots to begin a conflict, the issues of which were so extreme. Their policy, like that of the patriots—influencing it, and possibly influenced by it—was equally halting and indecisive. It was sufficiently satisfactory if, by the presence of such a force, the citizens should be overawed and kept from action.

This condition of things could not continue. The very nature of the movement was adverse to indecision. It needed but a first step—a first stroke—and this was to be taken by the patriots. They brooked impatiently the humiliating position in which the city stood, controlled by an inferior enemy; and it was resolved that Fort Johnson should be subdued. It was on this occasion that Marion first drew his sword against the British. He was one of those Captains who, with their companies, were despatched on this expedition. The command was given to Col. Moultrie. A strong resistance was expected, as, but a short time before, the garrison had been reinforced from the armed vessels. At midnight on the fourteenth of September, 1775, the detachment crossed to James Island. The disembarkation was effected with delay and difficulty, occasioned by the inadequate size and number of the boats. The forlorn hope, consisting of a detachment from the grenadiers of Capt. Pinckney, joined by the Cadets, and led by Lieut. Mouatt, were to scale the walls of the fort on its south bastion; Col. Moultrie with the rest of Pinckney's Grenadiers, and Marion's Light Infantry, were to enter or force the gates over the ravelin; while Capt. Elliott, with his grenadiers, penetrated the lower battery over the left flank. It was broad daylight before the landing was effected; and on making the assault they were surprised by an easy victory. The fort was abandoned. The enemy had probably been apprised of the attack. A detachment from the ships had landed some hours before—had dismantled the fort, dismounted the cannon, and withdrawn the garrison; retreating in safety to the ships. A gunner and three men only, fell into the hands of the provincials. The very day that this event occurred, Lord William Campbell, the Governor, fled to the Tamar sloop of war. His flight was no doubt hastened by a proceeding so decisive. That evening he dispatched his secretary to Fort Johnson, which he was not permitted to enter. He was met at the water-side by Capt. Pinckney, of whom he demanded, in the name of the Governor, by what authority he had taken and held possession of the fortress. The answer to this demand brought up the vessels of war, which, on the seventeenth of September, presented themselves within point blank shot of the fort. Up to this time, but three of the dismantled cannon had been remounted and put in order for action. With these, the provincials prepared for battle, relying, however, less upon their cannon than upon their ability to oppose the landing of any body of men. But the demonstration of the squadron was without fruits. They hauled off without a shot, and resumed their former less offensive position.

Here, however, the popular leaders were not disposed to suffer them to remain. Still they hesitated at coming to blows. They adopted a middle course, which, in such cases, is generally the worst. They ordered that the ships should not be victualled or supplied with water from the city, except from day to day. This produced a threat from Captain Thornborough that, unless supplied as before, he should prevent the ingress, or departure, of any vessel from the harbor. A menace of this kind, to have been properly met, should have been answered from the eighteen pounders of Fort Johnson. And, but for the reluctance of several highly esteemed patriots, such would have been the mode of answer. This temporizing policy continued to prevail until the 9th November, 1775, when the Provincial Congress resolved, "by every military operation, to oppose the passage of any British Armament." Such were the orders issued to the officer commanding at Fort Johnson. This fort had now been in possession of the popular party for nearly two months. It was in some degree prepared for use. It was well manned with a portion of those brave fellows who afterwards fought the good fight of Fort Sullivan. They would have done as good service here. The resolution of the Province once adopted, it was communicated as well to the commanders of the British vessels, as to the officers of the fort. There was still an open passage, through Hog-Island channel, by which the British vessels might approach the town without incurring any danger from the Fort. This passage it was determined to obstruct; and an armed schooner, called the Defence, fitted up for the occasion, was ordered to cover and protect a party which was employed to sink a number of hulks in that narrow strait. This drew upon them the fire of the British. It was returned by the "Defence," but with little injury to either side. The garrison at Fort Johnson endeavored to take part in this little action, but the distance was too great for any decisive results from its fire. Some of the shots took effect, but after a few rounds the fire was discontinued. Meanwhile, the alarm was beat in Charleston, where the troops stood to their arms, and every heart throbbed with the expectation of a close and bloody fight. But the time was not yet. Indecisive in itself, this brief combat was of great importance in one point of view. It was the beginning of the game. The blow for which all parties had been waiting, was now fairly struck. The sword had been drawn from the scabbard, not again to be sheathed, till the struggle was concluded. The local Congress proceeded vigorously. Ships were impressed for the purpose of war, new troops were enlisted and armed, and bills of credit issued. The British vessels, meanwhile, became more than ever troublesome, and, carrying out the menace of Captain Thornborough, proceeded to the seizure of all vessels within their reach, whether going from or returning to the port. It became necessary to drive them from the roadstead. To effect this, Col. Moultrie, with a party of newly raised Provincials and the Charleston Artillery, took post on Haddrill's Point, and, mounting a few pieces of heavy artillery, opened upon them with a well-directed fire, which drove them out to sea. This step was followed by one of preparation. The fortifications at Fort Johnson and Haddrill's Point were completed—the city was fortified—a new fort was raised on James and another begun on Sullivan's Island. The militia were diligently trained, the provincial troops augmented and disciplined, and all means within the power of the Colony were put in requisition to prepare it for defence. Among other preparations a military post was established at the town of Dorchester, and strongly fortified. This post was nearly at the head of navigation, on Ashley river, about twenty miles from Charleston. Though now utterly desolate, Dorchester was, prior to the Revolution, a town of considerable population and importance. Its abandonment may be ascribed to the Revolution, during which it was maintained as a military post by the Americans or British. To this place the public stores and records were in great part transferred from Charleston, as to a place of safe-keeping. The command was given to Marion. While in this command we do not find the occurrence of any events of importance. A couple of his original letters, dated from this post, lie before us. They refer only to ordinary events, but contain some expressions which denote the ardency of his patriotism, and the disappointments to which it was not unfrequently subjected in consequence of the apathy of others. Referring to the reluctance shown by many, of whom the utmost patriotism was expected, to rally around the flag of the country, he exclaims—in a partial perversion of Scripture language, but without irreverence, "Tell this not in the streets of Charleston," &c.

From this post Marion was removed to Charleston, very probably at his own solicitation. Events were ripening in that quarter, of a nature calculated to give becoming employment to a mind always active, and desiring nothing more than to serve his country. From Charleston, he was dispatched to Fort Johnson, where he was busily employed in completing the defences of that place. Weems preserves an anecdote of him, while in command of this fort, in January, 1776, which pleasantly describes the quiet and not unamiable sort of humor in which Marion was frequently said to indulge. While exceedingly busy in his preparations for defence, there came to him a thoughtless young officer, who loved the cockpit much better than consisted entirely with his duties. Christmas and New Year's Holidays were famous at that early period, for the exercise of this cruel sport in some parts of Carolina. To obtain leave of absence, however, on any holiday pretence, the young officer very well knew was impossible. Approaching his Commander with a lie in his mouth, he obtained the desired permission, in order to receive the last blessing of a dying father; and, exulting in the unworthy artifice, he hurried to Dorchester, which, on that occasion, was to be the scene of his recreation. During his absence, Marion arrived at the truth of the story, but said nothing. When the youth returned, which he did after two weeks' absence, he proceeded to the marquee of his Commander, to report himself, and began a tedious apology for having stayed, so long. Marion gently interrupted him, and, with a smile, in the presence of all the officers, replied—"Never mind it, Lieutenant— there's no harm done—we never missed you." The effect of this sarcasm is said to have been admirable; and to have resulted in the complete reform of the offender, who, from being a trifling, purposeless, and unscrupulous young man, grew considerate equally of his duties and his word, and, by a career of industry, sobriety and modesty, made ample amends, in future days, for all the errors of the past.

With the formation of new regiments, under the resolves of the Council of Safety, Marion was promoted to a Majority. This appointment materially enlarged the sphere of his duties. But he was one of those remarkable men, who, without pretension, prove themselves equal to any trust which may be imposed upon them. Without the presence of an actual enemy, he addressed himself to the task of preparing his men, for the encounter with them. He was constantly on parade, at the drill, closely engaged in the work of training, in which business, while very gentle, he was very exact; and, in such a degree had he improved the officers and men immediately under his charge, that they were very soon regarded as a model for all the rest. He was called the "architect of the Second Regiment. Weems, speaking for Col. Horry, says, "Indeed, I am not afraid to say that Marion was the *architect of* the Second Regiment, and laid the foundation of that excellent discipline and confidence in themselves, which gained them such reputation whenever they were brought to face their enemies." The value of this training was very soon to be subjected to the most thorough of all possible tests. He was ordered with his Regiment, under command of Col. Wm. Moultrie, to take post at Fort Sullivan, on the island of that name, which stands at the entrance of Charleston harbor, and within point blank shot of the channel. The difficulties and deficiencies of this post, furnished some admirable preparatory lessons for the great conflict which was to follow. They imposed the necessity of diligent industry and hard labor, equally on men and soldiers. This was one of the famous schools of Roman discipline. Fort Sullivan, better known as Fort Moultrie—was yet to be built. When the Second Regiment entered it, it was little more than an outline. Its shape was described upon the sand, and the palmetto rafts lay around it, waiting to be moulded into form. The structure was an inartificial one—a simple wall, behind which young beginners might train guns to do mischief to a veteran enemy in front. Its form was square, with a bastion at each angle, sufficiently large, when finished, to cover a thousand men. If was built of logs, laid one upon another in parallel rows, at a distance of sixteen feet, bound together at frequent intervals with timber, dove-tailed and bolted into the logs. The spaces between were filled up with sand. The merlons were walled entirely by palmetto logs, notched into one another at the angles, well bolted together and strengthened with pieces of massy timber. Such was the plan of the work; but, with all the diligence of the officers, and all the industry of the men, it remained unfinished at the perilous moment when a powerful British fleet appeared before its walls. The defence was confided to Col. Moultrie. The force under his command was four hundred and thirty-five men, rank and file, comprising four hundred and thirteen of the Second Regiment of Infantry, and twenty-two of the Fourth Regiment of Artillery. The whole number of cannon mounted on the fortress was thirty-one, of these, nine were French twenty-sixes; six English eighteens; nine twelve and seven nine pounders.[22]

General Charles Lee, who had been dispatched by the Continental Congress, to take command of the Army of the South, would have abandoned the fortress even before the appearance of the enemy. He was unwilling, in such a position, to abide the conflict. He seems, naturally enough for an officer brought up in a British Army, to have had an overweening veneration for a British fleet, in which it is fortunate for the country that the Carolinians did not share. In the unfinished condition of the fort, which really presented little more than a front towards the sea, his apprehensions were justifiable, and, could the fort have been enfiladed, as the British designed, it certainly would have been untenable. From the moment of his arrival, to the very moment when the action was raging, his chief solicitude seems to have been to ensure the defenders of the fortress a safe retreat. It is to their immortal honor that this mortifying measure was unnecessary.

On the 20th of June, 1776, a day ever memorable in the annals of Carolina, the British ships of war, nine in number,[23] commanded by Sir Peter Parker, drew up abreast of the fort, let go their anchors, with springs upon their cables, and commenced a terrible bombardment. The famous battle which followed makes one of the brightest pages in our history. Its events, however, are too generally known to make it necessary that we should dwell upon them here. A few, however, belong properly and especially to our pages. The subject of this memoir was a conspicuous sharer in its dangers and in its honors. The fire of the enemy was promptly answered, and with such efficiency of aim as to be long remembered by the survivors. Having but five thousand pounds of powder, with which to maintain a conflict that raged for eleven hours, with unabated violence, it became necessary, not only that the discharge from the fort should be timed, but that every shot should be made to do execution. In order to do this the guns were trained by the field officers in person; hence, perhaps, the terrible fatality of their fire. The Bristol, 50 gun ship, Commodore Sir Peter Parker, lost 44 men killed and thirty[24] wounded. Sir Peter himself lost an arm. The Experiment, another 50 gun ship, had 57 killed and 30 wounded.[25] To these two vessels in particular, the attention of the fort was directed. The words, passed along the line by officers and men, were—"Look to the Commodore—look to the fifty gun ships."[26] The smaller vessels suffered comparatively little. Their loss of men was small. The injury to the vessels themselves was greater, and one of them, the Acteon, run aground, and was subsequently burnt. The Carolinians lost but twelve men killed and twice that number wounded. One of the former was the brave fellow Macdonald, of whom we have already spoken. When borne from the embrasure where he received his mortal wound, he cried out to those around him—"Do not give up—you are fighting for liberty and country." The want of powder was severely felt. But for this, judging from the effects of the fire from the fort, the British Commodore must have struck, or his fleet must have been destroyed. So slow, at one time, were the discharges—so great the interval of time between them,—that the British were of opinion that the place was abandoned. But a new supply of powder was obtained by Marion, who, with a small party, leaving the fort, proceeded to the armed schooner Defence, lying in Stop Gap Creek, and seized upon her powder, by which the fire was kept up until a supply of five hundred weight was received from the city.[27] This caused a renewal of the conflict in all its fury. The garrison fought with a coolness which would have done honor to veterans. The day was very warm, and the men partially stripped to it. Moultrie says, "When the action begun (it being a warm day), some of the men took off their coats and threw them upon the top of the merlons. I saw a shot take one of them and throw it into a small tree behind the platform. It was noticed by our men, and they cried out, "look at the coat!" A little incident that speaks volumes for their coolness. Moultrie himself and several of his officers smoked their pipes during the action, only removing them when it became necessary to issue orders. In the hottest fire of the battle the flag of the fort was shot away, and fell without the fort. Jasper, with whom we have already brought the reader acquainted as one of Marion's men, instantly sprang after it upon the beach, between the ramparts and the enemy, and binding it to a sponge staff, restored it to its place, and succeeded in regaining his own in safety. We shall hear more hereafter, of this gallant fellow.[28] The coolness—nay the cavalier indifference—displayed by the Carolinians throughout the combat, is not its least remarkable feature. There is something chivalric in such deportment, which speaks for larger courage than belongs to ordinary valor. Mere bull-dog resolution and endurance is here lifted, by a generous ardor of soul, into something other than a passive virtue. The elasticity of spirit which it shows might be trained to any performance within the compass of human endowment.

Tradition ascribes to the hand and eye of Marion, the terrible effect of the last shot which was fired on this bloody day. It was aimed at the Commodore's ship, which had already received something more than her due share of the attention of the fort. This shot, penetrating the cabin of the vessel, cut down two young officers who were drinking, we may suppose, to their fortunate escape from a conflict which seemed already over—then ranging forward, swept three sailors from the maindeck into eternity, and finally buried itself in the bosom of the sea. This curious particular was derived from five sailors who deserted from the fleet that very night.

CHAPTER VI

1777–8–9 † FROM THE BATTLE OF FORT MOULTRIE TO THAT OF SAVANNAH † ANECDOTE OF JASPER † HIS DEATH

The battle of Fort Sullivan was of immense importance, not merely to Carolina, but to all the confederated colonies. It saved the former, for three years, from the calamities of invasion; a respite of the last value to a country so greatly divided in public feeling and opinion. The battle preceded the declaration of Independence, and, though not generally known to have taken place before that decisive measure was resolved upon, it came seasonably to confirm the patriots in those principles which they had so solemnly and recently avowed. Its farther effect was to dissipate that spell of invincibility, which, in the minds of the Americans, seemed to hover about a British armament;—to heighten the courage of the militia, and to convince the most sceptical, that it needed only confidence and practice, to make the American people as good soldiers as any in the world. The Carolina riflemen were not a little elated to discover that they could handle twenty-six pounders as efficiently as the smaller implements of death, to which their hands were better accustomed. To the defenders of the fortress, their victory brought imperishable laurels. They had shown the courage and the skill of veterans, and their countrymen gloried in the reputation in which they necessarily shared. Moultrie received the thanks of Congress, of the Commander in Chief, and of his fellow citizens. The fort was thenceforth called by his name, and he was made a Brigadier-General. His Major, Marion, necessarily had his share in these public honors, and was raised by Congress to the rank of Lieut.-Colonel in the regular service. Two days after the battle, General Lee reviewed the garrison at Fort Moultrie, and thanked them "for their gallant defence of the fort against a fleet of eight men-of-war and a bomb, during a cannonade of eleven hours, and a bombardment of seven." At the same time, Mrs. Barnard Elliott presented an elegant pair of embroidered colors to the Second Regiment, with a brief address, in which she expressed her conviction that they would "stand by them as long as they can wave in the air of liberty." It was in fulfilling the pledge made by General Moultrie, on this occasion, in behalf of the regiment, that the brave Jasper lost his life before the walls of Savannah.

The three years' respite from the horrors of war, which this victory secured to Carolina, was not, however, left unemployed by her citizen soldiery. The progress of events around them kept their services in constant requisition. While a part of them, in the interior, were compelled to take arms against the Cherokee Indians, the troops of the lower country were required against the Tories in Florida and Georgia. Governor Tonya of the former, an active loyalist, proved a formidable annoyance to the patriots of the latter province. Florida, under his administration, was the secure refuge and certain retreat for all the malcontents and outlaws of the neighboring colonies. He gave them ample encouragement, put arms into their hands, and even issued letters of marque against the property of the colonists, in anticipation of the act for that purpose, in the British parliament. General Lee marched upon Florida with the Virginia and North Carolina troops. He was subsequently joined by those of South Carolina; but, owing to his own ill-advised and improvident movements, the expedition was a total failure.[29] This result necessarily gave encouragement to the Tories; and, though in too small numbers to effect any important objects without the co-operation of a British force, they were yet sufficiently active to invite the presence of one. They formed themselves into little squads, and, moving through the country with celerity, pursued their marauding habits at little risk, as they sought only unsuspecting neighborhoods, and promptly fled to the fastnesses of Florida on the approach of danger. To direct and properly avail themselves of these parties, the British commanders in America addressed their attention to Georgia. The infancy of that colony necessarily led them to hope for an easy conquest in attempting it. In February, 1777, General Howe, then commanding the troops in North Carolina and Georgia, was advised of the approach of Colonel Fuser, to the invasion of Georgia. He hurried on immediately to prepare Savannah for defence; while Marion, with a force of 600 men, in several vessels, provided with cannon and ammunition, was dispatched, by the inland passage, to his assistance. Marion left Charleston on the 28th of February, but his approach had no farther effect than to precipitate the flight of the enemy, who, meeting with a stout opposition from Colonel Elbert, at Ogechee ferry, had already desisted from farther advance. The British attempts on Georgia were deferred to a later period. But the loyalists were busy, particularly that portion of them, which took the name of Scopholites, after one Scophol, a militia Colonel, whom Moultrie describes as an "illiterate, stupid, noisy blockhead." He proved not the less troublesome because of his stupidity.

Marion was more or less employed during this period, in various situations. He was never unemployed. We find him at length in command of the fort which he had formerly contributed to defend and render famous. He was placed in charge of the garrison at Fort Moultrie. The value of this fort was estimated rather according to its celebrity, than its real usefulness. Subsequent events have shown that its capacity was not great in retarding the approach of an enemy's fleet to the city. It was the error of Sir Peter Parker—obeying an old but exploded military maxim, not to leave an armed post of the enemy in his rear—to pause before a fortress, the conquest of which could in no wise contribute to his success,—and defeat before which, must necessarily endanger his final objects. It was still the impression of the Carolinians that Fort Moultrie must be assailed as a preliminary step to the conquest of Charleston, and the post, as one of the highest honor and danger, was conferred upon Marion.[30] It was not known, indeed, at what moment the gallantry of the garrison might he put to the proof. The British were known to be making large marine and military preparations at New York, intended, as it was generally understood, for the south. Charleston or Savannah, were supposed indifferently to be the places of its destination. It might be very well supposed that the enemy would seek, at the former place, to recover those honors of war of which its gallant defenders had deprived him.

But, any doubt as to the destination of the British fleet was soon removed. In December, 1778, thirty-seven sail appeared before Savannah, and four thousand British regulars were disembarked. The American force left in defence of Savannah was a feeble one, of six or seven hundred men, under General Howe. General Howe was but little of a soldier. Instead of withdrawing this force, he suffered it to be sacrificed. Badly posted, he was surprised, and his troops beaten and dispersed with little difficulty. Savannah fell at once into the hands of the enemy, and the whole colony very shortly after. General Prevost was in command of the British. Opposed to him was Major-General Lincoln, of the Continental army. While Prevost occupied the posts of Savannah, Ebenezer, Abercorn, and other places, he was active in pushing select parties forward to Augusta, and other commanding points in the interior. The force under Lincoln did not enable him to offer any active opposition to their progress. His head-quarters were at Purysburg, on the Savannah river, but a few miles from Abercorn, where Colonel Campbell lay with the main body of the enemy. General Ashe, of the Americans, occupied the post at Brier Creek, and, thus placed, the opposing commanders seemed disposed for a while to rest upon their arms, waiting events and reinforcements.

It was while the second North Carolina regiment lay at Purysburg, that an adventure occurred, which has so often been repeated in connection with the name and life of Marion, that we should scarcely be excused from introducing it here, as properly in place in this memoir. Weems asserts that Marion was present at this time with his regiment at Purysburg. It is impossible to say whether he was or not. It is not improbable that he was with his regiment, and yet the weight of evidence inclines us to the opinion that he was still at Fort Moultrie. It is not unlikely, however, that, when the direction of the British fleet was known, and it was ascertained that Savannah and not Charleston was its object, he immediately joined his regiment at Purysburg, leaving Fort Moultrie in the charge of some less distinguished officer. At all events the point is not of importance to the anecdote we have to relate. Personally, Marion had nothing to do with it. It was only because the actors in the adventure belonged to his regiment, and were of "Marion's men," that tradition has insisted on associating his name with theirs. It is not for us to have it otherwise. The reader is already so acquainted with the name of William Jasper—perhaps Sergeant Jasper is the better known. This brave man possessed remarkable talents for a scout. He could wear all disguises with admirable ease and dexterity. Garden styles him "a perfect Proteus."[31] He was equally remarkable for his strategy as for his bravery; and his nobleness and generosity were, quite as much as these, the distinguishing traits of his character. Such was the confidence in his fidelity and skill that a roving commission was granted him, with liberty to pick his associates from the Brigade. Of these he seldom chose more than six. "He often went out," says Moultrie, "and returned with prisoners, before I knew that he was gone. I have known of his catching a party that was looking for him. He has told me that he could have killed single men several times, but he would not; he would rather let them get off. He went into the British lines at Savannah, as a deserter, complaining, at the same time, of our ill-usage of him; he was gladly received (they having heard of his character) and caressed by them. He stayed eight days, and after informing himself well of their strength, situation and intentions, he returned to us again; but that game he could not play a second time. With his little party he was always hovering about the enemy's camp, and was frequently bringing in prisoners."[32] We have seen what reason was alleged by this brave fellow for not accepting the commission tendered to him by Governor Rutledge, for his gallantry in the battle of Fort Moultrie. The nature of his services was no less a reason why he should reject the commission. The fact that he seldom allowed himself a command of more than six men declared sufficiently the degree of authority to which he thought his talents were entitled.

It was while in the exercise of his roving privileges that Jasper prepared to visit the post of the enemy at Ebenezer. At this post he had a brother, who held the same rank in the British service, that he held in the American. This instance was quite too common in the history of the period and country, to occasion much surprise, or cause any suspicion of the integrity of either party. We have already considered the causes for this melancholy difference of individual sentiment in the country, and need not dwell upon them here. William Jasper loved his brother and wished to see him: it is very certain, at the same time, that he did not deny himself the privilege of seeing all around him. The Tory was alarmed at William's appearance in the British camp, but the other quieted his fears, by representing himself as no longer an American soldier. He checked the joy which this declaration excited in his brother's mind, assuring him that, though he found little encouragement in fighting for his country, "he had not the heart to fight against her." Our scout lingered for two or three days in the British camp, and then, by a *detour*, regained that of the Americans; reporting to his Commander all that he had seen. He was encouraged to repeat his visit a few weeks after, but this time he took with him a comrade, one Sergeant Newton, a fellow quite as brave in spirit, and strong in body as himself. Here he was again well received by his brother, who entertained the guests kindly for several days. Meanwhile, a small party of Americans were brought into Ebenezer as captives, over whom hung the danger of "short shrift and sudden cord." They were on their way to Savannah for trial. They had taken arms with the British, as hundreds more had done, when the country was deemed reconquered; but, on the approach of the American army, had rejoined their countrymen and were now once more at the mercy of the power with which they had broken faith. "It will go hard with them," said the Tory Jasper to his Whig brother; but the secret comment of the other was, "it shall go hard with me first." There was a woman, the wife of one of the prisoners, who, with her child, kept them company. William Jasper and his friend were touched by the spectacle of their distress; and they conferred together, as soon as they were alone, as to the possibility of rescuing them. Their plan was soon adopted. It was a simple one, such as naturally suggests itself to a hardy and magnanimous character. The prisoners had scarcely left the post for Savannah, under a guard of eight men, a sergeant and corporal, when they took leave of their host, and set forth also, though in a different direction from the guard. Changing their course when secure from observation, they stretched across the country and followed the footsteps of the happy captives. But it was only in the pursuit that they became truly conscious of the difficulty, nay, seeming impossibility, of effecting their object. The guard was armed and ten in number; they but two and weaponless. Hopeless, they nevertheless followed on. Two miles from Savannah there is a famous spring, the waters of which are well known to travellers. The conjecture that the guard might stop there, with the prisoners, for refreshment, suggested itself to our companions; here, opportunities might occur for the rescue, which had nowhere before presented themselves. Taking an obscure path with which they were familiar, which led them to the spot before the enemy could arrive, they placed themselves in ambush in the immediate neighborhood of the spring. They had not long to wait. Their conjecture proved correct. The guard was halted on the road opposite the spring. The corporal with four men conducted the captives to the water, while the sergeant, with the remainder of his force, having made them ground their arms near the road, brought up the rear. The prisoners threw themselves upon the earth—the woman and her child, near its father. Little did any of them dream that deliverance was at hand. The child fell asleep in the mother's lap. Two of the armed men kept guard, but we may suppose with little caution. What had they to apprehend, within sight of a walled town in the possession of their friends? Two others approached the spring, in order to bring water to the prisoners. Resting their muskets against a tree they proceeded to fill their canteens. At this moment Jasper gave the signal to his comrade. In an instant the muskets were in their hands. In another, they had shot down the two soldiers upon duty; then clubbing their weapons, they rushed out upon the astonished enemy, and felling their first opponents each at a blow, they succeeded in obtaining possession of the loaded muskets. This decided the conflict, which was over in a few minutes. The surviving guard yielded themselves to mercy before the presented weapons. Such an achievement could only be successful from its audacity and the operation of circumstances. The very proximity of Savannah increased the chances of success. But for this the guard would have taken better precautions. None were taken. The prompt valor, the bald decision, the cool calculation of the instant, were the essential elements which secured success. The work of our young heroes was not done imperfectly. The prisoners were quickly released, the arms of the captured British put into their hands, and, hurrying away from the spot which they have crowned with a local celebrity not soon to be forgotten, they crossed the Savannah in safety with their friends and foes. This is not the last achievement of the brave Jasper which we shall have occasion to record. The next, however, though not less distinguished by success, was unhappily written in his own blood.

The campaign which followed was distinguished by several vicissitudes, but the general result was the weakening and dispiriting of the American forces. Brigadier General Ashe was surprised in his camp and utterly

Jasper and Sergeant Newton rescuing the Prisoners

defeated, and the British army not only penetrated into Georgia, but made its appearance at Beaufort in South Carolina. Here it was met by Moultrie in a spirited encounter, which resulted in a drawn battle. Meanwhile, General Lincoln found the militia refractory. They refused to submit to the articles of war, and desired to serve only under those laws by which the militia was governed. Chagrined with this resistance, Lincoln transferred the militia to Moultrie, and, at the head of about 2000 troops of the regular service, he marched up the country to Augusta, proposing by this course to circumscribe the progress of the enemy in that quarter. Taking advantage of this movement, by which regular troops were withdrawn from the seaboard, the British General, Prevost, immediately crossed the Savannah with the intention of surprising Moultrie, who, with 1200 militia-men, lay at Black Swamp. But Moultrie, advised of his enemy, retired to Coosawhatchie, where he placed his rear guard; his head quarters being pitched on the bill, east of Tuliffinnee, two miles in advance, and on the route to Charleston. Here the rear-guard, under Colonel Laurens, engaged the enemy's advance, and was driven before it. Moultrie gradually retired as Prevost advanced, and the contest which followed between the two, seemed to be which should reach Charleston first. The defenceless condition of that city was known to the British General, whose object was to take it by *coup de main*. Moultrie erred in not making continued fight in the swamps and strong passes, the thick forests and intricate defiles, which were numerous along the route of the pursuing army. His policy seems to have been dictated by an undue estimate of the value of the city, and the importance of its safety to the state. But for this, even an army so much inferior as his, could have effectually checked the enemy long before the city could have been reached. Moultrie continued in advance of Prevost, and reached Charleston a few hours before him; just in season to establish something like order, and put the place in a tolerable state of defence. The fire from the lines arrested the British advance. The place was summoned, and defiance returned. Night followed, and the next morning the enemy had disappeared. His object had been surprise. He was unprepared for the assault, having no heavy artillery, and his departure was hastened by intercepted advices from Lincoln and Governor Rutledge, which announced to the garrison the approach of the regular troops and the country militia. Prevost retired to the neighboring islands, and established himself in a strong fort at Stono ferry. Here he was attacked by General Lincoln in a spirited but unsuccessful affair, in which the latter was compelled to retreat. The attack of Lincoln was followed by one of Moultrie, in galleys. The situation of the British became unpleasant, and they did not wait a repetition of these assaults, but retreated along the chain of islands on the coast, until they reached Beaufort and Savannah. Both of these places they maintained; the latter with their main army, the former with a strong body of troops, apart from their sick, wounded and convalescent. Here they were watched by General Lincoln, in a camp of observation at Sheldon, until the appearance of a French fleet on the coast led to renewed activity, and hopes, on the part of the Americans, which were destined to bitter disappointment.

Marion was certainly with his regiment at Sheldon, and when it became probable that there was some prospect of battle, we find him at Fort Moultrie, when Prevost was in possession of the contiguous islands. But a junction of the French and American forces, necessarily compelling the concentration of the whole of the southern invading army at Savannah, lessened the necessity of his remaining at a post which stood in no manner of danger.

Early in September, 1779, the French admiral, Count D'Estaign, with a fleet of twenty sail, appeared upon the coast. As soon as this was certainly known, General Lincoln put his army in motion for Savannah. But the French forces had disembarked before his arrival, and the impatience and imprudence of their admiral did not suffer him to wait the coming of the American. He was a rash man, and, as it appears, on bad terms with his subordinate officers, who were, indeed, not subordinate.[33] He proceeded to summon the place. The answer to his demand was, a request of twenty-four hours for consideration. By a singular error of judgment the French admiral granted the time required. His only hope had been in a *coup de main*. He had neither the time nor the material necessary for regular approaches; nor, had he acted decisively, do these seem to have been at all necessary. The place was not tenable at the period of his first summons. The prompt energies of the British commander soon made it so. Instead of considering, he consumed the twenty-four hours in working. The arrival of Lieutenant-Colonel Cruger, with a small command, from Sunbury, and the force of Lieutenant-Colonel Maitland, from Beaufort, soon put the fortress in such a condition of defence as to enable its commander to return his defiance to the renewed summons of the combined armies. There seems to have been but one opinion among the Americans as to the mistake of D'Estaign, in granting the required indulgence. Weems, speaking for General Horry, says, "I never beheld Marion in so great a passion. I was actually afraid he would have broken out on General Lincoln. 'My God!' he exclaimed, 'who ever heard of anything like this before? First allow an enemy to entrench, and then fight him! See the destruction brought upon the British at Bunker's Hill—yet our troops there were only militia; raw, half-armed clodhoppers, and not a mortar, or carronade, not even a swivel—only their ducking-guns! What, then, are we to expect from regulars, completely armed, with a choice train of artillery, and covered by a breastwork."'

The anticipations of Marion were fully realized. When the junction of the French and American armies was effected, it was determined to reduce the place by siege. Batteries were to be erected and cannon brought from the ships, a distance of several miles. Meanwhile, the works of the besieged were undergoing daily improvements, under an able engineer. Several hundred negroes were busy, day and night, upon the defences, stimulated, when necessary, to exertion, by the lash. On the 4th of October the besiegers opened with nine mortars and thirty-seven pieces of cannon from the land side, and sixteen from the water. They continued to play for several days, with little effect, and the anxiety of the French admiral to leave the coast, at a season of the year when it is particularly perilous to shipping to remain, determined the besiegers to risk everything upon an assault. The morning of the 9th October was fixed upon for the attack. The American army was paraded at one o'clock that morning, but it was near four before the head of the French column reached the front. "The whole army then marched towards the skirt of the wood in one long column, and as they approached the open space, was to break off into the different columns, as ordered for the attack. But, by the time the first French column had arrived at the open space, the day had fairly broke; when Count D'Estaign, without waiting until the other columns had arrived at their position, placed himself at the head of his first column, and rushed forward to the attack."[34] This was creditable to his gallantry, if not to his judgment. But it was valor thrown away. "The column was so severely galled by the grape-shot from the batteries, as they advanced, and by both grape-shot and musketry, when they reached the abbatis, that, in spite of the efforts of the officers, it got into confusion, and broke away to their left, toward the wood in that direction; the second and third French columns shared, successively, the same fate, having the additional discouragement of seeing, as they marched to the attack, the repulse and loss of their comrades who had preceded them. Count Pulaski, who, with the cavalry, preceded the right column of the Americans, proceeded gallantly, until stopped by the abbatis; and before he could force through it received his mortal wound."[35] The American column was much more successful. It was headed by Colonel Laurens, with the Light Infantry, followed by the Second South Carolina Regiment, of which Marion was second in command, and the first battalion of Charleston militia. This column pressed forward, in the face of a heavy fire, upon the Spring Hill redoubt, succeeded in getting into the ditch, and the colors of the second regiment were planted upon the berm. But the parapet was too high to be scaled under such a fire as proceeded from the walls, and, struggling bravely but vainly, the assailants were, after suffering severe slaughter, driven out of the ditch. This slaughter was increased in the effort to retain and carry off in safety the colors of the regiment.

These colors, as we have seen, were the gift of a lady. Moultrie, in the name of the regiment, had promised to defend them to the last. The promise was faithfully remembered in this moment of extremity. One of them was borne by Lieutenant Bush, supported by Sergeant Jasper; the other by Lieutenant Grey, supported by Sergeant Mc'Donald. Bush being slightly wounded early in the action delivered his standard to Jasper, for better security. Jasper a second time and now fatally wounded, restored it to the former. But at the moment of taking it, Bush received a mortal wound. He fell into the ditch with his ensign under him, and it remained in possession of the enemy. The other standard was more fortunate. Lieutenant Grey, by whom it was borne, was slain, but Mc'Donald plucked it from the redoubt where it had been planted, the moment the retreat was ordered, and succeeded in carrying it off in safety. The repulse was decisive. The slaughter, for so brief an engagement, had been terrible, amounting to nearly eleven hundred men; 637 French, and 457 Americans. Of the former, the Irish Brigade, and of the latter the 2d South Carolina Regiment, particularly distinguished themselves and suffered most. The loss of the British was slight; the assailants made no impression on their works. "Thus was this fine body of troops sacrificed by the imprudence of the French General, who, being of superior grade, commanded the whole.[36] In this battle Jasper was mortally wounded. He succeeded in regaining the camp of the Americans. The fatal wound was received in his endeavor to secure and save his colors. Another distinguished personage who fell in this fatal affair, was Col. Count Pulaski, a brave and skilful captain of cavalry, better known in history for his attempt upon the life of Stanislaus Poniatowski, King of Poland.

CHAPTER VII

FROM THE BATTLE OF SAVANNAH TO THE
DEFEAT OF GATES AT CAMDEN

The failure of the combined forces of France and America before the walls of Savannah, left the cause of the latter, in the South, in much worse condition than before. The event served to depress the Carolinians, and in the same degree, to elevate and encourage the enemy. The allies withdrew to their ships, and, shortly after, from the coast. General Lincoln, with the American army, retreated to the heights of Ebenezer, and thence to Sheldon. Proceeding from this place to Charleston, he left Marion in command of the army. On the thirty-first of January, 1780, he writes to the latter as follows: "The state of affairs is such as to make it necessary that we order our force to a point as much and as soon as possible. No troops will be kept in the field except two hundred Light Infantry and the Horse (Washington's). You will therefore please to select from the three regiments with you, two hundred of your best men, and those who are best clothed, and organize them into corps, with proper officers. All the remainder, with the baggage of the whole (saving such as is absolutely necessary for light troops), will march immediately for this town. You will please take command of the light infantry until Lieut. Col. Henderson arrives, which I expect will be in a few days. After that, I wish to see you as soon as possible in Charleston."

In the February following, Marion was dispatched to Bacon's Bridge on Ashley river, where Moultrie had established a camp for the reception of the militia of the neighborhood, as well as those which had been summoned from the interior. It was to Marion that Lincoln chiefly looked for the proper drilling of the militia. In his hands they lost the rude and inefficient character, the inexpert and spiritless manner, which, under ordinary commanders, always distinguish them. Feeling sure of their Captain, he, in turn, rendered them confident of themselves. Speaking of Marion's "*patience* with the militia"—a phrase of great importance in this connection—Horry, in his own memoirs, which now lie before us, adds, "No officer in the Union was better calculated to command them, and to have done more than he did."[37] Lincoln knew his value. The admirable training of the Second South Carolina Regiment had already done high honor to his skill as a disciplinarian. He discovered the secret which regularly bred military men are slow to discern, that, without patience, in the training of citizen soldiers for immediate service, they are incorrigible; and patience with them, on the part of a commanding officer, is neither inconsistent with their claims nor with their proper efficiency.

The accumulation of troops at Bacon's Bridge was made with the view to the defence of Charleston, now threatened by the enemy. Many concurring causes led to the leaguer of that city. Its conquest was desirable on many accounts, and circumstances had already shown that this was not a matter of serious difficulty. The invasion of Prevost the year before, which had so nearly proved successful; the little resistance which had been offered to him while traversing more than one hundred miles of country contiguous to the Capital; and the rich spoils which, on his retreat, had been borne off by his army, betrayed at once the wealth and weakness of that region. The possession of Savannah, where British Government had been regularly re-established, and the entire, if not totally undisturbed control of Georgia, necessarily facilitated the invasion of the sister province. South Carolina was now a frontier, equally exposed to the British in Georgia, and the Tories of Florida and North Carolina. The means of defence in her power were now far fewer than when Prevost made his attempt on Charleston. The Southern army was, in fact, totally broken up. The Carolina regiments had seen hard service, guarding the frontier, and contending with the British in Georgia. They were thinned by battle and sickness to a mere handful. The Virginia and North Carolina regiments had melted away, as the term for which they had enlisted, had expired. The Georgia regiment, captured by the British in detail, were perishing in their floating prisons. The weakness of the patriots necessarily increased the audacity, with the strength, of their enemies. The loyalists, encouraged by the progress of Prevost, and the notorious inefficiency of the Whigs, were now gathering in formidable bodies, in various quarters, operating in desultory bands, or crowding to swell the columns of the British army. All things concurred to encourage the attempt of the enemy on Charleston. Its possession, with that of Savannah, would not only enable them to complete their ascendency in the two provinces to which these cities belonged, but would probably give them North Carolina also. Virginia then, becoming the frontier, it would be easy, with the co-operation of an army ascending the Chesapeake, to traverse the entire South with their legions, detaching it wholly from the federal compact. Such was the British hope, and such their policy. There was yet another motive for the siege of Charleston, considered without reference to collateral or contingent events.

Esteemed erroneously as a place of great security—an error that arose in all probability from the simple fact of the successful defence of Fort Moultrie—it was crowded with valuable magazines. As a trading city, particularly while the commerce of the North remained interrupted, it had become a place of great business. It was a stronghold for privateers and their prizes, and always contained stores and shipping of immense value.

The temptations to its conquest were sufficiently numerous. Ten thousand choice troops, with a large and heavy train of artillery, were accordingly dispatched from New York for its investment, which was begun in February, 1780, and conducted by the Commander-in-Chief of the British forces, Sir Henry Clinton, in person. He conducted his approaches with a caution highly complimentary to the besieged. The fortifications were only field works, and might have been overrun in less than five days by an audacious enemy. The regular troops within the city were not above two thousand men. The citizen militia increased the number to nearly four thousand. For such an extent of lines as encircled the place, the adequate force should not have been less than that of the enemy. The fortifications, when the British first landed their materiel, were in a dilapidated and unfinished state, and, at that time, the defenders, apart from the citizens, scarcely exceeded eight hundred men; while the small pox, making its appearance within the walls, for the first time for twenty years—an enemy much more dreaded than the British,—effectually discouraged the country militia from coming to the assistance of the citizens. Under these circumstances, the conquest would have been easy to an active and energetic foe. But Sir Henry does not seem to have been impatient for his laurels. He was willing that they should mature gradually, and he sat down to a regular and formal investment.

It was an error of the Carolinians, under such circumstances, to risk the fortunes of the State, and the greater part of its regular military strength, in a besieged town; a still greater to do so in defiance of such difficulties as attended the defence. The policy which determined the resolution was a concession to the citizens, in spite of all military opinion. The city might have been yielded to the enemy, and the State preserved, or, which was the same thing, the troops. The loss of four thousand men from the ranks of active warfare, was the great and substantial loss, the true source, in fact, of most of the miseries and crimes by which the very bowels of the country were subsequently torn and distracted.

It was the great good fortune of the State that Francis Marion was not among those who fell into captivity in the fall of Charleston. He had marched into the city from Dorchester, when his active services were needed for its defence; but while the investment was in progress, and before it had been fully completed, an event occurred to him, an accident which was, no doubt, very much deplored at the time, by which his services, lost for the present, were subsequently secured for the country. Dining with a party of friends at a house in Tradd-street, the host, with that mistaken hospitality which has too frequently changed a virtue to a vice, turned the key upon his guests, to prevent escape, till each individual should be gorged with wine. Though an amiable man, Marion was a strictly temperate one. He was not disposed to submit to this too common form of social tyranny; yet not willing to resent the breach of propriety by converting the assembly into a bull-ring, he adopted a middle course, which displayed equally the gentleness and firmness of his temper. Opening a window, he coolly threw himself into the street. He was unfortunate in the attempt; the apartment was on the second story, the height considerable, and the adventure cost him a broken ancle. The injury was a severe and shocking one, and, for the time, totally unfitted him for service. He left the city in a litter, while the passage to the country still remained open for retreat, in obedience to an order of General Lincoln for the departure of all idle mouths, "all supernumerary officers, and all officers unfit for duty." Marion retired to his residence in St. John's parish. Here, suffering in mind and body, he awaited with impatience the progress of events, with which, however much he might sympathize, he could not share. His humiliation at this unavoidable but melancholy inaction, may be imagined from what we know of his habits and his patriotism.

The siege of Charleston, in consequence of the firm bearing of the besieged, and the cautious policy of the British Government, was protracted long after the works had been pronounced untenable. It was yielded unwillingly to the conqueror, only after all resistance had proved in vain. It fell by famine, rather than by the arms of the enemy. The defence was highly honorable to the besieged. It lasted six weeks, in which they had displayed equal courage and endurance. The consequences of this misfortune leave it somewhat doubtful, whether the determination to defend the city to the last extremity, was not the result of a correct policy; considering less its own loss, and that of the army, than the effect of the former upon the rustic population. Certainly, the capture of the army was a vital misfortune to the southern States; yet the loss of the city itself was of prodigious effect upon the scattered settlements of the country. The character and resolve of the capital cities, in those days, were very much the sources of the moral strength of the interior. Sparsely settled, with unfrequent opportunities of communion with one another, the minds of the forest population turned naturally for their tone and direction to the capital city. The active attrition of rival and conflicting minds, gives, in all countries, to the population of a dense community, an intellectual superiority over those who live remote, and feel none of the constant moral strifes to which the citizen is subject. In South Carolina, Charleston had been the seat of the original *movement*, had incurred the first dangers, achieved the first victories, and, in all public proceedings where action was desirable, had always led off in the van. To preserve intact, and from overthrow, the seat of ancient authority and opinion, was surely a policy neither selfish nor unwise. Perhaps, after all, the grand error was, in not making the preparations for defence adequate to the object. The resources of the State were small, and these had been diminished wofully in succoring her neighbors, and in small border strifes, which the borderers might have been taught to manage for themselves. The military force of the State, under any circumstances, could not have contended on equal terms with the ten thousand well-appointed regulars of Sir Henry Clinton. The assistance derived from Virginia and North Carolina was little more than nominal, calculated rather to swell the triumph of the victor than to retard his successes.

If the movements of the British were slow, and deficient in military enterprise, where Sir Henry Clinton commanded in person, such could not be said of them, after the conquest of Charleston was effected. The commander-in-chief was succeeded by Earl Cornwallis, and his career was certainly obnoxious to no such reproaches. We shall have more serious charges to bring against him. Of the gross abuse of power, wanton tyrannies, cruel murders, and most reckless disregard of decency and right, by which the course of the British was subsequently distinguished, we shall say no more than will suffice to show, in what dangers, through what difficulties, and under what stimulating causes, Francis Marion rose in arms, when everything appeared to be lost.

Charleston in possession of the enemy, they proceeded with wonderful activity to use all means in their power, for exhausting the resources, and breaking down the spirit of the country. Their maxim was that of habitual tyranny—"might is right." They seemed to recognize no other standard. The articles of capitulation, the laws of nations, private treaty, the dictates of humanity and religion, were all equally set at naught. The wealth of private families,—slaves by thousands,—were hurried into the waists of British ships, as the legitimate spoils of var. The latter found a market in the West India islands; the prisoners made by the fall of Charleston were, in defiance of the articles of capitulation, crowded into prison-ships, from whence they were only released by death, or by yielding to those arguments of their keepers which persuaded them to enlist in British regiments, to serve in other countries. Many yielded to these arguments, with the simple hope of escape from the horrors by which they were surrounded. When arts and arguments failed to overcome the inflexibility of these wretched prisoners, compulsion was resorted to, and hundreds were forced from their country, shipped to Jamaica, and there made to serve in British regiments.[38] Citizens of distinction, who, by their counsel or presence, opposed their influence over the prisoners, or proved themselves superior to their temptations, were torn from their homes without warning, and incarcerated in their floating dungeons. Nothing was forborne, in the shape of pitiless and pitiful persecution, to break the spirits, subdue the strength, and mock and mortify the hopes, alike, of citizen and captive.

With those who kept the field the proceedings were more summary, if not more severe. The fall of Charleston seems necessarily to have involved the safety of the country from the Savannah to the Pedee. In a few weeks after the capture of the city, the British were in peaceable possession of the space between these limits, from the seaboard to the mountains. They had few opponents—an isolated body of continentals, a small squad of militia, for the first time drilling for fixture service, or a little troop of horse—and these were quickly overcome. On these occasions the British were generally led by Lieutenant-Colonel Tarleton. This officer acquired for himself an odious distinction in his progress through the South in the campaigns which followed. He was rather an active than a skilful commander. Rapid in his movements, he gave little heed to the judicious disposition of his troops, and aiming more at impressing the fears of his enemy, than overcoming him by science, his chief success were the result of the panic which his surprises and his butcheries inspired. He seems never to have been successful against an equal and resolute foe. But, as courage and activity are, perhaps, after all, and before all, the most necessary requisites for a soldier, Turleton's services were inappreciable to the invading army. In one month after its arrival, his legion was mounted and began its career of slaughter. While yet the city was sustaining the siege, he penetrated the country, in pursuit of those bands of militia horse, which, by direction of the American commander, still kept the open field. On the 1 of March, he surprised a company of militia at Salkehatchie Bridge, killed and wounded several and dispersed the rest. Five days after, another party at Pon-Pon shared the same fortune. He was not so successful at Rantowles on the 23d of the same month, where in a rencounter with Col. Washington, his dragoons were roughly handled, and retreated with loss. He avenged himself, however, on Washington, in less than a month after, by surprising him at Monk's Corner. Col. White soon after took command of the southern cavalry, and obtained some trifling successes, but suffered himself to be surprised at Lenud's ferry on the Santee. These events all took place prior to the surrender of the city. The activity of Tarleton, with the general remissness, and want of ordinary military precautions on the part of the militia which opposed itself to him, made his progress easy, and thus enabled him to cut off every party that was embodied in the field. He was now to succeed in a much more important and much more bloody enterprise. A Continental force from Virginia of four hundred men, under Col. Beaufort, had been dispatched to the relief of Charleston. Beaufort had reached Camden before he was apprised of the surrender of that city. This event properly determined him to retreat. Earl Cornwallis, meanwhile, had taken the field with a force of twenty-five hundred men, and was then in rapid progress for the Santee. Hearing of the advance of Beaufort, he dispatched Tarleton in quest of him, with a select body of infantry and cavalry, in all, seven hundred men. Beaufort was overtaken near the Warsaw settlements, and summoned to surrender. This person does not seem to have been designed by nature for military operations. He halted at the summons, hesitated awhile, sent his wagons ahead, consulted with his officers, and did little or nothing farther, either for flight or conflict. While thus halting and hesitating he was attacked by the impetuous Tarleton, offered a feeble resistance, unmarked by conduct or spirit, suffered the enemy to gain his rear, and finally grounded his arms. He either did this too soon or too late. His flag was disregarded in the flush of battle, the bearer of it cut down by the hand of Tarleton, and the British infantry, with fixed bayonets, rushed upon the inactive Americans. Some of Beaufort's men, seeing that their application for quarter was disregarded, resolved to die like men, and resumed their arms. Their renewed fire provoked the massacre of the unresisting. A terrible butchery followed. The British gave no quarter. From that day, "Tarleton's Quarters," implying the merciless cutting down of the suppliant, grew into a proverbial phrase, which, in the hour of victory, seemed to embitter the hostility with which the American strove to avenge his slaughtered comrades.

The defeat of Beaufort, with the only regular force remaining in the State, following so close upon the fall of Charleston, paralyzed the hopes of the patriots. The country seemed everywhere subdued. An unnatural and painful apathy dispirited opposition. The presence of a British force, sufficient to overawe the neighborhood, at conspicuous points, and the awakened activity of the Tories in all quarters, no longer restrained by the presence in arms of their more patriotic countrymen, seemed to settle the question of supremacy. There was not only no head against the enemy, but the State, on a sudden, appeared to have been deprived of all her distinguished men. Moultrie and others who might have led, were prisoners of war. Governor Rutledge, a noble spirit and famous orator—the Patrick Henry of Carolina,—had withdrawn to the North State, to stimulate the energies of the people in that quarter and gain recruits. His example was followed by Sumter, Horry and others,—by all, in fact, who, escaping captivity, were in condition to fly. The progress of Cornwallis and Tarleton left mere distinction, unsupported by men, with few places of security. Marion, meanwhile, incapable of present flight, was compelled to take refuge in the swamp and forest. He was too conspicuous a person; had made too great a figure in previous campaigns, and his military talents were too well known and too highly esteemed, not to render him an object of some anxiety as well to friends as foes. Still suffering from the hurts received in Charleston, with bloody and malignant enemies all around him, his safety depended on his secrecy and obscurity alone. Fortunately he had "won golden opinions from all sorts of people. He had friends among all classes, who did not permit themselves to sleep while he was in danger. Their activity supplied the loss of his own. They watched while he slept. They assisted his feebleness. In the moment of alarm, he was sped from house to house, from tree to thicket, from the thicket to the swamp. His "hair-breadth 'scapes" under these frequent exigencies, were, no doubt, among the most interesting adventures of his life, furnishing rare material, could they be procured, for the poet and romancer. Unhappily, while the chronicles show the frequent emergency which attended his painful condition, they furnish nothing more. We are without details. The melancholy baldness and coldness with which they narrate events upon which one would like to linger is absolutely humbling to the imagination; which, kindled by the simple historical outline, looks in vain for the satisfaction of those doubts and inquiries, those hopes and fears, which the provoking narrative inspires only to defraud. How would some old inquisitive Froissart have dragged by frequent inquiry from contemporaneous lips, the particular fact, the whole adventure, step by step, item by item,—the close pursuit, the narrow escape,—and all the long train of little, but efficient circumstances, by which the story would have been made unique, with all its rich and numerous details! These, the reader must supply from his own resources of imagination. He must conjecture for himself the casual warning brought to the silent thicket, by the devoted friend, the constant woman, or the humble slave; the midnight bay of the watch dog or the whistle of the scout; or the sudden shot, from friend or foe, by which the fugitive is counselled to hurry to his den. A thousand events arise to the imagination as likely to have occurred to our partisan, in his hours of feebleness and danger, from the rapid cavalry of Tarleton, or the close and keen pursuit of the revengeful Tories. To what slight circumstances has he been indebted for his frequent escape! What humble agents have been commissioned by Providence to save a life, that was destined to be so precious to his country's liberties!

How long he remained in this situation is not exactly known,—probably several months. As soon as he was able to mount his horse, he collected a few friends, and set out for North Carolina. A Continental force was on its way from Virginia under Baron De Kalb. His purpose was to join it. It was while on this route, and with this object, that he encountered his old friend and long tried associate in arms, Col. P. Horry.[39]

Horry describes his uncle, at this meeting, as still "very crazy"—so much so that it required his help and that of Marion's servant to lift him from his horse. But his spirits were good. He was still cheerful, and possessed that rare elasticity of character which never loses its tone under privations and disappointments. Weems, who, we are compelled to admit, very frequently exercised the privilege of the ancient historian, of putting fine speeches into the mouth of his hero, tells us that he jeered at the doleful expressions of his companion, Horry, who, discussing the condition of the country, lamented that their "happy days were all gone." "Our happy days all gone, indeed!" answered Marion—"on the contrary, they are yet to come. The victory is still sure. The enemy, it is true, have all the trumps, and if they had but the spirit to play a generous game, they would certainly ruin us. But they have no idea of that game. They will treat the people cruelly, and that one thing will ruin them and save the country." Weems, speaking for Horry, describes in ludicrous terms, their journey through North Carolina,—through a region swarming with Tories, but, fortunately for our travellers, who were venomous without being active. Our fugitives were without money and without credit, and "but for carrying a knife, or a horse fleam, or a gun-flint, had no more use for a pocket than a Highlander has for a knee-buckle. As to hard money we had not seen a dollar for years." In this resourceless condition—a condition, which, it may be well to say in this place, continued throughout the war, they made their way with difficulty until they joined the Continental army. Gates had superseded De Kalb in its command, and was pressing forward, with the ambition, seemingly, of writing a despatch like Cæsar's, announcing, in the same breath, the sight and conquest of his enemy. Marion and his little troop of twenty men, made but a sorry figure in the presence of the Continental General. Gates was a man of moderate abilities, a vain man, of a swelling and ostentatious habit, whose judgment was very apt to be affected by parade, and the external show of things. Some of his leading opinions were calculated to show that he was unfit for a commander in the South. For example, he thought little of cavalry, which, in a plain country, sparsely settled, was among the first essentials of success, as well in securing intelligence, as in procuring supplies. It was not calculated therefore to raise the troop of our partisan in his esteem, to discover that they were all good riders and well mounted. Marion, himself, was a man equally modest in approach and unimposing in person. His followers may have provoked the sneer of the General, as it certainly moved the scorn and laughter of his well-equipped Continentals. We have a description of them from the pen of an excellent officer, the Adjutant General of Gates' army. He says, "Col. Marion, a gentleman of South Carolina, had been with the army a few days, attended by a very few followers, distinguished by small leather caps, and the wretchedness of their attire; their number did not exceed twenty men and boys, some white, some black, and all mounted, but most of them miserably equipped; their appearance was in fact so burlesque, that it was with much difficulty the diversion of the regular soldiery was restrained by the officers; and the General himself was glad of an opportunity of detaching Col. Marion, at his own instance, towards the interior of South Carolina, with orders to watch the motions of the enemy and furnish intelligence."[40]

From such small and insignificant beginnings flow greatness and great performances. We, who are in possession of all the subsequent events—who see this proud, vain Commander, hurrying on with the rapidity of madness to his own ruin—can but smile in the perusal of such a narrative, not at the rags of Marion's men, but at the undiscerning character of those who could see, in the mean equipment, the imperfect clothing, the mixture of man and boy, and white and black, anything but a noble patriotism, which, in such condition, was still content to carry on a war against a powerful enemy. The very rags and poverty of this little band, which was afterwards to become so famous, were so many proofs of their integrity and virtue, and should have inspired respect rather than ridicule. They were so many guarantees of good service which they were able and prepared to render. It was in defiance of the temptations and the power of the foe, that these men had taken the field against him, and had Gates been a wise commander, he would have seen even through their rags and destitution, the small but steady light of patriotism; which, enkindled throughout the State by the example of Marion, Sumter, and a few others, was to blaze out finally into that perfect brightness before which the invader was to shrink confounded.

Gates was wise enough to take counsel of Marion, if nothing more; and even this might not have been done, but for the suggestions of Governor Rutledge, who, at that time in the camp of the Continentals, might very well have informed him of the value of the man whose followers inspired only ridicule. It was with Marion that the plan was concerted, and not improbably at his suggestion, for moving into the very heart of the State. This, subsequently, was the policy of Greene, and had Gates adopted the deliberate caution of that commander, his successes would unquestionably have been the same. The object of such a movement was to give an opportunity to the native patriots to rally—to compel the British to concentrate their scattered forces, call in their detached parties, and thus circumscribe their influence, within the State, to the places where they still remained in force. To effect these objects, the Fabian maxims of warfare should have been those of the American General. Few of his militia had ever seen an enemy. He had but recently joined his troops, knew nothing of them, and they as little of him. Their march had been a fatiguing one. Time and training were necessary pre-requisites for their improvement and his success. Unhappily, these were the very agents with which the vanity of the unfortunate commander made him most willing to dispense. The victory at Saratoga had spoiled him for ever, and thinking too much of himself, he committed the next great error of a military man, of thinking too lightly of his foe. It would be idle and perhaps impertinent, to suggest that if Marion had been suffered to remain with him, the issue of this march night have been more fortunate. Gates was quite too vain-glorious to listen and Marion quite too moderate to obtrude his opinions; and yet Marion was a man of equal prudence and adroitness. He could insinuate advice, so that it would appear to self-conceit the very creature of its own conceptions. Had Marion remained, could Gates have listened, we are very sure there would have been no such final, fatal disaster as suddenly stopped the misdirected progress of the Continental army. There would have been some redeeming circumstances to qualify the catastrophe. All would not have been lost. At all events, with Marion at their head, the militia would have fought awhile,—would have discharged their pieces, once, twice, thrice, before they fled. They would have done for the born-leader of militia, what they refused to do for a commander who neither knew how to esteem, nor how to conduct them.

It was while Marion was in the camp of Gates, that a messenger from the Whigs of Williamsburg, then newly risen in arms, summoned him to be their leader. It was in consequence of this invitation, and not because of the awkwardness of his position there, that he determined to penetrate into South Carolina, in advance of the American army. Such an invitation was not to he neglected. Marion well knew its importance, and at once accepted the commission conferred upon him by Governor Rutledge. He took leave of Gates accordingly, having received, as is reported, certain instructions from that unhappy commander, to employ his men in the destruction of all the scows, boats, ferry-flats and barges on the route, by which the enemy might make his escape. The fancy of the American General already beheld the army of Lord Cornwallis in full flight. His great solicitude seems to have been how to secure his captives. He had, strangely enough for a military man, never taken counsel of the farm-yard proverb, which we need not here repeat for the benefit of the reader. With the departure of Marion, his better genius left him,—the only man who, in command of the militia, might have saved him from destruction. Leaving our partisan, with his little squad, to make his way cautiously through a country infested with Tories, we follow for the present the progress of the Continental army. On the night of the fifteenth of August, 1780 the Americans moved from Rugely's Mills. At midnight without dreaming of an enemy, they encountered him. The first intelligence communicated to either army of the presence of the other, was from the fire of the British advance upon the Americans. The two armies recoiled and lay upon their arms the rest of the night. So far the affair was indecisive. The Americans had sustained themselves in the face of some disadvantages, chiefly the result of their leader's imprudence. A night march of raw militia in the face of a foe, and in column of battle, was itself an error which a sagacious commander would never have made it is not to be denied, that the Americans were not satisfied with their situation. Some of their officers openly declared their discontent. But it was too late for a retrograde movement, nor is it likely, feeling as he did and sanguine as he was, that Gates would have believed any such movement necessary. The ground was equally unknown to both commanders; but Cornwallis had one advantage: he was in the command of veterans, who are generally cool enough in such situations to look about them, and make the most of their exigencies. The American line was soon formed and in waiting for the dawn and the enemy. The first Maryland division, including the Delawares under De Kalb, was posted on the right; the Virginia militia under Stevens on the left; the North Carolinians, led by Caswell in the centre; and the artillery, in battery, upon the road. Both wings rested on morasses, and the second Maryland brigade was posted as a reserve, a few hundred yards in the rear of the first. The British formed a single line, with each wing covered and supported by a body in reserve. They were much less numerous than the Americans, but they were picked men, the choice of the regiments in Charleston and Camden. The American militia, of which the greater part of Gates' army consisted, had never felt an enemy's fire. The Maryland and Delaware troops were good soldiers, well trained and in confidence of their leaders. With the break of day, and the advance of the American left, the action began. This division of the army consisted of Virginia militia under Stevens. Handled with unexpected severity by the British fire, they yielded before it and fled in panic, many of them without even discharging their pieces. The wretched example was followed by the North Carolina militia, with the exception of a single corps, commanded by Major Dixon. The cavalry under Armand, a foreign adventurer, broke at nearly the same moment; and a charge of the British cavalry, happily timed, put an end to all hope of rallying the terror-stricken fugitives. The devoted

Continentals alone kept their ground and bore the brunt of the action. They were led by the veteran De Kalb—the Commander in Chief having hurried from the field in a vain attempt to bring the militia back. The artillery was lost, the cavalry dispersed;—the regulars, numbering but nine hundred men, were required to bear the undivided pressure of two thousand of the best troops in the British service. With the example before them, the desertion of their General, and their own perfect isolation, they would have been justified by the necessity of the case, in instant flight. But, as if the cowardice of their countrymen had stung them into a determination to show, at all hazards, that they, at least, were made of very different stuff, they not only resisted the attack of the enemy, but carried the bayonet into his ranks. The combatants rushed and reeled together with locked weapons. But this struggle could not last. The conflict was prolonged only until the British cavalry could return from pursuing the fugitives. Their sabres gave the finishing stroke to the affair. De Kalb had fallen under eleven wounds, and nothing remained, but flight, to save this gallant body from the mortification of surrender on the field of battle. It was no consolation to Gates, while fleeing to North Carolina, to be overtaken by messengers from Sumter, announcing a gallant achievement of that brave partisan, by which forty wagons of booty and nearly three hundred prisoners had fallen into his hands. Such tidings only mocked his own disaster. He could only, in reply, relate his own irretrievable defeat, point to his fugitives, and counsel Sumter to immediate retreat from his triumphant and now returning enemy. Unhappily, ignorant of Gates' disaster, and of a bold, incautious temper, Sumter was approaching, rather than hastening from, danger. His flight, when he did retire, was not sufficiently rapid, nor sufficiently prudent. He was one of those men who too quickly feel themselves secure. He was surprised by Tarleton, but two days after, his troops utterly dispersed, he, too, a fugitive like Gates, with all the fruits of his late victory taken from his grasp. In almost every instance where the Americans suffered defeat, the misfortune was due to a want of proper caution—an unobservance of some of the simplest rules of military prudence. In a brilliant sortie, a manful charge, a sudden onslaught, no troops could have surpassed them—nay, we find as many examples of the sternest powers of human endurance, under the severest trials of firmness, in their military history, as in that of any other people. But to secure what they had won—to be consistently firm—always on their guard and beyond surprise,—were lessons which they were slow to acquire—which they learned at last only under the heaviest penalties of blood. Marion was one of the few Captains of American militia, that never suffered himself to be taken napping.

CHAPTER VIII

ORGANIZATION OF "MARION'S BRIGADE" †
SURPRISE OF TORIES UNDER GAINEY†
DEFEAT OF BARFIELD † CAPTURE OF BRITISH GUARD
WITH PRISONERS AT NELSON'S FERRY

The people of Williamsburg, by whom Marion was summoned from the camp of Gates, were sprung generally from Irish parentage. They inherited, in common with all the descendants of the Irish in America, a hearty detestation of the English name and authority. This feeling rendered them excellent patriots and daring soldiers, wherever the British Lion was the object of hostility. Those of whom we are now to speak, the people of Williamsburg, were men generally of fearless courage, powerful frame, well-strung nerves, and an audacious gallantry that led them to delight in dangers, even where the immediate objects by no means justified the risk. They felt that "rapture of the strife," in which the Goth exulted. In addition to these natural endowments for a brave soldiery, they were good riders and famous marksmen—hunters, that knew the woods almost as well by night as by day—could wind about and through the camp of an enemy, as free from suspicion as the velvet-footed squirrel, who, from the lateral branches of the pine, looks over their encampment. They possessed resources of knowledge and ingenuity, while in swamp and thicket, not merely to avoid the danger, but, in not unfrequent instances, to convert it to their own advantage. Nothing but the training and direction of such a mind as Marion's was needed to make, of these men, the most efficient of all partisan soldiery. The formation of the brigade of which he now prepared to take command, has a history of its own which is worth telling. The fame which it subsequently acquired in connection with its leader's name, and which the local traditions will not willingly let die, will justify us in the narration. Some few preliminary facts are necessary.

The fall of Charleston, and the dispersion or butchery of those parties which had kept the field after that event, necessarily depressed the spirits and discouraged the attempt of the scattered patriots who still yearned to oppose the invaders. The captivity of many of the leaders to whom they were accustomed to look for counsel and direction, and the flight of others, served still further to dissipate any hopes or purposes which they might have had of concentration. Thousands fled to the North, and embodied themselves under Washington and other American Generals, despairing of the cause at home. Everything appeared to be lost, and a timely proclamation of Sir Henry Clinton, a few days after the surrender of Charleston, tended yet more to subdue the spirit of resistance. The proclamation proffered "pardon to the inhabitants" with some few exceptions, "for their past treasonable offences, and a reinstatement in their rights and immunities heretofore enjoyed, exempt from taxation, except by their own legislature." This specious offer, made at a moment when his power was at its height, everywhere unquestioned and unopposed, indicated a degree of magnanimity, which in the case of those thousands in every such contest, who love repose better than virtue, was everywhere calculated to disarm the inhabitants. To many indeed it seemed to promise all for which they had been contending. It offered security from further injury, protection against the Tories who were using the authority of the British for their own purposes of plunder and revenge, a respite from their calamities, and a restoration of all their rights. With the immunities thus proffered, with the further conviction that further struggle against British power was hopeless, with the assurance, indeed, which was industriously conveyed to them from all quarters, that Congress, not able to assist, had resolved upon yielding the provinces of South Carolina and Georgia to the enemy, as considerations for the independence of the other colonies—they accepted the terms thus offered them by the British commander, and, in great numbers, signed declarations of allegiance, received protection as subjects of the crown, or, as prisoners of war, were paroled to their plantations. Could the British have persevered in this policy, had they kept faith with the inhabitants, they might much longer have held possession of the country. But, either they were not sincere in their first professions, or their subsequent necessities compelled them to adopt a less rational policy. Twenty days had not elapsed from the publication of the first proclamation when it was followed by another, which so entirely qualified and impaired the character of the former, as to revolt the people whom it had invited, and to impress them with the conviction that they had been imposed upon—that the first measure was a mere decoy,—a trap involving their pledges, yet withholding the very securities for which they had been given. This second proclamation, premising that it was necessary for all good citizens to uphold his Majesty's Government, proceeded to discharge from protection and parole all persons to whom such papers had been accorded. All persons not absolutely prisoners of war, taken in arms, were to be reinstated in their former positions as citizens—but, as citizens of the British Empire. In this relation the farther inferences were inevitable. They were now actually to support his Majesty's Government. The proclamation ended with the usual penalties—all who neglected to return to their allegiance were to be treated as rebels.

The policy thus adopted by the British commander soon made them so. The object of the Carolinians, in taking protections and paroles, was to avoid further warfare. The second proclamation of the British General required them to take up arms for his Majesty, and against their countrymen. This was a hopeful plan by which to fill the British regiments, to save farther importations of Hessians, farther cost of mercenaries, and, as in the case of the Aborigines, to employ the Anglo-American race against one another. The loyalists of the South were to be used against the patriots of the North, as the loyalists of the latter region had been employed to put down the liberties of the former. It was a short and ingenious process for finishing the rebellion; and, could it have entirely succeeded, as in part it did, it would have entitled Sir Henry Clinton to very far superior laurels, as a civilian, than he ever won as a soldier. The value of the Americans, as soldiers, was very well known to the British General. Some of the most sanguinary battles of the Revolution were those in which the combatants on both sides were chiefly natives of the soil, upon which a portion of them but too freely shed their blood in a sincere desire to holster up that foreign tyranny that mocked the generous valor which it employed.

The effect of this second proclamation of the British commander was such as he scarcely anticipated. The readiness with which numbers of the people had accepted paroles and protections, declared, at most, nothing but their indifference to the contest—declared no preference for British domination. In this lay the error of the conqueror. The natural feeling of the people, thus entrapped, was that of indignation. Their determination might have been conjectured by any reasoning mind. Compelled to take up arms—not permitted to enjoy that repose with their families, for which they sought the offered immunities of the British—it was more easy to espouse the cause of their countrymen, to which their affections were really given, than that of the invader. They had committed a great and humbling error in the endeavor to escape the conflict—in taking the proffered protection of a power which had seized with violence upon their native land. It was with some eagerness, therefore, that they threw aside its obligations, and, as opportunity presented itself, girded on their armor, and sallied forth to join their countrymen. Among the first to do so were the men by whom Marion was summoned from the camp of Gates. These brave fellows, occupying a portion of the country stretching from the Santee to the Pedee, including the whole of the present district of Williamsburg, and a part of Marion, were not altogether prepared to understand these British proclamations. They were no great politicians, had no love of blind vassalage, and naturally suspected all liberality of British origin. They wished for certain explanations before they sent in their adhesion. Not that they calculated upon resistance. This, no doubt, seemed to them as hopeless as it appeared in all other parts of the State. But their insulated position which left them uninformed as to the true condition of things, was, at the same time, a source of their courage and indifference. As yet, the arms of the British had not penetrated into their settlements. They were naturally anxious to prevent their doing so. Under these circumstances, they held a gathering of their best men for the purpose of consulting upon their affairs. The twin proclamations—how unlike!—of the British commander, were before them: and, in their primitive assembly, they sat down to discuss their separate merits. These confused rather than enlightened them, and it was resolved to send one of their number, in whom they had most confidence, to the nearest British authority, in order that their difficulties should be explained and their doubts satisfied. There was one sterling family among them of the name of James. Of this family there were five brothers, John, William, Gavin, Robert and James. No men under Marion were braver or truer than these. Fearless, strong and active, they were always ready for the foe; the first in attack, the last in retreat. There were other branches of this family who partook largely of the qualities of the five brothers. Of these, the eldest, Major John James, was chosen the representative of the men of Williamsburg. This gentleman had been their representative in the provincial assembly—he was in command of them as State militia. They gave him their fullest confidence, and he deserved it.

Under this appointment, Major James repaired to Georgetown, the nearest British post, which was then under the command of one Captain Ardesoif. Attired as a plain backwoodsman, James obtained an interview with Ardesoif, and, in prompt and plain terms, entered at once upon the business for which he came. But when he demanded the meaning of the British protection, and asked upon what terms the submission of the citizens was to be made, he was peremptorily informed that "the submission must be unconditional." To an inquiry, whether the inhabitants were to be allowed to remain upon their plantations, he was answered in the negative. "His Majesty," said Ardesoif, "offers you a free pardon, of which you are undeserving, for you all ought to be hanged; but it is only on condition that you take up arms in his cause." James, whom we may suppose to have been very far from relishing the tone and language

Major John James attacking Capt. Ardesoif.

in which he was addressed, very coolly replied, that "the people whom he came to *represent*, would scarcely submit on such conditions." The republican language of the worthy Major provoked the representative of Royalty. The word 'represent,' in particular, smote hardly on his ears; something, too, in the cool, contemptuous manner of the Major, may have contributed to his vexation. "*Represent!*" he exclaimed in a fury—"You d——d rebel, if you dare speak in such language, I will have you hung up at the yard-arm!" Ardesoif, it must be known, was a sea captain. The ship which he commanded lay in the neighboring river, he used only an habitual form of speech when he threatened the "yard-arm," instead of the tree. Major James gave him no time to make the correction. He was entirely weaponless, and Ardesoif wore a sword; but the inequality, in the moment of his anger, was unfelt by the high-spirited citizen. Suddenly rising, he seized upon the chair on which he bad been sitting, and floored the insolent subordinate at a blow; then hurrying forth without giving his enemy time to recover, he mounted his horse, and made his escape to the woods before pursuit could be attempted.

His people were soon assembled to hear his story. The exactions of the British, and the spirit which James had displayed, in resenting the insolence of Ardesoif, at once aroused their own. Required to take the field, it did not need a moment to decide "under which king." The result of their deliberations was the formation of "Marion's Brigade." Four captains were chosen for as many companies. These were, Captains William M'Cottry, Henry Mouzon, John James (of the Lake, a cousin of Major James), and John M'Cauley. These were all under the one command of our representative to Ardesoif. He instantly put them into motion, and, after some petty successes against small parties of British and Tories, he advanced one of the four companies, M'Cottry's, to the pass of Lynch Creek, at Witherspoon Ferry. Here M'Cottry heard of Col. Tarleton, and proceeded to encounter him. Tarleton had been apprised of the gatherings at Williamsburg, and, at the head of some seventy men, was pressing forward with the hope of surprising James. M'Cottry, more brave perhaps than prudent, after sending back to James for a reinforcement, set forward to give Tarleton battle. The British Colonel had taken post at Kingstree. M'Cottry approached him at midnight. It happened, perhaps fortunately for the former, that Tarleton had received some very exaggerated accounts of M'Cottry's force, which the boldness of his approach seemed to confirm. Taking the alarm accordingly, he disappeared in season, leaving to M'Cottry the *éclât* which necessarily attended his attempt. The excesses of Tarleton, while on this progress, and the crimes committed in the same neighborhood by other British captains about the same time, completed the movement which the native spirit of patriotism in the men of Williamsburg had so happily begun. The whole country was soon awakened—individuals and groups everywhere beginning to show themselves in arms, and nothing was needed but an embodied force of the Americans, upon which they could concentrate themselves and rally with effect.

It was on the 10th or 12th of August, some four days before the defeat of Gates, that Marion reached the post at Lynch's Creek, where M'Cottry had taken his position. He was commissioned by Governor Rutledge to take command of the country in this quarter, and we will henceforth distinguish him as General Marion, although it is not so certain at what period he actually received this promotion;—we find him in possession of it in the following December.

Of his personal appearance at this time we have a brief but striking account from the hands of the venerable Judge James—a son of the Major—who had the honor to serve under Marion at the age of fifteen.

"He was a stranger," says the Judge, "to the officers and men, and they flocked about him to obtain a sight of their future commander. He was rather below the middle stature, lean and swarthy. His body was well set, but his knees and ancles were badly formed, and he still limped upon one leg. He had a countenance remarkably steady; his nose was aquiline, his chin projecting; his forehead large and high, and his eyes black and piercing. He was then forty-eight years of age, with a frame capable of enduring fatigue and every privation." Of his dress, by which we may form some idea of that costume which had provoked the laughter of Gates' veterans, we have a description also, furnished us by the same excellent authority. We know not but that this description will provoke the smile of the reader. But, of such persons, in the language of the Judge, "even trifles become important." "He (Marion) was dressed in a close round-bodied crimson jacket, of a coarse texture, and wore a leather cap, part of the uniform of the second regiment, with a silver crescent in front, inscribed with the words, 'Liberty or Death!'"

Such regimentals show rather the exigencies than the tastes of our partisan. This scarlet cloth, of which his vest was made, was almost the only kind of color which the Carolinians could procure after the conquest of Charleston. The British seemed to distribute it with the protections and pardons, perhaps as a popular mode of disseminating their principles. Moultrie somewhere tells a ludicrous anecdote of some Americans (prisoners on parole) who were nearly cut to pieces by a party of their countrymen, in consequence of their scarlet jackets. They had taken the precaution to dye them with some native roots, but the dye had disappeared, leaving the original color nearly as vivid as before.

According to Weems, Marion made rather a theatrical display on taking command of his brigade. He swore them in a circle upon their swords, never to yield the contest until they had secured their own and the liberties of their country. There is no authority for this statement, either in the work of James, in the MS. of Horry, or in any of the authorities. There is no doubt that such were his own sentiments, and such the sentiments which he strove to impart to all his followers; but the scene as described by the reverend historian was quite too artificial and theatrical for the tastes of Marion. It does not accord with what we know of his modesty, his unaffected nature, and the general simplicity of his manners. He instilled his lessons by examples rather than by speeches. His words were usually very few. He secured the fidelity of his men by carrying them bravely into action, and bringing them honorably out of it.

Marion's career of activity commenced with his command. Though always prudent, he yet learned that prudence in military life must always imply activity. The insecurity of the encampment, with a militia force, is always greater than that of battle. The Roman captains of celebrity were particularly aware of this truth. But the activity of Marion was necessarily straitened by the condition in which he found his men They were wretchedly deficient in all the materials of service. His first effort to supply some of their wants; was in sacking the saw-mills. The saws were wrought and hammered by rude blacksmiths into some resemblance to sabres, and thus provided, Marion set his men in motion, two days after taking the command. Crossing the Pedee at Port's Ferry, he advanced upon a large body of Tories commanded by Major Gainey, who held a position upon Britton's Neck. Gainey was considered by the British an excellent partisan officer, but he was caught napping. Marion moved with equal secrecy and celerity. After riding all night, he came upon the enemy at dawn in the morning. The discovery and the attack were one. The surprise was complete. A captain and several privates were slain, and the party dispersed. Marion did not lose a man, and had but two wounded. In this engagement, our representative, Major James, distinguished himself, by singling out Major Gainey for personal combat. But Gainey shrank from his more powerful assailant, and sought safety in flight. James pursued for a distance of half a mile. In the eagerness of the chase he did not perceive that he was alone and unsupported. It was enough that he was gaining upon his enemy, who was almost within reach of his sword, when the chase brought them suddenly upon a body of Tories who had rallied upon the road. There was not a moment to be lost. Hesitation would have been fatal. But our gallant Major was not to be easily intimidated. With great coolness and presence of mind, waving his sword aloft, he cried out, "come on, boys! here they are!" and rushed headlong upon the group of enemies, as if perfectly assured of support. The *ruse* was successful. The Tories broke once more, and sought safety from their individual enemy in the recesses of Pedee swamp.

Marion did not suffer the courage of his men to cool. In twenty-four hours after this event, he was again in motion. Hearing of the proximity of another body of Tories, under Captain Barfield, he advanced against him with as much celerity and caution as before. But he found Barfield strongly posted, in greater force than he expected; warned of his approach and waiting for him. It was no part of Marion's practice to expose his men unnecessarily. He had too few, to risk the loss of any precious lives, where this was to be avoided. He determined upon a different mode of managing his enemy, and resorted to a stratagem, which, subsequently, he frequently made use of. Putting a select party of his men in ambush near the Blue Savannah, he feigned retreat with another, and thus beguiled his enemy from his strong position. The result accorded with his wishes. Barfield followed and fell into the snare. The defeat was equally complete with that of Gainey.

The conduct and skill, in managing his raw militia-men, which these two achievements displayed, naturally inspired his followers with confidence in themselves and their leader. They produced a corresponding effect upon the people of the country, and were productive of no small annoyance to the Tories, who were thus suddenly reminded that there might be retribution for crime even when sheltered under the dragon folds of England. Another benefit from these occurrences was in better providing the brigade with some of the proper weapons and munitions of war.

Among the recent captures of Marion were two old field-pieces. Returning to Port's Ferry, he threw up a redoubt on the east bank of the Pedee, upon which he mounted them. He seldom troubled himself with such heavy baggage, and probably disposed of them in this way, quite as much to disencumber himself of them, as with any such motive, as was alleged, when placing them in battery, of overawing the Tories by their presence. Movements of so rapid a kind, and so frequently made as his, requiring equal dispatch and secrecy, forbade the use of artillery; and he very well knew, that, to employ men for the maintenance of isolated posts—such posts as he could establish,—would have no other effect than to expose his brigade to the chances of being cut up in detail.

On the 17th August, the day following the defeat of Gates,—of which event he was as yet wholly ignorant—he dispatched Col. Peter Horry, with orders to take command of four companies, Bonneau's, Mitchell's, Benson's and Lenud's, near Georgetown, on the Santee; to destroy all the boats and canoes on the river from the lower ferry to Lenud's—to break up and stop all communications with Charleston, and to procure, if possible, supplies of gunpowder, flints and bullets. "Twenty-five weight of gunpowder, ball or buckshot," is the language of his orders. This will show how scanty were the supplies which were to be procured of the material upon which everything depended. Marion frequently went into action with less than three rounds to a man—half of his men were sometimes lookers on because of the lack of arms and ammunition—waiting to see the fall of friends or enemies, in order to obtain the necessary means of taking part in the affair. Buck-shot easily satisfied soldiers, who not unfrequently advanced to the combat with nothing but swan-shot in their fowling-pieces.

While Horry proceeded towards Georgetown, Marion marched to the upper Santee. On this march he was advised of the defeat of Gates; but, fearing its effect upon his men, without communicating it, he proceeded immediately toward Nelson's Ferry. This was a well known pass on the great route, the "war-path", from Charleston to Camden. Here his scouts advised him of the approach of a strong British guard, with a large body of prisoners taken from Gates. The guards had stopped at a house on the east side of the river. Informed of all necessary particulars, Marion, a little before daylight, detached Col. Hugh Horry, with sixteen men, to gain possession of the road, at the pass of Horse Creek, in the swamp, while the main body under himself was to attack the enemy's rear. The attempt was made at dawn, and was perfectly successful. A letter from Marion himself, to Col. P. Horry, thus details the event:—"On the 20th inst. I attacked a guard of the 63d and Prince of Wales' Regiment, with a number of Tories, at the Great Savannah, near Nelson's Ferry; killed and took twenty-two regulars, and two Tories prisoners, and retook one hundred and fifty Continentals of the Maryland line, one wagon and a drum; one captain and a subaltern were also captured. Our loss is one killed, and Captain Benson is slightly wounded on the head."

It will scarcely be believed that, of this hundred and fifty Continentals, but three men consented to join the ranks of their liberator. It may be that they were somewhat loth to be led, even though it were to victory, by the man whose ludicrous equipments and followers, but a few weeks before, had only provoked their merriment. The reason given for their refusal, however, was not deficient in force. "They considered the cause of the country to be hopeless. They were risking life without an adequate object." The defeat of Gates, and his bad generalship, which they had so recently witnessed, were, perhaps, quite sufficient reasons to justify their misgivings.

This disastrous event did not produce like despondency in our partisan or his followers, though it furnished reasons for the greatest circumspection. At this moment Marion's was the only body of American troops in the State, openly opposed to the triumphant progress of the British. The Continentals were dispersed or captured; the Virginia and North Carolina militia scattered to the four winds; Sumter's legion cut up by Tarleton, and he himself a fugitive, fearless and active still, but as yet seeking, rather than commanding, a force. Though small and seemingly insignificant, the force of Marion had shown what might be done, with the spirit and the *personnel* of the country, under competent leaders. The cruelties of the British, who subjected the vanquished to the worst treatment of war, helped his endeavors. Shortly after the victory over Gates, Lord Cornwallis addressed an order to the British commandants at the several posts throughout the country, of which the following are extracts:

"I have given orders that all of the inhabitants of this province who have subscribed, and have taken part in this revolt, should be punished with the greatest rigor; and also those who will not turn out, that they may be imprisoned and their whole property taken from them or destroyed...I have ordered in the most positive manner that every militia man, who has borne arms with us, and afterwards joined the enemy, shall be immediately hanged!"

This gentleman has been called, by some of the American writers, the "amiable Cornwallis." It is rather difficult to say for which of his qualities this dulcet epithet was bestowed. The preceding may well justify us in the doubt we venture to express, whether it was not given as much in mockery as compliment. But, lest his commands should not be understood, as not sufficiently explicit, his Lordship proceeded to furnish examples of his meaning, which left his desires beyond reasonable question. Immediately after his return to Camden, he stained the laurels of his recent victory, and celebrated his triumph over Gates, by hanging some twelve or fifteen wretched prisoners, old men and boys, who were only suspected of treachery to the royal cause. Similar barbarities were practised by subordinate officers, emulative of this example of their superior, or in obedience to his orders. But, fortunately for the country, even this brutality, which was intended to alarm the fears of the people, and do that which the arts of their conqueror had failed to effect, was not productive of the desired results. It drove the indignant into the field—it shamed the unwilling into decision—it spurred on the inert and inactive to exertion, and armed the doubtful and the timid with resolution. It sent hundreds, whom nothing had moved before, into the ranks of Marion and Sumter. The moment of defeat and greatest despondency—the dark before the dawn—was that when the people of the country were preparing to display the most animating signs of life. The very fact that the force of Marion was so insignificant, was something in favor of that courage and patriotism, that confidence in his own resources and his men, which, defying all the inequalities of force, could move him to traverse the very paths of the conqueror, and pluck his prisoners from his very grasp. The audacity and skill of Marion, exhibited in numerous small achievements of which history furnishes no particulars, extorted a reluctant confession from the enemy, whose unwilling language will suffice for our own. Tarleton writes: "*Mr.* Marion,[41] by his zeal and abilities, showed himself capable of the trust committed to his charge. He collected his adherents at the shortest notice, and, after snaking excursions into the friendly districts, or threatening the communications, to avoid pursuit he disbanded his followers. The alarms occasioned by these insurrections, frequently retarded supplies on their way to the army; and a late report of Marion's strength delayed the junction of the recruits who had arrived from New York for the corps in the country." The 64th Regiment of Infantry was ordered to Nelson's Ferry from Charleston, and directions were given to Lieut. Col. Tarleton to pass the Wateree to awe the insurgents.[42] Cornwallis writes to Tarleton: "I most sincerely hope that you will get at *Mr.* Marion." In short, to use the further language of the British Colonel, Marion completely overran the lower districts. He cut off supplies from the army, broke up the Tories, destroyed recruiting parties, intercepted and interrupted communications, and, darting to and fro between the British posts, which he had not the power to overcome, showed that nothing but that power was necessary to enable him to challenge with them the possession of the soil. That he should disband his men at one moment, and be able by a word to bring them together when they were again wanted, proves a singular alliance between the chieftain and his followers, which is characteristic only of the most romantic history. It shows a power, on the part of the former, such as we ascribe to the winding of the magic born of Astolfo, which few commanders of militia have ever had the skill to produce. Evidently, the personal and patriotic influences were very equally strong, to occasion such prompt fidelity, in his case, on the part of his followers.

CHAPTER IX

MARION RETREATS BEFORE A SUPERIOR FORCE †
DEFEATS THE TORIES AT BLACK MINGO †
SURPRISES AND DISPERSES THE FORCE OF COL.
TYNES AT TARCOTE † IS PURSUED BY TARLETON

The solicitude manifested by the British commander in the South to get
Marion from his path, soon set the legion of Tarleton, and a strong force
under Major Wemyss, in motion for his retreats. The progress of Tarleton
was somewhat delayed, and his co-operation with Wemyss prevented. The
latter pushed his advance with equal spirit and address. Marion had with
him but one hundred and fifty men, when he heard of the approach of his
enemies. His force, it must be remembered, was of a peculiar kind, and was
constantly fluctuating. His men had cares other than those of their country's
liberties. Young and tender families were to be provided for and guarded in
the thickets where they found shelter. These were often threatened in the
absence of their protectors by marauding bands of Tories, who watched the
moment of the departure of the Whigs, to rise upon the weak, and rob and
harass the unprotected. The citizen soldiery were thus doubly employed,
and had cares to endure, and duties to perform, from which regular troops
are usually exempt, and for which regular officers seldom make allowance.
The good judgment of Marion, taking these necessities into consideration,
exercised that patience with the militia which secured their fidelity. When he
found this or that body of men anxious about their families, he yielded most
generally without reluctance to their wishes. This indulgence had its effects.
Their return was certain. They seldom lingered beyond the time at which
they had pledged themselves to reappear.

It was in consequence of this indulgence that his force was thus reduced
when the British approach was known. Wemyss was in command of the
63d regiment. He was accompanied by a large body of Tories under Major
Harrison. They moved with caution and speed, but the American General
was on the alert. He dispatched Major James with a select body of volunteers

to reconnoitre. His various outposts were called in, and with his whole present strength, thus united, Marion followed on the footsteps of James, prepared, if the chances promised him success, for doing battle with his enemy.

Major James, meanwhile, who was equally bold and skilful, pressed forward fearlessly till he became aware of the proximity of the British. He was resolved to make sure of his intelligence. He placed himself in a thicket on their line of march, and by a bright moon, was readily enabled to form a very correct notion of their character and numbers. But as the rear-guard passed by, his courageous spirit prompted further performances. He was not content to carry to his general no other proofs of his vigilance but the tidings which he had obtained. His perfect knowledge of the ground, his confidence in the excellent character of his men, and the speed of their horses, moved him to greater daring; and, bursting from his hiding-place, with a terrible shout, he swooped down with his small party upon the startled stragglers in the rear of the Tory march, carrying off his prisoners in the twinkling of an eye, without stopping to slay, and without suffering the loss of a man. Before the enemy could rally, and turn upon his path, the tread of the partisan's horse no longer sounded in his ears.

The intelligence which James bore to his commander was scarcely so encouraging. He reported the British regulars to be double their own force in number, while the Tories in the rear were alone estimated at five hundred men. Retreat, perhaps dispersion, was now inevitable. This was the sort of game, which, in his feebleness, and under the pressure of a very superior foe, our partisan was compelled to play. It was sometimes a humiliating one, and always attended with some discouragements. The evil effects, however, were only temporary. His men never retired beyond his reach. They came again at a call, refreshed by the respite, and assured by the conviction that their commander was quite as careful of their lives as themselves. Such a game was not without its interest, and its peculiarities were such as to give animation to the valor which it exercised. In these peculiarities of his warfare, lies that secret charm which has made tradition, in the southern country, linger so long and so fondly upon the name of Marion.

Judge James gives us, in few words, a lively idea of the consultation which followed the return and the report of Major James. "About an hour before day, Marion met the Major half a mile from his plantation. The officers immediately dismounted and retired to consult; the men sat on their horses in a state of anxious suspense. The conference was long and animated. At the end of it, an order was given to direct the march back to Lynch's Creek (the route to North Carolina), and no sooner was it given than a bitter groan might have been heard along the whole line. A bitter cup had now been mingled for the people of Williamsburg and Pedee, and they were doomed to drain it to the dregs, but in the end it proved a salutary medicine."

The evil here deplored was the temporary abandonment, for the first time, of this particular section of country. Hitherto, the enemy had never appeared in their neighborhood with such a force as enabled them to overrun it without fear of opposition. Now, they were destined to suffer from those tender mercies of British and Tories, which had written their chronicles in blood and flame, wherever their footsteps had gone before. Bitter, indeed, was the medicine, to whom its taste was new. But, as writes the venerable biographer, it was salutary in the end. It strengthened their souls for the future trial. It made them more resolute in the play. With their own houses in smoking ruins, and their own wives and children homeless and wandering, they could better feel what was due to the sufferings of their common country.

It was at sunset the next evening that Marion commenced his flight to North Carolina. He kept with him only sixty men. The rest dropped off by degrees as they approached their several hiding-places, lying snug, until they again heard the signal of their commander,—frequently nothing but a whisper,—which once more brought them forth, to turn the pursuit upon their enemies and avenge themselves by sudden onslaught for the ruin of their homesteads. On this retreat, Marion took with him the two field-pieces which we found him placing in battery on the Pedee a short time before. His desire to save these pieces was due rather to the supposed effect which their possession had upon the minds of the Tories, than because of any real intrinsic use which they possessed in his hands. They encumbered his flight, however, and he disposed of them, finally, without compunction. Wheeling them into a swamp he left them, where, possibly, they remain to this day, the object of occasional start and wonderment to the stalking deer-hunter. This, says Judge James, "was the last instance of military parade evinced by the General." Marching day and night he arrived at Amy's Mill, on Drowning Creek. From this place, he sent forth his parties, back to South Carolina, to gain intelligence and rouse the militia. He himself continued his march. He pitched his camp finally, on the east side of the White Marsh, near the head of the Waccamaw. There may have been a motive, other than the desire for safety, which led Marion to choose and retain this position. The borders of North Carolina swarmed with Tories, chiefly descendants of the Scotch, who constituted, on frequent subsequent occasions, the perplexing enemies with whom our partisan had to contend. It is not improbable, though history does not declare the fact, that he chose the present occasion for overawing the scattered parties, who were always stretching with lawless footsteps from Cape Fear to the Great Pedee. It was while he lay at this place, that the venerable Judge James, then a boy of sixteen, had the honor, for the first time, to dine with Marion. It was in the absence of Major James, the father of the boy, who was one of the volunteers sent back to South Carolina. The artless description which the Judge has given us of this event, so characteristic of Marion, and of the necessities to which he was habitually compelled to submit, will better please than a much more elaborate narrative.

"The dinner was set before the company by the General's servant, Oscar, partly on a pine log and partly on the ground. It consisted of lean beef, without salt, and sweet potatoes. The author had left a small pot of boiled hominy in his camp, and requested leave of his host to send for it, and the proposal was gladly acquiesced in. The hominy had salt in it, and proved, though eaten out of the pot, a most acceptable repast. The General said but little, and that was chiefly what a son would be most likely to be gratified by, in the praise of his father. We had nothing to drink but bad water; and all the company appeared to be rather grave."

That the party should be rather grave, flying from their homes and a superior foe, eating unsalted pottage, and drinking bad water, was, perhaps, natural enough. That this gravity should appear doubly impressive to a lad of sixteen, in a presence which he was taught to venerate, was still more likely to be the case. But Marion, though a cheerful man, wore ordinarily a grave, sedate expression of countenance. Never darkened by gloom, it was seldom usurped by mere merriment. He had no uproarious humor. His tastes were delicate, his habits gentle, his sensibilities warm and watchful. At most a quiet smile lighted up his features, and he could deal in little gushes of humor, of which there was a precious fountain at the bottom of his heart. That he was capable of a sharp sarcasm, was also generally understood among his friends. Horry remarks, that few men ever excelled him at retort. But he was singularly considerate of the sensibilities of others, and had his temper under rare command. His powers of forbearance were remarkable. His demeanor, whether in triumph or despondency, was equally quiet and subdued. He yielded to few excitements, was seldom elevated by successes to imprudence—as seldom depressed by disappointments to despondency. The equable tone of his mind reminds us again of Washington.

It was while Marion remained at White Marsh, that one of his captains, Gavin Witherspoon, whom he had sent out with four men, achieved one of those clever performances, that so frequently distinguished the men of Marion. He had taken refuge in Pedee Swamp from the pursuit of the enemy, and, while hiding, discovered one of the camps of the Tories who had been in pursuit of him. Witherspoon proposed to his four comrades to watch the enemy camp, until the Tories were asleep. But his men timidly shrunk from the performance, expressing their dread of superior numbers. Witherspoon undertook the adventure himself. Creeping up to the encampment, he found that they slept at the butt of a pine tree, which had been torn up by the roots. Their guns were piled against one of its branches at a little distance from them. These he first determined to secure, and, still creeping, with the skill and caution of an experienced scout, he succeeded in his object. The guns once in his possession, he aroused the Tories by commanding their surrender. They were seven in number, unarmed, and knew nothing of the force of the assailant. His own more timid followers drew near in sufficient time to assist in securing the prisoners. There was another Witherspoon with Marion, John, a brother of Gavin, and like him distinguished for great coolness, strength, and courage. Both of the brothers delighted in such adventures, and were always ready to engage in them,—the rashness of the attempt giving a sort of relish to the danger, which always sweetened it to the taste of our partisans.

The return of the various scouting parties which Marion sent out, soon set his little brigade in motion. The intelligence which they brought was well calculated to sting his soldiers, as well as himself, into immediate activity. The medicine which the British had administered to the country they abandoned, had not been suffered to lose any of its bitterness. As had been feared, the Tories had laid waste the farms and plantations. The region through which Major Wemyss had passed, for seventy miles in length and fifteen in breadth, displayed one broad face of desolation. It had been swept by sword and fire. Havoc had exercised its most ingenious powers of destruction. On most of the plantations the houses were given to the flames, the inhabitants plundered of all their possessions, and the stock, especially the sheep, wantonly shot or bayoneted. Wemyss seems to have been particularly hostile to looms and sheep, simply because they supplied the inhabitants with clothing. He seldom suffered the furniture to be withdrawn from a dwelling which he had doomed to be destroyed: Presbyterian churches he burnt religiously, as so many "sedition-shops." It was fortunate for the wretched country, thus ravaged, that the corn was not generally housed it was only in part destroyed. Had the Tories played the same game in the cornfields of the patriots, that Grant's men had done in those of the Cherokees, as recorded in an early page of this volume,[43] the devastation would have been complete. They had not limited their proceedings to these minor crimes. They had added human butchery and hanging to those other offences for which vengeance was in store. The wife and children of one Adam Cusack, threw themselves across the path of Wemyss to obtain the pardon of the husband and the father. The crime of Cusack was in having taken arms against the enemy. Their prayers were in vain. But for the interference of his own officers, the ruthless Briton would have ridden over the kneeling innocents. This was not the only savage murder of the same description which this wretched people had to endure. But such atrocities were sharp medicines, benefits in disguise, good against cowardice, selfishness, double-dealing, and deficient patriotism. They worked famously upon the natives, while they proved the invader to be as little capable of good policy, as of ordinary humanity. They roused the spirit of the militia, whet their anger and their swords together, and, by the time that Marion reappeared, they were ready for their General. He asked for nothing more. He re-entered South Carolina by a forced march. Travelling night and day, he hurried through the Tory settlements on Little Pedee, a space of sixty miles, on the second day of his journey. At Lynch's Creek he was joined by Captains James and Mouzon, with a considerable body of men. He was prepared to give them instant employment. Major Wemyss had retired to Georgetown, but Marion was advised of a large body of Tories at Black Mingo, fifteen miles below, under the command of Capt. John Coming Ball. Marion was in expectation, every moment, of additional troops, but he determined not to wait for them. He found his men in the proper mood for fight, and at such times small inequalities of force are not to be regarded. He resolved to give the humor vent, and at once commenced his march for the enemy's encampment. He found the Tories strongly posted at Shepherd's Ferry, on the south side of the Black Mingo, on a deep navigable stream, the passage of which they commanded. There was but one other approach to them, about a mile above their position, through a boggy causeway, and over a bridge of planks. It was nearly midnight when Marion's troops reached this pass. While the horses were crossing the bridge, an alarm-gun was heard from the Tory camp. Celerity now became as necessary to success as caution, and Marion ordered his men to follow him at full gallop. When they reached the main road, about three hundred yards from the enemy, the whole force, with the exception of a small body acting as cavalry, dismounted. A body of picked men, under Captain Waties, was ordered down the road to attack Bollard's house, where the Tories had been posted. Two companies, under Col. Hugh Horry, were sent to the right, and the cavalry to the left, to support the attack, Marion himself bringing up the reserve. It so happened, however, that the Tories had taken the alarm, and having withdrawn from the house, had chosen a strong position in an old field near it. Here they encountered Horry's command, on the advance, with a fire equally severe and unexpected. The effect was that of a surprise upon the assailants. Horry's troops fell back in confusion, but were promptly rallied and brought to the charge. The battle was obstinate and bloody, but the appearance of the corps under

Marion crossing the Black Mingo.

Waties, suddenly, in the rear of the Tories, soon brought it to a close. Finding themselves between two fires, the enemy gave way in all directions, and fled for refuge to the neighboring swamp of Black Mingo. So warmly contested was this affair, that, though soon over, fully one third of the men brought into the field were put *hors de combat.* The loss of Marion was proportionably very considerable. Captain Logan was among his slain; and Captain Mouzon and Lieut. Scott so severely wounded as to be unfit for future service. The force of the Tories was almost twice as great as that of the Whigs. They lost their commander, and left nearly half their number, killed and wounded, on the ground. But for the alarm given by the tread of Marion's horses, while crossing the neighboring bridge, the Tories would most probably have been surprised. At any rate, the affair would have been settled without subjecting the brigade to the severe loss which it sustained. After this event Marion adopted the precaution, whenever about to cross a bridge by night, with an enemy near, to cover the planks with the blankets of his men. But he generally preferred fords, where they could possibly be had, to bridges.

This victory was very complete. Many of the Tories came in, and joined the ranks of the conqueror. Those who did not, were quite too much confounded to show much impatience in taking up arms against him. His uniform successes, whenever he struck, had already strongly impressed the imaginations of the people. His name was already the rallying word throughout the country. To join Marion, to be one of Marion's men, was the duty which the grandsire imposed upon the lad, and to the performance of which, throwing aside his crutch, he led the way.

We have already shown why the force of Marion was so liable to fluctuation. The necessity of providing for, and protecting destitute families, starving wives and naked children, was more imperative than that of a remote and fancied liberty. These cases attended to, the militia came forth, struck a few blows, and once more returned to their destitute dependants. The victory over the Tories of Black Mingo, was, from this cause, followed by a more than usually prolonged inactivity of our partisan. His men demanded a respite to go and see their families. He consented, with some reluctance, for the business of the campaign was only beginning to open itself before him. They promised him, as usual, to return in season; but remained so long absent, that, for the first time, he now began to doubt and despair of them. This feeling was not natural with him. It was probably only due now to some derangement of his own health, some anxiety to achieve objects which presented themselves prominently to his mind. He had probably heard of the advance of General Greene, who, having succeeded to Gates, was pressing forward with fresh recruits, and the remnant of the fugitives who survived, in freedom, the fatal battle of Camden. A laudable anxiety to be active at such a time, to show to the approaching Continentals that there was a spirit in the State which they came to succor, of which the most happy auguries might be entertained, prompted his morbid impatience at the long delay of his absentees. There were other causes which led him to feel this delay more seriously now than at other times. The Tories were again gathering in force around him. Under these circumstances, and with these feelings, he consulted with his officers whether they should not leave the State and join the approaching army of Greene. Hugh Horry counselled him strenuously against it. His counsel was seconded by the rest. They prevailed with him. It was fortunate that they did so; for the great efficiency of Marion was in the independence of his command. While the matter was yet in debate, the militia began to re-appear. He had not sufficiently allowed for their exigencies, for the scattered homes and hiding-places of famishing hundreds, living on precarious supplies, in swamp and thicket. How could he reproach them—fighting as they were for love of country only, and under such privations—that country yielding them nothing, no money, no clothes, no provisions,—for they were nothing but militia. They were not enrolled on the Continental pay list. That they should seek the field at all, thus circumstanced, will be ever a wonder to that class of philosophers who found their systems upon the simple doctrine of human selfishness.

True to their chief, he rejoiced once more in their fidelity and, marching into Williamsburg, he continued to increase his numbers with his advance. His present object was the chastisement of Col. Harrison, who was in force upon Lynch's Creek; but his progress in this direction was suddenly arrested by his scouts, who brought him tidings of large gatherings of Tories in and about Salem and the fork of Black River. In this quarter, one Colonel Tynes had made his appearance, and had summoned the people generally, as good subjects of his majesty, to take the field against their countrymen. It was necessary to check this rising, and to scatter it before it gained too much head; to lessen the influence of Tynes and his party, over those who were doubtful, and afford the friends of the patriots an opportunity to come out on the proper side. There were other inducements to the movement. Col. Tynes had brought with him from Charleston, large supplies of the materials of war and comfort—commodities of which the poor patriots stood grievously in need. They hungered at the tidings brought by the scouts, of new English muskets and bayonets, broad-swords and pistols, saddles and bridles, powder and ball, which the provident Colonel had procured from Charleston for fitting out the new levies. To strike at this gathering, prevent these new levies, and procure the supplies which were designed for them, were controlling objects to which all others were made to yield. The half-naked troops of the brigade found new motives to valor in the good things which the adventure promised. Tynes lay at Tarcote, in the forks of Black River, and, as Marion was advised, without exercising much military watchfulness. The head of his column was instantly turned in this direction. Crossing the lower ford of the northern branch of Black River, at Nelson's plantation, he came upon the camp of Tynes at midnight. A hurried, but satisfactory survey, revealed the position of the enemy. No preparation had been made for safety, no precautions taken against attack. Some of the Tories slept, others feasted, and others were at cards—none watched. Marion made his arrangements for the attack without obstacle or interruption. The surprise was complete,—the panic universal. A few were slain, some with the cards in their hands. Tynes, with two of his officers, and many of his men, were made prisoners, but the greater number fled. Few were slain, as scarcely any resistance was offered, and Tarcote Swamp was fortunately nigh to receive and shelter the fugitives, many of whom shortly after made their appearance and took their places in the ranks of the conqueror. Marion lost not a man. The anticipations of his people were gratified with the acquisition of no small store of those supplies, arms and ammunition, of which they had previously stood in so much need.

These spirited achievements, however small, were so cleverly executed, so unexpectedly, and with such uniform success, as to occasion a lively sensation through the country. Hope everywhere began to warm the patriots of the State, bringing courage along with it. The effect upon the enemy, of an opposite temper and tendency, was quite as lively. Cornwallis, whom we have already seen urging Tarleton to the pursuit of our partisan, frankly acknowledged his great merits, and was heard to say that "he would give a good deal to have him taken."[44] His language to Sir Henry Clinton, in a letter dated from his camp at Winnsborough, December 3d, 1780, of a different tone, indeed, was of like tenor. It spoke for the wonderful progress and influence of our hero—a progress and influence not to be understood by the reader, from the meagre account which we are enabled to give of the battles, skirmishes and happy stratagems, in which his men were constantly engaged. Cornwallis writes,—"Col. Marion had so wrought on the minds of the people, partly by the terror of his threats and cruelty of his punishments, and partly by the promise of plunder, that *there was scarcely an inhabitant between the Santee and Pedee, that was not in arms against us. Some parties had even crossed the Santee, and carried terror to the gates of Charleston.*"

Where his lordship speaks of the successes of Marion, his great influence over the people, and the audacity with which they urged their progress through all parts of that section of country, which had been yielded to his control by Governor Rutledge, his statement is true to the very letter. It sums up very happily the results of his activity and conduct. But, when his lordship alleges cruelty and threats, and the hopes of plunder, as the means by which these results were produced, we meet his assertion with very flat denial. All the testimonies of the time, but his own, show that, in this respect, he wandered very widely from the truth. No single specification of cruelty was ever alleged against the fair fame of Francis Marion. His reputation, as a humane soldier, is beyond reproach, and when questioned, always challenged and invited investigation. The charge made by Cornwallis was urged by Lt.-Col. Balfour, commandant of Charleston, in a correspondence with General Moultrie. The latter answered it in a frank and confident manner, which showed what he thought of it. "I am sorry," he writes to Balfour, "to hear that General Marion should use his prisoners ill. *It is contrary to his natural disposition: I know him to be generous and humane.*"[45] He adds elsewhere: "General Marion always gave orders to his men that there should be no waste of the inhabitants' property, and no plundering."[46] Marion had lived in the family of Moultrie,[47] had repeatedly served under him, and if any man knew thoroughly his true disposition, the hero of Fort Sullivan was certainly that man. But the testimony of all who knew him was to the same effect. Indeed, the gentleness of his nature made him a favorite wherever known. Touching the lessons and hopes of plunder, which his men are said to have received, this scarcely requires any answer. We have seen, and shall see hereafter, the state of poverty and privation in which the brigade of Marion subsisted. A few little facts will better serve to show what their condition was. During the whole period in which we have seen him engaged, and for some months later, Marion himself, winter and summer, had slept without the luxury of a blanket. He had but one, on taking command of the "Brigade," and this he lost by accident. Sleeping soundly, after one of his forced marches, upon a bed of pine straw, it took fire, his blanket was destroyed, and he himself had an escape so narrow, that one half of the cap he wore was shrivelled up by the flames. His food was hominy or potatoes; his drink vinegar and water, of which he was fond. He had neither tea nor coffee, and seldom tasted wine or spirits. And this moderation was shown at a time when he held in his possession a power from Governor Rutledge, to impress and appropriate whatever he thought necessary to his purposes.[48] The charge against him of cruelty and plunder is perfectly absurd, and rests on the vague assertions of an enemy, who specifies no offence and offers no sort of evidence. It was but natural that such charges should be made by an astonished and disappointed foe—natural that the conqueror should ascribe to any but the right cause the reluctance of a people to submit to a monstrous usurpation, and their anxiety to avail themselves, by the presence of a favorite leader, of a principle and prospects to which their affections were really surrendered. Could the British commanders in America have really been brought to admit that the affections of the people were not with their sovereign, the war must have found a finish much sooner than it did. Their hopes were built upon this doubt; and hence their anxiety to show the coercive measures of the chieftains by whom this control, adverse to their wishes, was maintained over the minds of the people. The great influence of Marion was due to other acts. It was by the power of love, and not of terror, that he managed his followers. They loved him for himself, and loved his cause for their country. His rare command of temper, his bland, affectionate manner, his calm superiority, and that confidence in his courage and conduct, as a leader, without which militia-men are never led to victory,—these were the sources of his influence over them, and of their successes against the enemy. It was through these that he "carried terror to the very gates of Charleston." We shall see indeed, that, under Marion, the militia were never conducted to defeat.

Whatever may have been the causes of his victories, first over the minds of his people, and next over their foes, the British found it necessary that his influence should be restrained, and his farther progress arrested. Cornwallis, as we have seen, was willing to "give a good deal to have him taken." Tarleton is affectionately invoked to this pleasant duty, by the sincere hope that he would "get at Mr. Marion." This, however desirable, was no easy matter. Marion was a very "will o' the wisp" in military affairs, almost as difficult to find, at times, by his own followers, as by the enemy. He was the true model of a partisan in a country, like ours, of swamp and thicket; leading the pursuing foe, like Puck, "through bog and through briar," till he wearied out his patience, exhausted his resources, and finally laid him open for defeat. He seldom lingered long in any one spot, changing his ground frequently, with Indian policy; his scouts, well chosen, were always on the alert; and, by constant activity and enterprise, he not only baffled pursuit, but deprived retreat of its usual mortifications. The employment which he thus gave his men, not only hardened them against every turn of fortune, but kept them always in good spirits.

Tarleton rose from a sick bed to undertake his capture. He had been confined for some time in Charleston with fever. The first moment of convalescence was seized upon for carrying into effect the wishes of Cornwallis. He concerted his plans before he left the city. His legion, which was at Camden, were instructed to meet him, while with a troop of horse he set forward for some point upon the Wateree. From this point he was to descend the Wateree in quest of our partisan. His plan of pursuit, as furnished by his own pen, will be seen hereafter. Marion was not unadvised of his progress, but, either from the rapidity of Tarleton's movements, or some error in the report of his scouts, he failed of success in the object which he aimed at. This was the capture of Tarleton, while, with his troop of horse, he was on his way to join the legion. With this object he pressed his march for Nelson's Ferry on the Santee, and placed his men in ambush in the river swamp. He arrived too late. Tarleton had already crossed fully two days before. Marion passed the river in pursuit, advancing with some earnestness on the footsteps of his foe, still under the impression that Tarleton was only in command of the small troop with which he had marched from Charleston. But the British commander had already effected the junction with his legion, and was at hand in greater force than our partisan dreamed of. At night, having reached a strong position in the woods, Marion was taking his usual precautions for making his camp. He was suddenly struck with a great light, seemingly at the plantation of General Richardson. This awakened his anxieties, and led him at once to suspect the presence of his enemy in that quarter. The progress of the British was thus usually distinguished when they reached a settlement of the patriots. The suspicions of Marion were soon confirmed by the arrival of Colonel Richardson, from whom he learned that Tarleton was really at the plantation, the fires of which he saw, in force with his whole legion, and two field-pieces. The strength of the British was double his own, and, to increase his anxieties, it was discovered that one of his men,—probably one of the late converts, who had joined the ranks after the defeat of Tynes,—had deserted to the enemy. In command of a force so superior, and in possession of a guide well acquainted with the country, Tarleton was too strong to be withstood. The position of Marion was no longer safe. He at once fell back, and crossing in silence and darkness a dense and gloomy swamp of vast extent, called the "wood-yard," halted on Jack's creek, a distance of six miles from his late encampment. This post was temporarily a secure one. Tarleton, meanwhile, was conducted faithfully by the deserter into the "wood-yard,"—but the bird had flown. He pressed the pursuit the next day, with that hot haste by which he was quite as much distinguished as by his cruelties. But Marion knew his foe, and had already changed his ground. Pushing his way through a wild extent of country, full of bogs and swamps, he reached Benbow's Ferry, about ten miles above Kingstree, where, taking a strong position, he resolved to defend himself. The place was one with which himself and men were familiar. It was not only eligible in itself, commanding the passage of the river, but it was one in which defeat was not necessarily final. It had resources, and means of rally, which are always important considerations to a militia command. There were three difficult passes, through the swamp, in Marion's rear, at each of which, if driven by the enemy, his men could make a stubborn fight. His position taken, he proceeded promptly to strengthen its natural defences by art. Trees were felled across the track, and the post so improved as to reconcile the inequalities of his own with the pursuing force of Tarleton. Had the latter made his appearance, as Marion fully hoped and expected, the fatal rifles of the "Brigade" thus planted, would have very quickly emptied his best saddles. But the commander of the legion grew weary of the chase, at the very moment when it halted to await him. Of the pursuit he has given us a somewhat vain glorious description. He represents himself as having been nearly successful, by means of his great adroitness and the excellence of his strategy. He says—"According to the reports of the country, General Marion's numbers were hourly increasing, which induced Lt.-Col. Tarleton to move his corps, for a short time, in a very compact body, lest the Americans should gain any advantage over patrols or detachments. But as soon as he found that the account of numbers was exaggerated, and that the enemy declined an engagement, he divided his corps into several small parties, publishing intelligence that each was on patrol, and that the main body of the King's troops had countermarched to Camden. Notwithstanding the divisions scattered throughout the country, to impose upon the enemy, Lt.-Col. Tarleton took care that no detachment should be out of the reach of assistance; and that the whole formed after dark every evening a solid and vigilant corps during the night. This stratagem had not been employed more than three days, before General Marion was on the point of falling a sacrifice to it. He advanced on the 10th before day, with five hundred militia, to attack Lt.-Col. Tarleton (who had notice of his approach), and arrived within two miles of his post, when a person of the name of Richardson discovered to him his misconception of the British force."

But, as we have seen, Marion's advance upon Tarleton was only the continuation of the pursuit which he began under the impression that the latter was still forcing his way to Camden with the small force with which he had crossed the Santee. Of the descent of the legion from above, he knew nothing, and the three days' strategy of Tarleton were wasted upon him. The caution of the British Colonel in all this time might have been spared. It influenced the course of Marion in no respect. We have seen that, when the latter discovered his enemy, it was before day had closed, and not just before day. We have also seen that Tarleton's own bonfires had already revealed the secret of his presence, in strength, to his wary antagonist.

If Col. Richardson had never entered the camp of Marion, the blazing dwellings of the Richardson family would have led to such precautions, on the side of the partisan, as must have effectually baffled the objects of the British Colonel. This indulgence in the usual British passion for burning the homesteads of women and children, which Tarleton could not resist, even though his immediate aim required the utmost watchfulness and secrecy, at once revealed to Marion not only that his enemy was there, but that he was there, with a force, in the strength of which he had the utmost confidence. It is not to be supposed that a small detachment, a scouting party of horse, a troop sent out for intelligence,—such as the British Colonel represents his several parties to have been, when his force was broken up in detail, to beguile the partisan,—would be likely to commit such excesses as to draw the eye of the country suddenly upon them, at a time, too, when a wary adversary was within two miles with a force of five hundred men.

Tarleton proceeds: "A pursuit was immediately commenced, and continued for seven hours, through swamps and defiles. Some prisoners fell into the possession of the legion dragoons, who gained ground very fast, and must soon have brought the enemy to action, when an express from Earl Cornwallis, who had followed the tracks of the march, recalled Lt.-Col. Tarleton."

Such is the British narrative. We have reason to think it faulty in several respects. We doubt that it was the express of Earl Cornwallis that arrested the pursuit of our Legionary Colonel. We are disposed to ascribe it to his own weariness of the game. The dispatch of Cornwallis to which he refers, was dated at Winnsboro' on the 9th of the month. It was on the night of the 10th, as we see by Tarleton's own statement, that he commenced the close and earnest pursuit of Marion. The distance from Winnsboro' to the 'wood yard,' even allowing that the instincts and information of the express should bring him directly upon the trail of the Legion, would have employed him fully two days to overcome. These two days would have brought him to the close of the twelfth, up to which period, had Tarleton continued the chase, he might have enjoyed the satisfaction of shaking hands with his antagonist in his defences at Benbow's Ferry. There, at the first proper position in which he might, with any hopes of success, oppose his adversary, had Marion taken his stand. There, having entrenched himself, he was busy in bringing together his forces. "Had Tarleton," says Judge James, "proceeded with his jaded horses to Benbow's, he would have exposed his force to such sharp shooting as he had not yet experienced, and that in a place where he could not have acted with either his artillery or cavalry."

But Tarleton had tired of the adventure. After a pursuit of twenty-five miles, he found his progress arrested by a swamp, wide and deep, through which his eye could discern no beaten road. But this should have discouraged no resolute commander, having his enemy before him. Marion had already preceded him in the passage, and was then within ten miles, awaiting his approach. He could have reached him in three hours, and four might have sufficed for the march and conflict. The express of Cornwallis might have yielded that time, since it was not on the necessity of the Earl that he had written. Tarleton insinuates that the sole desire of Marion was to save himself. Now, one fact will suffice to show the incorrectness of this notion. For a distance of twelve miles on his retreat, the course of the partisan skirted the south branch of Black River. He could, at any time and in a few minutes, have plunged into it, and no regular body of cavalry could have followed him. Besides, so close, we are told, was the pursuit, that the dragoons were taking prisoners. The enemy must have been overtaken, but for the express. Under such circumstances it seems strange that Tarleton should show such singular deference to the express as to forbear the blow, when his sabre was already uplifted, and one of his most troublesome enemies was actually beneath it. It is scarcely possible that, with his dragoons so close on the heels of the fugitives and informed by prisoners of the proximity of his foe, he should not have heard that he was finally posted and in waiting for him. We will suppose, however, that he did not. He turned the head of his column at the very moment when his object was attainable. Popular tradition represents him as expressing himself discouraged at the sight of Ox swamp, and exclaiming, "Come, my boys! let us go back. We will soon find the *Game Cock* (meaning Sumter), but as for this d——d *Swamp*-fox, the devil himself could not catch him." From this speech of Tarleton, we are given to understand that the two popular names were derived, by which Sumter and Marion were ever after known by their followers.

Tarleton gained nothing by the pursuit of his wily antagonist. Marion remained in perfect mastery over the whole territory which he had been wont to overrun, with a strength somewhat increased by the fact that he had succeeded in baffling and eluding the attempts of one who had hitherto been successful in all his enterprises. From this moment the career of Tarleton ceased to be fortunate. His failure to capture Marion was the first in a long train of disappointments and disasters, some of which were also attended by the most disgraceful and humbling defeats.

CHAPTER X

MARION ATTEMPTS GEORGETOWN † HORRY DEFEATS MERRITT † MELTON DEFEATED BY BARFIELD † GABRIEL MARION TAKEN BY THE TORIES AND MURDERED † MARION RETIRES TO SNOW'S ISLAND

Failing to overtake Marion in his retreat, and unwilling to press upon him in his stronghold, Tarleton turned the heads of his columns in the search after the other famous partisan of Carolina, General Sumter. This gentleman, after the surprise and dispersion of his force, which had followed so closely the defeat of Gates, had fallen back, with the wreck of his command, to the neighborhood of the mountains. But, no sooner was it understood that a second Continental army was on its march for Carolina, than he emerged from his retreat, and renewed his enterprises with as much activity as ever. It was to direct his arms against this enemy, and to restrain his incursions, that Tarleton was recalled from the pursuit of Marion by Earl Cornwallis.

The force under Sumter had increased to about five hundred men when he approached, and took post within twenty-eight miles of the encampment of Cornwallis at Winnsboro'. This approach, particularly as Sumter, unlike Marion, was apt to linger some time in a favorite position, induced the British commander to attempt his surprise. Col. Wemyss was accordingly sent against him with a strong body of British infantry. But Wemyss was defeated, severely wounded himself, and fell into the hands of the Americans. The failure of Wemyss, and the audacity of Sumter, provoked the anxiety and indignation of Cornwallis. Tarleton promptly seconded the wishes of his superior, and rapidly advanced upon his adversary. Sumter, hearing of his approach, and with a force very far superior to his own, commenced his retreat, and threw the Tyger River between himself and his pursuer. Apprehensive only of losing his prey, and not at all doubtful of his victory, Tarleton continued the pursuit with about four hundred mounted men, leaving the main body of his infantry and artillery to follow. As soon as Sumter discovered that the whole of the British army was not at his heels, he discontinued his flight, and waited for his enemy at the house and farm of one Blackstock, on the banks of the Tyger. Here an action followed, in which the British were defeated Tarleton lost ninety-two slain and one hundred wounded. The Americans lost three men slain and as many wounded. But among the latter was their commander. The wound of Sumter was in the breast, and a very severe one. He was wrapped up in the raw hide of a bullock, suspended between two horses, and, guarded by a hundred faithful followers, was conveyed in safety to North Carolina, where, unhappily, he lay for some time totally incapacitated from active performance.

This event was preceded and followed by others quite as encouraging to the American cause. The battle of Ring's Mountain took place on the 7th October, 1780, in which the British, under Major Ferguson, experienced a total defeat; Ferguson being slain, and the killed, wounded and captured of his army, amounting to eleven hundred men. Meanwhile, the example of Marion and Sumter had aroused the partisan spirit in numerous other places; and every distinct section of the country soon produced its particular leader, under whom the Whigs embodied themselves, striking wherever an opportunity offered of cutting off the British and Tories in detail, and retiring to places of safety, or dispersing in groups, on the approach of a superior force. This species of warfare was, of all kinds, that which was most likely to try the patience, and baffle the progress, of the British commander. He could overrun the country, but he made no conquests. His great armies passed over the land unquestioned, but had no sooner withdrawn, than his posts were assailed, his detachments cut off, his supplies arrested, and the Tories once more overawed by their fierce and fearless neighbors. Marion's brigade, in particular, constantly in motion,—moving by night as frequently as by day, singularly well informed by its scouts, and appearing at the least expected moment, always ready to prevent the gathering, into force and strength, of the loyalists. And this activity was shown, and this warfare waged, at a time, when, not only was the State without an army, without any distinct embodiment of its own, or of its confederates, when it was covered everywhere with strong and well appointed posts of the enemy. The position of Earl Cornwallis at Winnsboro', completed his chain of posts from Georgetown to Augusta, in a circle, the centre of which would have been about Beaufort, in South Carolina, equidistant from Charleston and Savannah. These posts consisted of Georgetown, Camden, Winnsboro', Ninety-Six and Augusta. Within this circle was an interior chain, at the distance of half the radius, consisting of Fort Watson on the road to Camden, Motte's house, and Granby on the Congaree. Dorchester and Orangeburgh, on the road both to Ninety-six and Granby, were fortified as posts of rest and deposit, on the line of communication; as was Monk's Corner, or Biggin Church, and some other small posts on that to Camden. These posts were all judiciously chosen, both for arming the country and obtaining subsistence.[49]

Penetrating between these posts, and snatching their prey, or smiting the enemy's detachments, under the very jaws of their cannon, our partisans succeeded in embodying public opinion, through the very sense of shame, against their enemies. The courage of the Whigs was ennobled, and their timidity rebuked, when they beheld such a daring spirit, and one so crowned by frequent successes, in such petty numbers. The *esprit de corps*, which these successes, and this spirit, awakened in the brigade of Marion, necessarily imparted itself to the region of country in which he operated; and the admiration which he inspired in the friendly, and the fear which he taught to the adverse, uniting in their effects, brought equally the faithful and the doubtful to his ranks. From the moment that he eluded the arts, and baffled the pursuit of Tarleton, the people of that tract of country, on a line stretching from Camden, across, to the mouth of Black Creek on the Pedee, including generally both banks of the Wateree, Santee and Pedee, were now (excepting Harrison's party on Lynch's Creek) either ready, or preparing to join him. Under these auspices, with his brigade increasing, Marion began to prepare for new enterprises.

The British post at Georgetown was one of considerable strength and importance. It was of special importance to Marion. From this place he procured, or expected to procure, his supplies of salt, clothing, and ammunition. Of these commodities he was now grievously in want. To surprise Georgetown became as desirable as it was difficult. Marion determined to attempt it. It was only by a surprise that he could hope to be successful, and he made his plans accordingly. They were unfortunate, and the event was particularly and personally distressing to himself. To expedite his schemes, he crossed Black river, at a retired place, called Potato Ferry, and proceeded by the "Gap-way" towards the object of his aim. Three miles from the town there is an inland swamp, called "White's Bay," which, discharging itself by two mouths, the one into Black river, the other into Sampit, completely insulates the town, which stands on the north side of the latter river near its junction with Winyaw bay. Over the creek which empties into the Sampit, there is a bridge, two miles from Georgetown. In the rear of these swamps, Marion concealed himself with the main body of his force, sending out two parties to reconnoitre. One of these parties was commanded by Col. P. Horry, the other by Capt. Melton. These officers both encountered the enemy, but they were not both equally fortunate in the result. Horry may be allowed to tell his own story. "I was sent," he writes, "by Gen. Marion to reconnoitre Georgetown. I proceeded with a guide through the woods all night. At the dawn of day, I drew near the town. I laid an ambuscade, with thirty men and three officers, near the road. About sunrise a chair appeared with two ladies escorted by two British officers. I was ready in advance with an officer to cut them off, but reflecting that they might escape, and alarm the town, which would prevent my taking greater numbers, I desisted. The officers and chair halted very near me, but soon the chair went on, and the officers gallopped in retrograde into the town. Our party continued in ambush, until 10 o'clock A. M.

"Nothing appearing, and men and horses having eaten nothing for thirty-six hours, we were hungered, and retired to a plantation of my quarter-master's, a Mr. White, not far distant. There a curious scene took place. As soon as I entered the house…four ladies appeared, two of whom where Mrs. White and her daughter. I was asked what I wanted. I answered, food, refreshment. The other two ladies were those whom I had seen escorted by the British officers. They seemed greatly agitated, and begged most earnestly that I would go away, for the family was very poor, had no provisions of any sort,—that I knew that they were Whigs, and surely would not add to their distress. So pressing were they for my immediately leaving the plantation, that I thought they had more in view than they pretended. I kept my eye on Mrs. White, and saw she had a smiling countenance, but said nothing. Soon she left the room, and I left it also and went into the piazza, laid my cap, sword and pistols on the long bench, and walked the piazza;—when I discovered Mrs. White behind the house chimney beckoning me. I got to her undiscovered by the young ladies, when she said 'Colonel Horry, be on your guard; these two young ladies, Miss F— and M—, are just from Georgetown; they are much frightened, and I believe the British are leaving it and may soon attack you. As to provisions, which they make such a rout about, I have plenty for your men and horses in yonder barn, but you must affect to take them by force. Hams, bacon, rice, and fodder, are there. You must insist on the key of the barn, and threaten to split the door with an axe if not immediately opened.' I begged her to say no more, for I was well acquainted with all such matters—to leave the ladies and everything else to my management. She said 'Yes; but do not ruin us: be artful and cunning, or Mr. White may be hanged and all our houses burnt over our heads.' We both secretly returned, she to the room where the young ladies were, and I to the piazza I had just left."[50] This little narrative will give some idea of the straits to which the good whig matrons of Carolina were sometimes reduced in those days. But no time was allowed Horry to extort the provisions as suggested. He had scarcely got to the piazza when his videttes gave the alarm. Two shots warned him of the approach of the foe, and forgetting that his cap, sabre and pistols, lay on the long bench on the piazza, Horry mounted his horse, left the enclosure, and rushed into the melee. The British were seventeen in number, well mounted, and commanded by a brave fellow named Merritt. The dragoons, taken by surprise, turned in flight, and, smiting at every step, the partisans pursued them with fatal earnestness. But two men are reported to have escaped death or captivity, and they were their captain and a sergeant. It was in approaching to encounter Merritt that Horry discovered that he was weaponless. "My officers," says he, "in succession, came up with Captain Merritt, who was in the rear of his party, urging them forward. They engaged him. He was a brave fellow. Baxter, with pistols, fired at his breast, and missing him, retired; Postelle and Greene, with swords, engaged him; both were beaten off. Greene nearly lost his head. His buckskin breeches were cut through several inches...I almost blush to say that this one British officer beat off three Americans."[51] The honor of the day was decidedly with Merritt, though he was beaten. He was no doubt a far better swordsman then our self-taught cavalry, with broadswords wrought out of mill saws. Merritt abandoned his horse, and escaped to a neighboring swamp, from whence, at midnight, he got into Georgetown.[52] Two of Horry's prisoners proved to be American soldiers; "the sergeant belonged to the 3d Regiment of South Carolina Continentals, and a drummer formerly belonged to my own Regiment (the 5th.) The drummer was cruelly wounded on the head; the sergeant was of Virginia, and wounded on the arm. They said they had enlisted from the Prison Ship to have a chance of escaping and joining their countrymen in arms,"[53] and would have done so that day but that the British captain was in the rear, and they dared not. Horry rejoined Marion in safety with his prisoners.

Captain Melton was not so fortunate. He came in contact with a party of Tories, much larger than his own force, who were patrolling, under Captain Barfield, near White's Bridge. A sharp, but short action followed, in which Melton was compelled to retreat. But Gabriel Marion, a nephew of the General, had his horse shot under him, and fell into the hands of the Tories. As soon as he was recognized he was put to death, no respite allowed, no pause, no prayer. His name was fatal to him. The loss was severely felt by his uncle, who, with no family or children of his own, had lavished the greater part of his affections upon this youth, of whom high expectations had been formed, and who had already frequently distinguished himself by his gallantry and conduct. He had held a lieutenancy in the Second South Carolina Regiment, and was present at the battle of Fort Moultrie. Subsequently, he had taken part in most of the adventures of his uncle. Marion felt his privation keenly; but he consoled himself by saying that "he should not mourn for him. The youth was virtuous, and had fallen in the cause of his country!" But this event, with some other instances of brutality and murder on the part of the Tories, happening about this time, gave a more savage character than ever to the warfare which ensued. Motives of private anger and personal revenge embittered and increased the usual ferocities of civil war; and hundreds of dreadful and desperate tragedies gave that peculiar aspect to the struggle, which led Greene to say that the inhabitants pursued each other rather like wild beasts than like men. In the Cheraw district, on the Pedee, above the line where Marion commanded, the Whig and Tory warfare, of which we know but little beyond this fact, was one of utter extermination. The revolutionary struggle in Carolina was of a sort utterly unknown in any other part of the Union.

The attempt upon Georgetown was thus defeated. The British had taken the alarm, and were now in strength, and in a state of vigilance and activity, which precluded the possibility of surprise. Marion's wishes, therefore, with regard to this place, were deferred accordingly to a more auspicious season. He retired to Snow's Island, where he made his camp. This place acquired large celebrity as the "camp of Marion." To this day it is pointed out with this distinguishing title, and its traditionary honors insisted upon. It was peculiarly eligible for his purposes, furnishing a secure retreat, a depot for his arms, ammunition, prisoners and invalids— difficult of access, easily guarded, and contiguous to the scenes of his most active operations. "Snow's Island" lies at the confluence of Lynch's Creek and the Pedee. On the east flows the latter river; on the west, Clark's Creek, issuing from Lynch's, and a stream navigable for small vessels; on the north lies Lynch's Creek, wide and deep, but nearly choked by rafts of logs and refuse timber. The island, high river swamp, was spacious, and, like all the Pedee river swamp of that day, abounded in live stock and provision. Thick woods covered the elevated tracts, dense cane-brakes the lower, and here and there the eye rested upon a cultivated spot, in maize, which the invalids and convalescents were wont to tend.

Here Marion made his fortress. Having secured all the boats of the neighborhood, he chose such as he needed, and destroyed the rest. Where the natural defences of the island seemed to require aid from art, he bestowed it; and, by cutting away bridges and obstructing the ordinary pathways with timber, he contrived to insulate, as much as possible, the country under his command. From this fortress, his scouting parties were sent forth nightly in all directions. Enemies were always easy to be found. The British maintained minor posts at Nelson's Ferry and Scott's Lake, as well as Georgetown; and the Tories on Lynch's Creek and Little Pedee were much more numerous, if less skilfully conducted, than the men of Marion.

Marion's encampment implied no repose, no forbearance of the active business of war. Very far from it. He was never more dangerous to an enemy, than when he seemed quietly in camp. His camp, indeed, was frequently a lure, by which to tempt the Tories into unseasonable exposure. The post at Snow's Island gave him particular facilities for this species of warfare. He had but to cross a river, and a three hours' march enabled him to forage in an enemy's country. Reinforcements came to him daily, and it was only now, for the first time, that his command began to assume the appearance, and exhibit the force of a brigade.[54] He became somewhat bolder in consequence, in the tone which he used towards the Tories. We find him at this period,[55] sending forth his officers with orders of a peremptory nature. He writes to Adjutant Postelle: "You will proceed with a party down Black river, from Black Mingo to the mouth of Pedee, and come up to this place. You will take all the boats and canoes from Euhaney up, and impress negroes to bring them to camp—put some men to see them safe. You will take every horse, to whomsoever he may belong, whether friend or foe. You will take all arms and ammunition for the use of our service. You will forbid all persons from carrying any grains, stock, or any sort of provisions to Georgetown, or where the enemy may get them, on pain of being held as traitors, and enemies to the Americans. All persons who will not join you, you will take prisoners and bring to me, &c."

He then laid the country under martial law, the proper measure for straitening an enemy, and compelling sluggish and doubtful friends to declare themselves. In this proceeding he was justified by the authority of Governor Rutledge, from whom, with his brigadier's commission, he had received military command over a region of country of vast extent, which the indefatigable partisan contrived to compass and coerce, if not altogether to command and control. Similar orders with those which were given to Postelle, were addressed to Col. P. Horry; and they were both dispatched; the one, as we have seen, between Black and Pedee rivers, the other to Waccamaw Creek. Other parties were sent out in other quarters, with like objects; and, with the whole contiguous country thus placed under the keenest surveillance, Marion hailed the close of the year in his swamp fortress. All these parties were more or less engaged with the enemy, at different periods, while on their scouting expeditions. Several small, but spirited achievements, of which history condescends to furnish no details, occurred among them, in which, however, the partisans were not always successful. One instance may be mentioned. Lieutenant Roger Gordon had been dispatched with a small party to patrol on Lynch's Creek. He suffered himself, while taking refreshments at a house, to be surrounded by a party of Tories, under Capt. Butler. The enemy made good his approaches to the house, and set it on fire. Finding himself greatly outnumbered, and perceiving that resistance would be useless, Gordon surrendered upon terms; but as soon as his party had yielded up their arms, they were murdered to a man. These bloody events were accompanied and followed by others of a like character. Nor were the Tories always, or exclusively guilty. The sanguinary warfare began with them, but it was perpetuated by mutual excesses. Shortly after the murder of Gabriel Marion, the person who was supposed to have been guilty of the savage crime, was taken prisoner by Horry. While on the road, returning to the camp, environed by his guards, the prisoner was shot down by an officer, who escaped detection under cover of the night. Prisoners, after this, were seldom made on either side, where the Whigs and Tories came in conflict. No quarter was given. Safety lay in victory alone, and the vanquished, if they could not find refuge in the swamps, found no mercy from the conqueror. Even where, under the occasional influence of a milder mood, or milder captain, the discomfited were admitted to present mercy, there was still no security for their lives. There were a few infuriated men, who defied subordination, by who on both sides, the unhappy captives were sure to be sacrificed.

We need not say, in behalf of Marion, and his superior officers, that, where he or they commanded in person, no countenance was given to these bloody principles and performances. Marion was notoriously the most merciful of enemies. The death of the prisoner in the ranks of Horry, though the unhappy man was charged with the murder of his favorite nephew, was a subject of the greatest soreness and annoyance to his mind; and he warmly expressed the indignation which he felt, at an action which he could not punish.

CHAPTER XI

MARION'S CAMP AT SNOW'S ISLAND † THE CHARACTER OF HIS WARFARE † OF HIS MEN † ANECDOTES OF CONYERS AND HORRY † HE FEASTS A BRITISH OFFICER ON POTATOES † QUELLS A MUTINY

Marion's career as a partisan, in the thickets and swamps of Carolina, is abundantly distinguished by the picturesque; but it was while he held his camp at Snow's Island, that it received its highest colors of romance. In this snug and impenetrable fortress, he reminds us very much of the ancient feudal baron of France and Germany, who, perched on castled eminence, looked down with the complacency of an eagle from his eyrie, and marked all below him for his own. The resemblance is good in all respects but one. The plea and justification of Marion are complete. His warfare was legitimate. He was no mountain robber,—no selfish and reckless ruler, thirsting for spoil and delighting inhumanly in blood. The love of liberty, the defence of country, the protection of the feeble, the maintenance of humanity and all its dearest interests, against its tyrant—these were the noble incentives which strengthened him in his stronghold, made it terrible in the eyes of his enemy, and sacred in those of his countrymen. Here he lay, grimly watching for the proper time and opportunity when to sally forth and strike. His position, so far as it sheltered him from his enemies, and gave him facilities for their overthrow, was wonderfully like that of the knightly robber of the Middle Ages. True, his camp was without its castle—but it had its fosse and keep— its draw-bridge and portcullis. There were no towers frowning in stone and iron—but there were tall pillars of pine and cypress, from the waving tops of which the warders looked out, and gave warning of the foe or the victim. No cannon thundered from his walls; no knights, shining in armor, sallied forth to the tourney. He was fond of none of the mere pomps of war. He held no revels—"drank no wine through the helmet barred," and, quite unlike the baronial ruffian of the Middle Ages, was strangely indifferent to the feasts of gluttony and swilled insolence. He found no joy in the pleasures of the table. Art had done little to increase the comforts or the securities of his fortress. It was one, complete to his hands, from those of nature—such an one as must have delighted the generous English outlaw of Sherwood forest—isolated by deep ravines and rivers, a dense forest of mighty trees, and interminable undergrowth. The vine and briar guarded his passes. The laurel and the shrub, the vine and sweet scented jessamine, roofed his dwelling, and clambered up between his closed eyelids and the stars. Obstructions, scarcely penetrable by any foe, crowded the pathways to his tent;—and no footstep, not practised in the secret, and 'to the manner born,' might pass unchallenged to his midnight rest. The swamp was his moat; his bulwarks were the deep ravines, which, watched by sleepless rifles, were quite as impregnable as the castles on the Rhine. Here, in the possession of his fortress, the partisan slept secure. In the defence of such a place, in the employment of such material as he had to use, Marion stands out alone in our written history, as the great master of that sort of strategy, which renders the untaught militia-man in his native thickets, a match for the best drilled veteran of Europe. Marion seemed to possess an intuitive knowledge of his men and material, by which, without effort, he was led to the most judicious modes for their exercise. He beheld, at a glance, the evils or advantages of a position. By a nice adaptation of his resources to his situation, he promptly supplied its deficiencies and repaired its defects. Till this was done, he did not sleep;—he relaxed in none of his endeavors. By patient toil, by keenest vigilance, by a genius peculiarly his own, he reconciled those inequalities of fortune or circumstance, under which ordinary men sit down in despair. Surrounded by superior foes, he showed no solicitude on this account. If his position was good, their superiority gave him little concern. He soon contrived to lessen it, by cutting off their advanced parties, their scouts or foragers, and striking at their detachments in detail. It was on their own ground, in their immediate presence, nay, in the very midst of them, that he frequently made himself a home. Better live upon foes than upon friends, was his maxim and this practice of living amongst foes was the great school by which his people were taught vigilance.

The adroitness and address of Marion's captainship were never more fully displayed than when he kept Snow's Island; sallying forth, as occasion offered, to harass the superior foe, to cut off his convoys, or to break up, before they could well embody, the gathering and undisciplined Tories. His movements were marked by equal promptitude and wariness. He suffered no risks from a neglect of proper precaution. His habits of circumspection and resolve ran together in happy unison. His plans, carefully considered beforehand, were always timed with the happiest reference to the condition and feelings of his men. To prepare that condition, and to train those feelings, were the chief employment of his repose. He knew his game, and how it should be played, before a step was taken or a weapon drawn. When he himself, or any of his parties, left the island, upon an expedition, they advanced along no beaten paths. They made them as they went. He had the Indian faculty in perfection, of gathering his course from the sun, from the stars, from the bark and the tops of trees, and such other natural guides, as the woodman acquires only through long and watchful experience. Many of the trails, thus opened by him, upon these expeditions, are now the ordinary avenues of the country. On starting, he almost invariably struck into the woods, and seeking the heads of the larger water courses, crossed them at their first and small beginnings. He destroyed the bridges where he could. He preferred fords. The former not only facilitated the progress of less fearless enemies, but apprised them of his own approach. If speed was essential, a more direct, but not less cautious route was pursued. The stream was crossed sometimes where it was deepest. On such occasions the party swam their horses, Marion himself leading the way, though he himself was unable to swim. He rode a famous horse called Ball, which he had taken from a loyalist captain of that name. This animal was a sorrel, of high, generous blood, and took the water as if born to it. The horses of the brigade soon learned to follow him as naturally as their riders followed his master. There was no waiting for pontoons and boats. Had there been there would have been no surprises.

The secrecy with which Marion conducted his expeditions was, perhaps, one of the reasons for their frequent success. He entrusted his schemes to nobody, not even his most confidential officers. He consulted with them respectfully, heard them patiently, weighed their suggestions, and silently approached his conclusions. They knew his determinations only from his actions. He left no track behind him, if it were possible to avoid it. He was often vainly hunted after by his own detachments. He was more apt at finding them than they him. His scouts were taught a peculiar and shrill whistle, which, at night, could be heard at a most astonishing distance. We are reminded of the signal of Roderick Dhu:—

—*"He whistled shrill,*
And he was answered from the hill,
Wild as the scream of the curlew,
From crag to crag, the signal flew."

His expeditions were frequently long, and his men, hurrying forth without due preparation, not unfrequently suffered much privation from want of food. To guard against this danger, it was their habit to watch his cook. If they saw him unusually busied in preparing supplies of the rude, portable food, which it was Marion's custom to carry on such occasions, they knew what was before them, and provided themselves accordingly. In no other way could they arrive at their general's intentions. His favorite time for moving was with the setting sun, and then it was known that the march would continue all night. Before striking any sudden blow, he has been known to march sixty or seventy miles, taking no other food in twenty-four hours, than a meal of cold potatoes and a draught of cold water, the latter might have been repeated. This was truly a Spartan process for acquiring vigor. Its results were a degree of patient hardihood, as well in officers as men, to which few soldiers in any periods have attained. These marches were made in all seasons. His men were badly clothed in homespun, a light wear which afforded little warmth. They slept in the open air, and frequently without a blanket. Their ordinary food consisted of sweet potatoes, garnished, on fortunate occasions, with lean beef. Salt was only to be had when they succeeded in the capture of an enemy's commissariat; and even when this most necessary of all human condiments was obtained, the unselfish nature of Marion made him indifferent to its use. He distributed it on such occasions, in quantities not exceeding a bushel, to each Whig family; and by this patriarchal care, still farther endeared himself to the affection of his followers.

The effect of this mode of progress was soon felt by the people of the partisan. They quickly sought to emulate the virtues which they admired. They became expert in the arts which he practised so successfully. The constant employment which he gave them, the nature of his exactions, taught activity, vigilance, coolness and audacity. His first requisition, from his subordinates, was good information. His scouts were always his best men. They were generally good horsemen, and first rate shots. His cavalry were, in fact, so many mounted gunmen, not uniformly weaponed, but carrying the rifle, the carbine, or an ordinary fowling-piece, as they happened to possess or procure them. Their swords, unless taken from the enemy, were made out of mill saws, roughly manufactured by a forest blacksmith. His scouts were out in all directions, and at all hours. They did the double duty of patrol and spies. They hovered about the posts of the enemy, crouching in the thicket, or darting along the plain, picking up prisoners, and information, and spoils together. They cut off stragglers, encountered patrols of the foe, and arrested his supplies on the way to the garrison. Sometimes the single scout, buried in the thick tops of the tree, looked down upon the march of his legions, or hung perched over the hostile encampment till it slept, then slipping down, stole through the silent host, carrying off a drowsy sentinel, or a favorite charger, upon which the daring spy flourished conspicuous among his less fortunate companions. The boldness of these adventurers was sometimes wonderful almost beyond belief. It was the strict result of that confidence in their woodman skill, which the practice of their leader, and his invariable success, naturally taught them to entertain.

The mutual confidence which thus grew up between our partisan and his men, made the business of war, in spite of its peculiar difficulties and privations, a pleasant one. As they had no doubts of their leader's ability to conduct them to victory, he had no apprehension, but, when brought to a meeting with the enemy, that they would secure it. His mode of battle was a simple one; generally very direct; but he was wonderfully prompt in availing himself of the exigencies of the affair. His rule was to know his enemy, how posted and in what strength,—then, if his men were set on, they had nothing to do but to fight. They knew that he had so placed them that valor was the only requisite. A swamp, right or left, or in his rear; a thicket beside him;—any spot in which time could be gained, and an inexperienced militia rallied, long enough to become reconciled to the unaccustomed sights and sounds of war,—were all that he required, in order to secure a fit position for fighting in. He found no difficulty in making good soldiers of them. It caused him no surprise, and we may add no great concern, that his raw militia men, armed with rifle and ducking gun, should retire before the pushing bayonets of a regular soldiery. He considered it mere butchery to expose them to this trial. But he taught his men to retire slowly, to take post behind the first tree or thicket, reload, and try the effect of a second fire; and so on, of a third and fourth, retiring still, but never forgetting to take advantage of every shelter that offered itself. He expected them to fly, but not too far to be useful. We shall see the effect of this training at Eutaw, where the militia in the advance delivered seventeen fires, before they yielded to the press of the enemy. But, says Johnson, with equal truth and terseness, "that distrust of their own immediate commanders which militia are too apt to he affected with, never produced an emotion where Marion and Pickens commanded."[56] The history of American warfare shows conclusively that, under the right leaders, the American militia are as cool in moments of danger as the best drilled soldiery in the universe. But they have been a thousand times disgraced by imbecile and vainglorious pretenders.

Marion was admirably supported by his followers. Several officers of the brigade were distinguished men. Of Major John James we have already seen something. All the brothers were men of courage and great muscular activity. The Witherspoons were similarly endowed. His chief counsellors were the brothers Horry and Postelle,—all like himself descended from Huguenot stocks. To the two last (the brothers Postelle) it has been remarked, that "nothing appeared difficult."[57] Captains Baxter and Conyers were particularly distinguished,—the first for his gigantic frame, which was informed by a corresponding courage; the latter by his equal bravery and horsemanship. He was a sort of knight-errant in the brigade, and his behavior seemed not unfrequently dictated by a passion for chivalrous display. An anecdote, in connection with Conyers, is told, which will serve to show what was the spirit of the patriotic damsels of the revolution. Marion had environed Colonel Watson, at a plantation where Mary, the second daughter of John Witherspoon, was living at the time. She was betrothed to Conyers. The gallant captain daily challenged the British posts, skirmishing in the sight of his mistress. His daring was apparent enough—his great skill and courage were known. He presented himself frequently before the lines of the enemy, either as a single champion or at the head of his troop. The pride of the maiden's heart may be imagined when she heard the warning in the camp, as she frequently did—"Take care,—there is Conyers!" The insult was unresented: but, one day, when her lover appeared as usual, a British officer, approaching her, spoke sneeringly, or disrespectfully, of our knight-errant. The high spirited girl drew the shoe from her foot, and flinging it in his face, exclaimed, "Coward! go and meet him!" The chronicler from whom we derive this anecdote is particularly careful to tell us that it was a walking shoe and not a kid slipper which she made use of; by which we are to understand, that she was no ways tender of the stroke.

The Horrys were both able officers. Hugh was a particular favorite of Marion. For his brother he had large esteem. Of Peter Horry we have several amusing anecdotes, some of which we gather from himself. It is upon the authority of his MS. memoir that we depend for several matters of interest in this volume. This memoir, written in the old age of the author, and while he suffered from infirmities of age and health, is a crude but not uninteresting narrative of events in his own life, and of the war. The colonel confesses himself very frankly. In his youth he had a great passion for the sex, which led him into frequent difficulties. These, though never very serious, he most seriously relates. He was brave, and ambitious of distinction. This ambition led him to desire a command of cavalry rather than of infantry. But he was no rider—was several times unhorsed in combat, and was indebted to the fidelity of his soldiers for his safety.[58] On one occasion his escape was more narrow from a different cause. He gives us a ludicrous account of it himself. Crossing the swamp at Lynch's Creek, to join Marion, in the dark, and the swamp swimming, he encountered the bough of a tree, to which he clung, while his horse passed from under him. He was no swimmer, and, but for timely assistance from his followers, would have been drowned. Another story, which places him in a scarcely less ludicrous attitude, is told by Garden.[59] He was ordered by Marion to wait, in ambush, the approach of a British detachment. The duty was executed with skill; the enemy was completely in his power. But he labored under an impediment in his speech, which, we may readily suppose, was greatly increased by anxiety and excitement. The word stuck in his throat, as "amen" did in that of Macbeth. The emergency was pressing, but this only increased the difficulty. In vain did he make the attempt. He could say "fi—fi—fi!" but he could get no further—the "r" was incorrigible. At length, irritated almost to madness, he exclaimed, "*Shoot*, d——n you, *shoot!* you know what I would say! Shoot, and be d——d to you!" He was present, and acted bravely, in almost every affair of consequence, in the brigade of Marion. At Quinby, Capt. Baxter, already mentioned, a man distinguished by his great strength and courage, as well as size, and by equally great simplicity of character, cried out, "I am wounded, colonel!" "Think no more of it, Baxter," was the answer of Horry, "but stand to your post." "But I can't stand," says Baxter, "I am wounded a second time." "Lie down then, Baxter, but quit not your post." "They have shot me again, colonel," said the wounded man, "and if I stay any longer here, I shall be shot to pieces." "Be it so, Baxter, but stir not," was the order, which the brave fellow obeyed, receiving a fourth wound before the engagement was over.

It was while Marion was lying with his main force at the camp at Snow's Island, that two circumstances occurred which deserve mention, as equally serving to illustrate his own and the character of the warfare of that time and region. One of these occurrences has long been a popular anecdote, and, as such, has been made the subject of a very charming picture, which has done something towards giving it a more extended circulation.[60] The other is less generally known, but is not less deserving of the popular ear, as distinguishing, quite as much as the former, the purity, simplicity, and firmness of Marion's character. It appears that, desiring the exchange of prisoners, a young officer was dispatched from the British post at Georgetown to the swamp encampment of Marion, in order to effect this object. He was encountered by one of the scouting parties of the brigade, carefully blindfolded, and conducted, by intricate paths, through the wild passes, and into the deep recesses of the island. Here, when his eyes were uncovered, he found himself surrounded by a motley multitude, which might well have reminded him of Robin Hood and his outlaws. The scene was unquestionably wonderfully picturesque and attractive, and our young officer seems to have been duly impressed by it. He was in the middle of one of those grand natural amphitheatres so common in our swamp forests, in which the massive pine, the gigantic cypress, and the stately and ever-green laurel, streaming with moss, and linking their opposite arms, inflexibly locked in the embrace of centuries, group together, with elaborate limbs and leaves, the chief and most graceful features of Gothic architecture. To these recesses, through the massed foliage of the forest, the sunlight came as sparingly, and with rays as mellow and subdued, as through the painted window of the old cathedral, falling upon aisle and chancel. Scattered around were the forms of those hardy warriors with whom our young officer was yet destined, most probably, to meet in conflict,—strange or savage in costume or attitude—lithe and sinewy of frame—keen-eyed and wakeful at the least alarm. Some slept, some joined in boyish sports; some with foot in stirrup, stood ready for the signal to mount and march. The deadly rifle leaned against the tree, the sabre depended from its boughs. Steeds were browsing in the shade, with loosened bits, but saddled, ready at the first sound of the bugle to skirr through brake and thicket. Distant fires, dimly burning, sent up their faint white smokes, that, mingling with the thick forest tops, which they could not pierce, were scarce distinguishable from the long grey moss which made the old trees look like so many ancient patriarchs. But the most remarkable object in all this scene was Marion himself. Could it be that the person who stood before our visitor—"in stature of the smallest size, thin, as well as low"[61] that of the redoubted chief, whose sleepless activity and patriotic zeal had carried terror to the gates of Charleston; had baffled the pursuit and defied the arms of the best British captains; had beaten the equal enemy, and laughed at the superior? Certainly, if he were, then never were the simple resources of intellect, as distinguishable from strength of limb, or powers of muscle, so wonderfully evident as in this particular instance. The physical powers of Marion were those simply of endurance. His frame had an iron hardihood, derived from severe discipline and subdued desires and appetites, but lacked the necessary muscle and capacities of the mere soldier. It was as the general, the commander, the counsellor, rather than as the simple leader of his men, that Marion takes rank, and is to be considered in the annals of war. He attempted no physical achievements, and seems to have placed very little reliance upon his personal prowess.[62]

The British visitor was a young man who had never seen Marion. The great generals whom he was accustomed to see, were great of limb, portly, and huge of proportion. Such was Cornwallis, and others of the British army. Such, too, was the case among the Americans. The average weight

Marion inviting a British Officer to Dinner.

of these opposing generals, during that war, is stated at more than two hundred pounds. The successes of Marion must naturally have led our young Englishman to look for something in his *physique* even above this average, and verging on the gigantic. Vastness seems always the most necessary agent in provoking youthful wonder, and satisfying it. His astonishment, when they did meet, was, in all probability, not of a kind to lessen the partisan in his estimation. That a frame so slight, and seemingly so feeble, coupled with so much gentleness, and so little pretension, should provoke a respect so general, and fears, on one side, so impressive, was well calculated to compel inquiry as to the true sources of this influence. Such an inquiry was in no way detrimental to a reputation founded, like Marion's, on the successful exercise of peculiar mental endowments. The young officer, as soon as his business was dispatched, prepared to depart, but Marion gently detained him, as he said, for dinner, which was in preparation. "The mild and dignified simplicity of Marion's manners had already produced their effects, and, to prolong so interesting an interview, the invitation was accepted. The entertainment was served up on pieces of bark, and consisted entirely of roasted potatoes, of which the general ate heartily, requesting his guest to profit by his example, repeating the old adage, that "hunger is the best sauce." "But surely, general," said the officer, "this cannot be your ordinary fare." "Indeed, sir, it is," he replied, "and we are fortunate on this occasion, entertaining company, to have more than our usual allowance."[63] The story goes, that the young Briton was so greatly impressed with the occurrence, that, on his return to Georgetown, he retired from the service, declaring his conviction that men who could with such content endure the privations of such a life, were not to be subdued. His conclusion was strictly logical, and hence, indeed, the importance of such a warfare as that carried on by Marion, in which, if he obtained no great victories, he was yet never to be overcome.

The next anecdote, if less pleasing in its particulars, is yet better calculated for the development of Marion's character the equal powers of firmness and forbearance which he possessed, his superiority to common emotions, and the mingled gentleness and dignity with which he executed the most unpleasant duties of his command. Marion had placed one of his detachments at the plantation of a Mr. George Crofts, on Sampit Creek. This person had proved invariably true to the American cause; had supplied the partisans secretly with the munitions of war, with cattle and provisions. He was an invalid, however, suffering from a mortal infirmity, which compelled his removal for medical attendance to Georgetown, then in possession of the enemy.[64] During the absence of the family, Marion placed a sergeant in the dwelling-house, for its protection. From this place the guard was expelled by two officers of the brigade, and the house stripped of its contents. The facts were first disclosed to Marion by Col. P. Horry, who received them from the wife of Crofts. This lady pointed to the sword of her husband actually at the side of the principal offender. The indignation of Marion was not apt to expend itself in words. Redress was promised to the complainant and she was dismissed. Marion proceeded with all diligence to the recovery of the property. But his course was governed by prudence as well as decision. The offenders were men of some influence, and had a small faction in the brigade, which had already proved troublesome, and might be dangerous. One of them was a major, the other a captain. Their names are both before us in the MS. memoir of Horry, whose copious detail on this subject leaves nothing to be supplied. We forbear giving them, as their personal publication would answer no good purpose. They were in command of a body of men, about sixty in number, known as the Georgia Refugees. Upon the minds of these men the offenders had already sought to act, in reference to the expected collision with their general. Marion made his preparations with his ordinary quietness, and then dispatched Horry to the person who was in possession of the sword of Croft; for which he made a formal demand. He refused to give it up, alleging that it was his, and taken in war. "If the general wants it," he added, "let him come for it himself." When this reply was communicated to Marion he instructed Horry to renew the demand. His purpose seems to have been, discovering the temper of the offender, to gain the necessary time. His officers, meanwhile, were gathering around him. He was making his preparations for a struggle, which might be bloody, which might, indeed, involve not only the safety of his brigade, but his own future usefulness. Horry, however, with proper spirit, entreated not to be sent again to the offender, giving, as a reason for his reluctance, that, in consequence of the previous rudeness of the other, he was not in the mood to tolerate a repetition of the indignity, and might, if irritated, be provoked to violence. Marion then dispatched his orderly to the guilty major, with a request, civilly worded, that he might see him at head quarters. He appeared accordingly, accompanied by the captain who had joined with him in the outrage, and under whose influence he appeared to act. Marion renewed his demand, in person, for the sword of Croft. The other again refused to deliver it, alleging that "Croft was a Tory, and even then with the enemy in Georgetown."

"Will you deliver me the sword or not, Major ——?" was the answer which Marion made to this suggestion.

"I will not!" was the reply of the offender. "At these words," says Horry in the MS. before us, "I could forbear no longer, and said with great warmth, 'By G—d, sir, did I command this brigade, as you do, I would hang them both up in half an hour!' Marion sternly replied,—'This is none of your business, sir: they are both before me!—Sergeant of the guard, bring me a file of men with loaded arms and fixed bayonets!'—'I was silent!' adds Horry: 'all our field officers in camp were present, and when the second refusal of the sword was given, they all put their hands to their swords in readiness to draw. My own sword was already drawn!'

In the regular service, and with officers accustomed to, and bred up in, the severe and stern sense of authority which is usually thought necessary to a proper discipline, the refractory offender would most probably have been hewn down in the moment of his disobedience. The effect of such a proceeding, in the present instance, might have been of the most fatal character. The *esprit de corps* might have prompted the immediate followers of the offender to have seized upon their weapons, and, though annihilated, as Horry tells us they would have been, yet several valuable lives might have been lost, which the country could ill have spared. The mutiny would have been put down, but at what a price! The patience and prudence of Marion's character taught him forbearance. His mildness, by putting the offender entirely in the wrong, so justified his severity, as to disarm the followers of the criminals. These, as we have already said, were about sixty in number. Horry continues: "Their intentions were, to call upon these men for support—our officers well knew that they meant, if possible, to intimidate Marion, so as to [make him] come into their measures of plunder and Tory-killing." The affair fortunately terminated without bloodshed. The prudence of the general had its effect. The delay gave time to the offenders for reflection. Perhaps, looking round upon their followers, they saw no consenting spirit of mutiny in their eyes, encouraging their own; for, "though many of these refugees were present, none offered to back or support the mutinous officers;"—and when the guard that was ordered, appeared in sight, the companion of the chief offender was seen to touch the arm of the other, who then proffered the sword to Marion, saying, "General, you need not have sent for the guard."[65] Marion, refusing to receive it, referred him to the sergeant of the guard, and thus doubly degraded, the dishonored major of Continentals—for he was such—disappeared from sight, followed by his associate. His farther punishment was of a kind somewhat differing from those which are common to armies, by which the profession of arms is sometimes quite as much dishonored as the criminal. Marion endeavored, by his punishments, to elevate the sense of character in the spectators. He had some of the notions of Napoleon on this subject. He was averse to those brutal punishments which, in the creature, degrade the glorious image of the Creator. In the case of the two offenders, thus dismissed from his presence, the penalty was, of all others, the most terrible to persons, in whose minds there remained the sparks even of a conventional honor. These men had been guilty of numerous offences against humanity. Marion expelled them from his brigade. Subsequently, their actions became such, that he proclaimed their outlawry through the country.[66] By one of these men he was challenged to single combat, but he treated the summons with deserved contempt. His composure remained unruffled by the circumstance.

In this affair, as in numerous others, Marion's great knowledge of the militia service, and of the peculiar people with whom he sometimes had to deal, enabled him to relieve himself with little difficulty from troublesome companions. Of these he necessarily had many; for the exigencies of the country were such that patriotism was not permitted to be too nice in the material which it was compelled to employ. The refugees were from various quarters—were sometimes, as we have seen, adopted in his ranks from those of the defeated Tories, and were frequently grossly ignorant, not only of what was due to the community in which they found themselves, but still more ignorant of the obligations of that military law to which they voluntarily put themselves in subjection. Marion's modes of punishment happily reached all such cases without making the unhappy offender pay too dearly for the sin of ignorance. On one occasion, Horry tells us that he carried before him a prisoner charged with desertion to the enemy. "Marion released him, saying to me, 'let him go, he is too worthless to deserve the consideration of a court martial.'" Such a decision in such a case, would have shocked a military martinet, and yet, in all probability, the fellow thus discharged, never repeated the offence, and fought famously afterwards in the cause of his merciful commander. We have something yet to learn on these subjects. The result of a system in which scorn is so equally blended with mercy, was singularly good. In the case of the person offending (as is frequently the case among militia) through sheer ignorance of martial law, it teaches while it punishes, and reforms, in some degree, the being which it saves. Where the fault flows from native worthlessness of character the effect is not less beneficial. One of Marion's modes of getting rid of worthless officers, was to put them into coventry. In this practice his good officers joined him, and their sympathy and co-operation soon secured his object. "He kept a list of them," said Horry, "which he called his Black List. This mode answered so well that many resigned their commissions, and the brigade was thus fortunately rid of such worthless fellows." The value of such a riddance is well shown by another sentence from the MS. of our veteran. "I found the men seldom defective, were it not for the bad example set them by their officers."[67]

CHAPTER XII

GENERAL GREENE ASSUMES COMMAND OF THE
SOUTHERN ARMY † HIS CORRESPONDENCE WITH
MARION † CONDITION OF THE COUNTRY † MARION
AND LEE SURPRISE GEORGETOWN † COL. HORRY
DEFEATS GAINEY † MARION PURSUES MCILRAITH †
PROPOSED PITCHED BATTLE BETWEEN PICKED MEN

The year 1781 opened, with new interest, the great drama of war in South Carolina. In that State, as we have seen, deprived of a large portion of her military effectives, opposition had never entirely ceased to the progress of the invader. New and more strenuous exertions, on the part of Congress, were made to give her the necessary assistance. Without this, the war, prolonged with whatever spirit by the partisans, was not likely, because of their deficient *materiel* and resources, to reach any decisive results. We may yield thus much, though we are unwilling to admit the justice of those opinions, on the part of General Greene and other officers of the regular army, by which the influence of the native militia, on the events of the war, was quite too much disparaged. But for this militia, and the great spirit and conduct manifested by the partisan leaders in Carolina, no regular force which Congress would or could have sent into the field, would have sufficed for the recovery of the two almost isolated States of South Carolina and Georgia. Indeed, we are inclined to think that, but for the native spirit which they had shown in the conquest, no attempt would have been made for their recovery. We should be at a loss, unless we recognized the value of this native spirit, and the importance of its achievements, however small individually, to determine by what means these States were finally recovered to the American confederacy. In no single pitched battle between the two grand armies did the Americans obtain a decided victory. The fruits of victory inured to them, quite as much in consequence of the active combination of the partisan captains, as by the vigour of their own arms. By these the enemy were harassed with unparalleled audacity—their supplies and convoys cut off, their detachments captured or cut to pieces, their movements watched, and their whole influence so narrowed and restrained, as to be confined almost entirely to those places where they remained in strength. It is not meant by this, to lessen in any degree the value of the services rendered by the Continental forces. These were very great, and contributed in large measure to bring the war to an early and a happy issue. It is only intended to insist upon those claims of the partisans, which, unasserted by themselves, have been a little too irreverently dismissed by others. But for these leaders, Marion, Sumter, Pickens, Davie, Hampton, and some fifty more well endowed and gallant spirits, the Continental forces sent to Carolina would have vainly flung themselves upon the impenetrable masses of the British.

It was the vitality thus exhibited by the country, by the native captains and people, that persuaded Congress, though sadly deficient in materials and men, to make another attempt to afford to the South, the succor which it asked. The wreck of the army under Gates had been collected by that unfortunate commander at Charlotte, North Carolina. He was superseded in its command by General Greene, a soldier of great firmness and discretion, great prudence and forethought—qualities the very opposite of those by which his predecessor seems to have been distinguished. New hopes were awakened by this change of command, which, though slow of fruition, were not finally to be disappointed. Greene's assumption of command was distinguished by a happy augury. In a few hours after reaching camp Charlotte, he received intelligence of the success of Lt.-Col. Washington, against the British post held at Clermont, South Carolina, by the British Colonel Rugely. Rugely was well posted in a redoubt, which was tenable except against artillery. Washington's force consisted only of cavalry. A pleasant *ruse de guerre* of the latter, which produced some little merriment among the Americans at the expense of the British colonel, enabled Washington to succeed. A pine log was rudely hewn into the appearance of a cannon, and, mounted upon wagon wheels, was advanced with solemnity to the attack. The affair looked sufficiently serious, and Rugely, to avoid any unnecessary effusion of blood, yielded the post. Cornwallis, dryly commenting on the transaction, in a letter to Tarleton, remarks. "Rugely will not be made a brigadier."

Greene proceeded in the duties of his command with characteristic vigilance and vigour. He soon put his army under marching orders for the Pedee, which river he reached on the 26th of December. He took post near Hicks' Creek, on the east side of the river. Before leaving camp Charlotte, he had judiciously made up an independent brigade for General Morgan, composed of his most efficient soldiers. It consisted of a corps of light infantry, detached from the Maryland line, of 320 men; a body of Virginia militia of 200 men, and

Washington's cavalry, perhaps one hundred more. Morgan was to be joined, on reaching the tract of country assigned to his operations in South Carolina, by the militia lately under Sumter; that gallant leader being still *hors de combat*, in consequence of the severe wound received at Blackstock's. The force of Morgan was expected to be still farther increased by volunteer militia from North Carolina; and he received a powerful support in the co-operation of Col. Pickens, with the well exercised militia under his command.

The object of this detachment was to give confidence and encouragement to the country, to inspirit the patriots, overawe the Tories, and facilitate the accumulation of the necessary provisions. The main army at Hicks' Creek, meanwhile, formed a camp of repose. This was necessary, as well as time and training, to its usefulness. It was sadly deficient in all the munitions and materials of war—the mere skeleton of an army, thin in numbers, and in a melancholy state of nakedness. "Were you to arrive," says Greene, in a letter to Lafayette, dated December 29, "you would find a few ragged, half-starved troops in the wilderness, destitute of everything necessary for either the comfort or convenience of soldiers." The department was not only in a deplorable condition, but the country was laid waste. Such a warfare as had been pursued among the inhabitants, beggars description. The whole body of the population seems to have been in arms, at one time or another, and, unhappily, from causes already discussed, in opposite ranks. A civil war, as history teaches, is like no other. Like a religious war, the elements of a fanatical passion seem to work the mind up to a degree of ferocity, which is not common among the usual provocations of hate in ordinary warfare. "The inhabitants," says Greene, "pursue each other with savage fury…The Whigs and the Tories are butchering one another hourly. The war here is upon a very different scale from what it is to the northward. It is a plain business there. The geography of the country reduces its operations to two or three points. But here, it is everywhere; and the country is so full of deep rivers and impassable creeks and swamps, that you are always liable to misfortunes of a capital nature."

The geographical character of the country, as described by Greene, is at once suggestive of the partisan warfare. It is the true sort of warfare for such a country. The sparseness of its settlements, and the extent of its plains, indicate the employment of cavalry—the intricate woods and swamps as strikingly denote the uses and importance of riflemen. The brigade of Marion combined the qualities of both.

General Greene, unlike his predecessor, knew the value of such services as those of Marion. On taking command at Charlotte, the very day after his arrival, he thus writes to our partisan: "I have not," says he, "the honour of your acquaintance, but am no stranger to your character and merit. Your services in the lower part of South Carolina, in awing the Tories and preventing the enemy from extending their limits, have been very important. And it is my earnest desire that you continue where you are until farther advice from me. Your letter of the 22d of last month to General Gates, is before me. I am fully sensible your service is hard and sufferings great, but how great the prize for which we contend! I like your plan of frequently shifting your ground. It frequently prevents a surprise and perhaps a total loss of your party. Until a more permanent army can be collected than is in the field at present, we must endeavour to keep up a partisan war, and preserve the tide of sentiment among the people in our favour as much as possible. Spies are the eyes of an army, and without them a general is always groping in the dark, and can neither secure himself, nor annoy his enemy. At present, I am badly off for intelligence. It is of the highest importance that I get the earliest intelligence of any reinforcement which may arrive at Charleston. I wish you, therefore, to fix some plan for procuring such information and conveying it to me with all possible dispatch. The spy should be taught to be particular in his inquiries and get the names of the corps, strength and commanding officer's name—place from whence they came and where they are going. It will be best to fix upon somebody in town to do this, and have a runner between you and him to give you the intelligence; as a person who lives out of town cannot make the inquiries without being suspected. The utmost secrecy will be necessary in the business."

This letter found Marion at one of his lurking places on Black river. It was properly addressed to him. He was the man who, of all others, was not only best acquainted with the importance of good information, furnished promptly, but who had never been without his spies and runners, from the first moment when he took the field. He readily assumed the duty, and upon him Greene wholly relied for his intelligence of every sort. Every occurrence in Charleston, Georgetown, and the whole low country, was promptly furnished to the commander, to whom, however, Marion complains generally of the embarrassment in procuring intelligence, arising from the want of a little hard money—but this want was quite as great in the camp of Greene as in that of the partisan.

It is probable that Marion had communicated to General Gates a desire to strengthen his militia with a small force of regular troops. With such a force, it was expected that something of a more decisive nature could be effected. His eye was upon Georgetown. The capture of that post was particularly desirable on many accounts; and if his views and wishes were not communicated to Gates, they were to Greene, who subsequently made his dispositions for promoting them. While the latter was moving down to his camp at Hicks' Creek, Marion was engaged in some very active movements against a party under McArthur and Coffin, and between that and the High Hills of the Santee. To cut off his retreat by the Pedee, a strong detachment had been pushed on from Charleston to Georgetown, intended to intercept him by ascending the north bank of the Pedee river. But Marion, informed of the movement, readily divined its object, and, retiring across the country, took a strong position on Lynch's Creek, in the vicinity of his favourite retreat at Snow's Island, where he always kept a force to guard his boats and overawe the Tories. The moment his pursuers had left the ground, Marion resumed offensive operations upon it. In a short time, his parties were pushed down to the immediate neighbourhood of Georgetown, on all the rivers that flow into the bay of Winyaw. His smaller parties were actively busy in collecting boats and transferring provisions to Snow's Island. This was with the twofold purpose of straitening the enemy, and supplying the Continental army. In the meantime, with a respectable force of mounted infantry, he himself pressed closely upon the town, watching an opportunity when he might attempt something with a prospect of success. But the British confined themselves to their redoubts. Marion had neither bayonets nor artillery. With one hundred Continental troops—he writes with his usual modesty to Greene—he should be able to render important services. While thus employed, he received intelligence that the loyalists were embodying above him, in great force, under Hector McNeill. They were at Amy's Mill on Drowning Creek, and were emboldened by a knowledge of the fact that the main army was entirely destitute of cavalry. Marion was not able to detach a force sufficient for their dispersion, and it would have been fatal to his safety to suffer them to descend upon him while his detachments were abroad. His first measures were to call in his scattered parties. He then communicated to Greene the necessity of reinforcing him against his increasing enemies, and, in particular, of addressing himself to the movements of McNeill, as he supposed them to be directed, in part, against the country between the Waccamaw and the sea-coast, which had never been ravaged, and which, at this time, held abundance of provisions. To this communication Greene replies: "I have detached Major Anderson with one thousand regulars, and one hundred Virginia militia, to attack and disperse the Tories at Amy's Mill, on Drowning Creek. The party marched yesterday with orders to endeavour to surprise them; perhaps you might be able to make some detachment that would contribute to their success...I wish your answer respecting the practicability of surprising the party near Nelson's; the route, and force you will be able to detach. This inquiry is a matter that requires great secrecy."

Another letter of Greene's, three days after (January 22d), refers to some "skirmishes between your people and the enemy, which," says Greene, "do them honor," of which we have no particulars. The same letter begs for a supply of horses. "Get as many as you can, and let us have fifteen or twenty sent to camp without loss of time, they being wanted for immediate service." By another letter, dated the day after the preceding, Greene communicates to Marion the defeat of Tarleton by Morgan, at the celebrated battle of the Cowpens. "On the 17th at daybreak, the enemy, consisting of eleven hundred and fifty British troops and fifty militia, attacked General Morgan, who was at the Cowpens, between Pacolet and Broad rivers, with 290 infantry, eighty cavalry and about six hundred militia. The action lasted fifty minutes and was remarkably severe. Our brave troops charged the enemy with bayonets and entirely routed them, killing nearly one hundred and fifty, wounding upwards of two hundred, and taking more than five hundred prisoners exclusive of the prisoners with two pieces of artillery, thirty-five wagons, upwards of one hundred dragoon horses, and with the loss of only ten men killed and fifty-five wounded. Our intrepid party pursued the enemy upwards of twenty miles. About thirty commissioned officers are among the prisoners. Col. Tarleton had his horse killed and was wounded, but made his escape with two hundred of his troops."

Before receiving this grateful intelligence Marion had been joined by Lieut.-Col. Lee, at the head of a legion which acquired high reputation for its spirit and activity during the war. Lee tells us that it was no easy matter to find our partisan. "An officer, with a small party, preceded Lee a few days' march to find out Marion, who was known to vary his position in the swamps of the Pedee; sometimes in South Carolina, sometimes in North Carolina, and sometimes on the Black river. With the greatest difficulty did this officer learn how to communicate with the brigadier; and that by the accident of hearing among our friends on the south side of the Pedee, of a small provision party of Marion's being on the same side of the river. Making himself known to this party he was conveyed to the general, who had changed his ground since his party left him, which occasioned many hours' search even before his own men could find him."[68]

This anecdote illustrates the wary habits of our partisan, and one of the modes by which he so successfully baffled the numerous and superior parties who were dispatched in his pursuit. We have given, elsewhere, from Col. Lee's memoirs, a brief description of Marion and his mode of warfare, taken from the appendix to that work. But another occurs, in the text before us, which, as it is brief, differing somewhat in phrase, and somewhat more comprehensive, than the former, will no doubt contribute to the value and interest of our narrative. "Marion," says Lee, "was about forty-eight years of age, small in stature, hard in visage, healthy, abstemious and taciturn. Enthusiastically wedded to the cause of liberty, he deeply deplored the doleful condition of his beloved country. The common weal was his sole object; nothing selfish, nothing mercenary soiled his ermine character. Fertile in stratagem, he struck unperceived, and retiring to those hidden retreats selected by himself, in the morasses of Pedee and Black river, he placed his corps, not only out of the reach of his foe, but often out of the discovery of his friends. A rigid disciplinarian, he reduced to practice the justice of his heart; and during the difficult course of warfare though which he passed calumny itself never charged him with molesting the rights of person, property or humanity. Never avoiding danger, he never rashly sought it; and, acting for all around him as he did for himself, he risked the lives of his troops only when it was necessary. Never elated with prosperity, nor depressed by adversity, he preserved an equanimity which won the admiration of his friends and exalted the respect of his enemies."

Such were Lee's opinions of the partisan, to whose assistance he was dispatched by Greene, with his legion, consisting of near three hundred men, horse and foot.

The junction of Lee's troops with those of Marion led to the enterprise which the other had long since had at heart, the capture of the British garrison at Georgetown. Georgetown was a small village, the situation and importance of which have already been described. The garrison consisted of two hundred men commanded by Colonel Campbell. His defences in front were slight, and not calculated to resist artillery. "Between these defences and the town, anti contiguous to each, was an enclosed work with a frieze and palisade, which constituted his chief protection."[69] It was held by a subaltern guard. "The rest of the troops were dispersed in light parties in and near the town, and looking towards the country." It was planned by the assailants to convey a portion of their force secretly down the Pedee, and land them, in the water suburb of the town, which, being deemed secure, was left unguarded. This body was then to move in two divisions. The first was to force the commandant's quarters—the place of parade—to secure him, and all others who might flock thither on the alarm. The second was designed to intercept such of the garrison as might endeavour to gain the fort. The partisan militia, and the cavalry of the legion, led by Marion and Lee in person, were to approach the place in the night, to lie concealed, and when the entrance of the other parties into the town should be announced, they were to penetrate to their assistance, and put the finishing stroke to the affair.

The plan promised well, but the attempt was only partially successful. Captain Carnes, with the infantry of the legion, in boats, dropped down the Pedee, sheltered from discovery by the deep swamps and dense forests which lined its banks, until he reached an island at its mouth within a few miles of Georgetown. Here he landed, and lay concealed during the day. The night after, Marion and Lee proceeded to their place of destination, which they reached by twelve o'clock, when, hearing the expected signal, they rushed into the town, Marion leading his militia, and Lee his dragoons, prepared to bear down all opposition; but they found all the work already over which it was in the power of the present assailants to attempt. The two parties of infantry, the one led by Carnes the other by Rudolph, had reached their places, but perhaps not in good season. The surprise was incomplete. They delayed too long upon the way, instead of pushing up directly upon the redoubt. They were also delayed by the desire of securing the person of the commandant—an unimportant consideration, in comparison with the stronghold of the garrison, which, assailed vigorously at the first alarm, must have fallen into their hands. The commandant was secured, and Carnes judiciously posted his division for seizing such parties of the garrison as might flock to the parade-ground. Rudolph had also gained his appointed station in the vicinity of the fort, and so distributed his corps as to prevent all communication with it. But this was not probably achieved with sufficient rapidity and the garrison was strengthening itself while the Americans were busy in catching Campbell, and cutting down the fugitives. When Marion and Lee appeared, there was nothing to he done—no enemy to be seen. Not a British soldier appeared on parade—no one attempted either to gain the fort or repair to the commandant. The troops of the garrison simply hugged their respective quarters, and barricaded the doors. The assailants were unprovided with the necessary implements for battering or bombarding. The fort was in possession of the British, and daylight was approaching. And thus this bold and brilliant attempt was baffled—it is difficult, at this time of day, to say how. Lee was dissatisfied with the result. Marion, more modestly, in a letter to Greene, says: "Col. Lee informed you yesterday, by express, of our little success on Georgetown, which could not be greater without artillery." Lee says: "If, instead of placing Rudolph's division to intercept the fugitives, it had been ordered to carry the fort by the bayonet, our success would have been complete. The fort taken, and the commandant a prisoner, we might have availed ourselves of the cannon, and have readily demolished every obstacle and shelter." There were probably several causes combined, which baffled the perfect success of the enterprise: the guides are said to have blundered; there was too much time lost in capturing Campbell, and probably in the prosecution of some private revenges. A circuitous route was taken by Carnes, when a direct one might have been had, by which his entrance into the town was delayed until near daylight; and, by one account, the advance of Marion and Lee was not in season. The simple secret of failure was probably a want of concert between the parties, by which the British had time to recover from their alarm, and put themselves in a state of preparation. Many of the British were killed, few taken; among the former was Major Irvine, who was slain by Lieut. Cryer, whom, on a former occasion, he had subjected to a cruel punishment of five hundred lashes. Lieut.-Col. Campbell was suffered to remain on parole.

Though failing of its object, yet the audacity which marked the enterprise, and the partial success of the attempt, were calculated to have their effect upon the fears of the enemy. It was the first of a series of movements against their several fortified posts, by which their power was to be broken up in detail. Its present effect was to discourage the removal of forces from the seaboard to the interior, to prevent any accession of strength to the army of Cornwallis, who now, roused by the defeat of Tarleton, was rapidly pressing, with all his array, upon the heels of Morgan. The American plan of operations, of which this *coup de main* constituted a particular of some importance, had for its object to keep Cornwallis from Virginia—to detain him in South Carolina until an army of sufficient strength could be collected for his overthrow. This plan had been the subject of much earnest correspondence between Greene, Marion, and others of the American officers. That part of it which contemplated the conquest of Georgetown harmonized immediately with the long cherished objects of our partisan.

Halting but a few hours to rest their troops, Marion and Lee, after the attempt on Georgetown, moved the same day directly up the north bank of the Santee towards Nelson's Ferry. Their object was the surprise of Col. Watson, who had taken post there. But, though the march was conducted with equal caution and celerity, it became known to the threatened party. Watson, consulting his fears, did not wait to receive them; but, throwing a garrison of about eighty men into Fort Watson, five miles above the ferry, hurried off to Camden.

Upon the defeat of Tarleton by Morgan, General Greene hastened to put himself at the head of the force conducted by the latter, which was then in full flight before the superior army of Cornwallis. Orders from Greene to Lee found him preparing for further co-operations with Marion, which they arrested. Lee was summoned to join the commander-in-chief with his whole legion, and Marion was thus deprived of the further use, which he so much coveted, of the Continentals. But this diminution of force did not lessen the activity of the latter. On the 29ᵗʰ January, he sent out two small detachments of thirty men each, under Colonel and Major Postelle, to strike at the smaller British posts beyond the Santee. These parties were successful in several affairs. A great quantity of valuable stores were burnt at Manigault's Ferry, and in the vicinity. At Keithfield, near Monk's corner, Major Postelle captured forty of the British regulars without the loss of a man. Here also fourteen baggage wagons, with all their stores, were committed to the flames. The proceedings of these parties, conducted with caution and celerity, were exceedingly successful. In giving his instructions to the officers entrusted with these duties, Marion writes—"You will consider provisions of all kinds British property. The destruction of all the British stores in the above-mentioned places, is of the greatest consequence to us, and only requires boldness and expedition."

About this time Marion organized four new companies of cavalry. This proceeding was prompted by the scarcity of ammunition. His rifles were comparatively useless, and the want of powder and ball rendered it necessary that he should rely upon some other weapons. To provide broadswords for his troops, he was compelled once more to put in requisition the mill saws of the country, and his blacksmiths were busy in manufacturing blades, which, as we are told by a contemporary, were sufficiently keen and massy to hew a man down at a blow. This body of cavalry he assigned to the command of Col. P. Horry. Horry was an admirable infantry officer. His ability to manage a squadron of cavalry was yet to be ascertained. He labored under one disqualification, as he plainly tells us in his own manuscript. He was not much of a horseman. But he had several excellent officers under him. As the brigade was not strong enough to allow of the employment, in body, of his whole command, its operations were commonly by detachment. The colonel, at the head of one of his parties consisting of sixty men, had soon an opportunity of testing his capacity and fortune in this new command. We glean the adventure from his own manuscript. He was sent to the Waccamaw to reconnoitre and drive off some cattle. After crossing Socastee swamp, a famous resort for the Tories, he heard of a party of British dragoons under Colonel Campbell. Horry's men had found a fine English charger hid in a swamp. This he was prevailed upon to mount, in order to spare his own. It so happened, somewhat unfortunately for him, that he did so with an enemy at hand. With his own horse he was sufficiently familiar to escape ordinary accidents. It will be seen that he incurred some risks with the more spirited quadruped. His patrol had brought in a negro, whom he placed under guard. He had in his command a Captain Clarke, who, knowing the negro, set him free during the night. "Reader" says our colonel, with a serenity that is delightful, "behold a militia captain releasing a prisoner confined by his colonel commandant, and see the consequence!" The negro fell into the hands of the British, and conducted them upon the steps of our partisan. It so happened that the same Captain Clarke, who seems to have been a sad simpleton, and something of a poltroon, had been sent in front with five horsemen as an advanced guard. Near the great Waccamaw road, the bugles of the British were heard sounding the charge. Horry was fortunately prepared for the enemy, but such was not the case with Clarke. He confounded the martial tones of the bugle with the sylvan notes of the horn. "Stop," says our militia captain, to his men—"stop, and you will see the deer, dogs and huntsmen, as they cross the road." He himself happened to be the silly deer. The huntsmen were upon him in a few moments, and he discovered his mistake only when their broadswords were about his ears. He was taken, but escaped. A short encounter followed between Campbell and Horry, in which the former was worsted. Six of his men fell at the first fire, three slain, and as many wounded. Horry's pieces were common shot guns, and the only shot that he had were swan shot, or the mischief would have been greater. Campbell's horse was killed under him, and he narrowly escaped. Horry was dismounted in the encounter,—in what manner we are not told,—and would have been cut down by a British sergeant, but for his wearing a uniform that resembled that of a British colonel. He was helped to a horse at a most fortunate moment. He did not know, in consequence of the blunder of Clarke, that the dragoons whom he had fought and beaten, were only an advanced guard of a body of infantry. Horses and men were in his hands, and, dividing his force, he sent off one party of his men in charge of the prisoners and trophies. A sudden attack of the British infantry took the small party which remained with him totally by surprise. They broke and left him almost alone, with nothing but his small sword in his hand. It was at this moment that a brave fellow of the second regiment, named McDonald, yielded his own pony to his commander, by which he escaped. McDonald saved himself by darting into the neighboring swamp. The British, dreading an ambuscade, did not pursue, and Horry rallied his men, and returned, with a reinforcement sent by Marion, to the scene of battle; but the enemy had left it and retired to Georgetown. Horry proceeded to Sand Hill, where, finding himself in good quarters, among some rich and friendly Whigs, living well on their supplies, he proceeded to entrench himself in a regular redoubt. But from this imposing situation Marion soon and sensibly recalled him. "He wrote me," says Horry, "that the open field was our play—that the enemy knew better how to defend forts and entrenched places than we did, and that if we attempted it, we should soon fall into their hands." Marion's farther instructions were to join him immediately, with every man that he could bring, for that it was his purpose to attack the enemy as soon as possible. Horry admits that he quitted his redoubt and good fare very reluctantly. He set out with eighty men, but when he joined his commander in Lynch's Creek Swamp, they were reduced to eighteen. It seems that his force had been made up in part of new recruits, who had but lately joined themselves to Marion. Horry calls them "wild Tories or half-made new Whigs—volunteers, assuredly, not to fight, but plunder,—who would run at the sight of the enemy." His recent surprise and danger had rendered the colonel sore. It was on this occasion, that, as we have already related, he was nearly drowned, and only saved by clinging to the impending branches of a tree.

While Horry was skirmishing with Campbell, Major John Postelle, who was stationed to guard the lower part of the Pedee, succeeded in capturing Captain Depeyster, with twenty-nine grenadiers. Depeyster had taken post in the dwelling-house of Postelle's father. The latter had with him but twenty-eight militia, but he knew the grounds, and gaining possession of the kitchen, fired it, and was preparing to burn the house also, when Depeyster submitted.

We find, at this time, a correspondence of Marion with two of the British officers, in relation to the detention, as a prisoner, of Captain Postelle, who, it seems, though bearing a flag, was detained for trial by the enemy. Portions of these letters, in which Marion asserts his own humanity in the treatment of prisoners, we quote as exhibiting his own sense, at least, of what was the true character of his conduct in such matters. The reader will not have forgotten the charges made against him, in this respect, in an earlier part of this volume by Lt.-Col. Balfour, in a letter to General Moultrie. One of the present letters of Marion is addressed to Balfour.

"I am sorry to complain of the ill treatment my officers and men meet with from Captain Saunders. The officers are closely confined in a small place where they can neither stand nor lie at length, nor have they more than half rations. I have treated your officers and men who have fallen into my hands, in a different manner. Should these evils not be prevented in future, it will not be in my power to prevent retaliation. Lord Rawdon and Col. Watson have hanged three men of my brigade for supposed crimes, which will make as many of your men, in my hands, suffer."

Again, on the same subject, in a letter to Col. Watson—"The hanging of prisoners and the violation of my flag, will be retaliated if a stop is not put to such proceedings, which are disgraceful to all civilized nations. All of your officers and men, who have fallen into my hands, have been treated with humanity and tenderness, and I wish sincerely that I may not be obliged to act contrary to my inclination."

The British officers thus addressed, alleged against Postelle that he had broken his parole. If this were so, it was a just cause of detention; but it will be remembered that the British themselves revoked these paroles on the assumption that the province was conquered, and when, as citizens, they wished to exact military service from the people. In these circumstances the virtue of the obligation was lost, and ceased on the part of the citizen, because of the violation on the part of the conqueror, of the immunities which he promised. Marion took decisive measures for compelling the necessary respect to his flag, by seizing upon Captain Merritt, the bearer of a British flag, and putting him in close keeping as a security for Postelle. We do not know that he retaliated upon the British soldiers the cruel murders, by hanging, which had been practised upon his own. His nature would probably recoil from carrying his own threat into execution. In answer to one of Marion's reproaches, we are told by Col. Watson, that "the burning of houses and the property of the inhabitants, who are our enemies, is customary in all civilized nations." The code of civilisation is certainly susceptible of liberal constructions. Its elasticity is not the least of its many merits.

Cornwallis pursued Greene into North Carolina, and after much manoeuvering between the armies, they met at Guilford on the 15th of March, 1781. The honors of the victory, small as it was, lay with the British. Their loss, however, was such, that the advantages of the field inured to the Americans. From this field, Cornwallis took his way to Virginia, and his career as a commander in America was finally arrested at the siege of York. During the absence of Greene from South Carolina, Marion's was the only force in active operation against the British. An opportunity so favorable for harassing and distressing the enemy, as that afforded by the absence of their main army in North Carolina, was not neglected; and, calling in his detachments, he once more carried dismay into the heart of the Tory settlements, on both sides of the Santee. His incursions, and those of his officers, were extended as far as the confluence of the Congaree and Wateree, and as low down as Monk's Corner,—thus breaking up the line of communication between Charleston and the grand army, and intercepting detachments and supplies, sent from that place to the line of posts established through the country. This sort of warfare, which seldom reaches events such as those which mark epochs in the progress of great bodies of men, is yet one which calls for constant activity. We have details of but few of the numerous conflicts which took place between our partisan and the Tory leaders. These were scattered over the country, living by plunder, and indulging in every species of ferocity. Greene writes, "The Whigs and Tories are continually out in small parties, and all the middle country is so disaffected, that you cannot lay in the most trifling magazine or send a wagon through the country with the least article of stores without a guard." In addressing himself to this sort of warfare, Marion was pursuing a course of the largest benefit to the country. In overawing these plunderers, subduing the savage spirit, and confining the British to their strong places, he was acquiring an importance, which, if we are to estimate the merits of a leader only by the magnitude of his victories, will leave us wholly at a loss to know by what means his great reputation was acquired. But the value of his services is best gathered from the effect which they had upon the enemy. The insults and vexations which he unceasingly occasioned to the British, were not to be borne and Col. Watson was dispatched with a select force of five hundred men to hunt him up and destroy him. We have seen Tarleton and others engaged in the pursuit, but without success. Watson was destined to be less fortunate. In the meanwhile, and before Watson came upon his trail, Col. Peter Horry had been engaged in a series of petty but rather amusing skirmishes, in the neighborhood of Georgetown. A party of the British were engaged in killing beeves at White's bridge near Georgetown. Horry's men charged there while at this employment, and killing some, pursued the rest towards that place. The firing was heard in the town, and the facts of the case conjectured. This brought out a reinforcement, before which the detachment of Horry was compelled to retreat. But, on gaining the woods, they were joined also by their friends and the fight was resumed between the Sampit and Black river roads, with a dogged fierceness on both sides, that made it particularly bloody. In the course of the struggle, Horry at one moment found himself alone. His men were more or less individually engaged, and scattered through the woods around him. His only weapon was his small sword. In this situation he was suddenly assailed by a Tory captain, named Lewis, at the head of a small party. Lewis was armed with a musket, and in the act of firing, when a sudden shot from the woods tumbled him from his horse, in the very moment when his own gun was discharged. The bullet of Lewis took effect on Horry's horse. The shot which so seasonably slew the Tory, had been lent by the hands of a boy named Gwin. The party of Lewis, apprehending an ambush, immediately fell hack and put themselves in cover. The conflict lasted through the better part of the day, one side gaining ground, and now the other. It closed in the final defeat of the enemy, who were pursued with a savage and unsparing spirit. One half of their number were left dead upon the ground. Their leader was Major Gainey. Great expectations were formed

Sergant M'Donald pursuing Major Gainey.

of his ability to cope with Marion. On this occasion, though he made his escape, his mode of doing so was characterized by a peculiar circumstance, which rendered it particularly amusing to one side and annoying to the other. He was singled out in the chase by Sergeant McDonald, a fierce young fellow, who was admirably mounted. Gainey was fortunate in being well mounted also. McDonald, regarding but the one enemy, passed all others. He himself said that he could have slain several in the chase. But he wished for no meaner object than their leader. One man alone who threw himself in the way of the pursuit became its victim. Him he shot down, and, as they went at full speed down the Black river road, at the corner of Richmond fence, the sergeant had gained so far upon his enemy, as to be able to plunge his bayonet into his back. The steel separated from his gun, and, with no time to extricate it, Gainey rushed into Georgetown, with the weapon still conspicuously showing how close and eager had been the chase, and how narrow the escape. The wound was not fatal.

The next affair was with Col. Tynes, who had been defeated by Marion some time before, made prisoner and sent to North Carolina. But the North Carolina jailors seem to have been pretty generally Tories, for we find Horry complaining that they discharged the prisoners quite as fast as they were sent there; and it was the complaint of some of Marion's officers that they had to fight the same persons in some instances, not less than three or four times. Tynes had collected a second force, and, penetrating the forests of Black river, was approaching the camp of our partisan. Marion went against him, fell upon him suddenly, completely routed him, taking himself and almost his whole party prisoners. He made his escape a second time from North Carolina, and with a third and larger force than ever, re-appeared in the neighborhood of Marion's camp. Horry was sent against him with forty chosen horsemen. He travelled all night, and stopped the next day at the house of a Tory, where he obtained refreshments. His men succeeded in obtaining something more. The Tory most liberally filled their canteens with apple-brandy; and when the Colonel got within striking distance of Tyne and his Tories, scarcely one of his troops was fit for action. He prudently retreated, very much mortified with the transaction. Marion captured a part of Tynes' force a few days after, and this luckless loyalist seems to have disappeared from the field from that moment.

Watson's march against Marion was conducted with great caution. The operations of the partisan, meanwhile, were continued without interruption. About the middle of February, he was apprised of the march of Major McIlraith from Nelson's Ferry, at the head of a force fully equal to his own. This British officer seems to have been singularly unlike his brethren in some remarkable particulars. He took no pleasure in burning houses, the hospitality of which he had enjoyed; he destroyed no cattle wantonly, and hung no unhappy prisoner. The story goes that while Marion was pressing upon the steps of the enemy, he paused at the house of a venerable lady who had been always a friend to the Whigs, and who now declared her unhappiness at seeing him. Her reason being asked, she declared that she conjectured his purpose—that he was pursuing McIlraith, and that so honorable and gentle had been the conduct of that officer, on his march, that she was really quite unwilling that he should suffer harm, though an enemy. What he heard did not impair Marion's activity, but it tended somewhat to subdue those fiercer feelings which ordinarily governed the partisans in that sanguinary warfare. He encountered and assailed McIlraith on the road near Half-way Swamp, first cutting off two picquets in his rear in succession, then wheeling round his main body, attacked him at the same moment in flank and front. McIlraith was without cavalry, and his situation was perilous in the extreme. But he was a brave fellow, and Marion had few bayonets. By forced marches and constant skirmishing, the British major gained an open field upon the road. He posted himself within the enclosure upon the west of the road. Marion pitched his camp on the edge of a large cypress pond, which lay on the east, and closely skirted the highway. Here McIlraith sent him a flag, reproaching him with shooting his picquets, contrary, as he alleged, to all the laws of civilized warfare, and concluded with defying him to combat in the open field. The arguments of military men, on the subject of the laws of civilized warfare, are sometimes equally absurd and impertinent. Warfare itself is against all the laws of civilisation, and there is something ludicrous in the stronger reproaching the feebler power, that it should resort to such means as are in its possession, for reconciling the inequalities of force between them. Marion's reply to McIlraith was sufficiently to the purpose. He said that the practice of the British in burning the property of those who would not submit and join them, was much more indefensible than that of shooting picquets, and that while they persisted in the one practice, he should certainly persevere in the other. As to the challenge of McIlraith, he said that he considered it that of a man whose condition was desperate; but concluded with saying that if he, McIlraith, wished to witness a combat between twenty picked soldiers on each side, he was not unwilling to gratify him.

Here was a proposal that savored something of chivalry. McIlraith agreed to the suggestion, and an arrangement was made for a meeting. The place chosen for the combat was in a part of a field, which is very well known, south of an old oak tree, which was still, up to the year 1821, pointed out to the stranger. It may be standing to this day, for the oak outlasts many generations of brave men. Marion chose for the leader of his band, Major John Vanderhorst, then a supernumerary officer in his brigade. The second in command was Capt. Samuel Price, of All Saints. The names of the men were written on slips of paper and handed to them severally. Gavin Witherspoon received the first. The names of the others are not preserved. Not one of them refused. When they were separated from their comrades, they were paraded near the fence, and Marion addressed them in the following language:

"My brave soldiers! You are twenty men picked this day out of my whole brigade. I know you all, and have often witnessed your bravery. In the name of your country, I call upon you once more to show it. My confidence in you is great. I am sure it will not be disappointed. Fight like men, as you have always done—and you are sure of the victory."

The speech was short, but it was effectual. It was, perhaps, a long one for Marion. His words were usually few, but they were always to the purpose. More words were unnecessary here. The combatants heard him with pride, and hailed his exhortations with applause. While their cheers were loudest, Marion transferred them to their leader.

Vanderhorst now asked Witherspoon, "at what distance he would prefer, as the most sure to strike with buckshot?"

"Fifty yards, for the first fire," was the answer.

"Then," said Vanderhorst, "when we get within fifty yards, as I am not a good judge of distances, Mr. Witherspoon will tap me on the shoulder. I will then give the word, my lads, and you will form on my left opposite these fellows. As you form, each man will fire at the one directly opposite, and my word for it, few will need a second shot."

Nothing, indeed, was more certain than this; and how McIlraith proposed to fight with any hope of the result, knowing how deadly was the aim of the Americans, is beyond conjecture. If he relied upon the bayonet, as perhaps he did, his hope must have rested only upon those who survived the first fire; and with these, it was only necessary for the Americans to practise the game of the survivor of the Horatii, in order to gain as complete a victory. They had but to scatter and re-load—change their ground, avoid the push of the bayonet, till they could secure a second shot, and that certainly would have finished the business. But McIlraith had already reconsidered the proceeding. His men were formed in a straight line in front of the oak. Vanderhorst was advancing and had got within one hundred yards, when a British officer was seen to pass hurriedly to the detachment, and the next moment the men retreated, with a quick step, towards the main body. Vanderhorst and his party gave three huzzas, but not a shot was fired.

McIlraith committed two errors. He should not have made the arrangement, but, once made, he should have suffered it to go on at all hazards. The effect was discreditable to himself, and detrimental to the efficiency of his men. Marion would have fought his enemy all day on the same terms. His followers were on their own ground, with a familiar weapon, while the soldiers of the British were deprived of all their usual advantages—the assurance of support after the fire of the enemy was drawn. The militia seldom stood the encounter of the bayonet, but they as seldom failed to do famous execution with the first two or three discharges.

That night McIlraith abandoned his heavy baggage, left fires burning, and retreating silently from the ground, hurried, with all dispatch, along the river road towards Singleton's Mills, distant ten miles. Marion discovered the retreat before daylight, and sent Col. Hugh Horry forward with one hundred men, to get in advance of him before he should reach the mill. But Horry soon found this to be impossible, and he detached Major James, at the head of a select party, well mounted on the swiftest horses, with instructions to cross the mill-pond above, and take possession of Singleton's houses. These standing on a high hill, commanded a narrow defile on the road between the hill and the Wateree swamp. James reached the house as the British advanced to the foot of the hill. But here he found a new enemy, which his foresters dreaded much more than the British or Tories—the small-pox. Singleton's family were down with it, and James shrank from availing himself of any advantage offered by the situation. But before he retired, one of his men, resting his rifle against a tree, shot the commander of the British advance. He was mortally wounded, and died the next day. Marion was displeased with this achievement. The forbearance of McIlraith, while passing through the country, had touched his heart. He withdrew his forces, not displeased that his enemy had secured a stronghold in Singleton's Mill. The conscientiousness of the British officer is said to have incurred the displeasure of his commander, and that of his brother officers. When he reached Charleston he was put into coventry. Our authorities ascribe this to his gratuitous humanity, his reluctance to burn and plunder, with such excellent examples before him, as Cornwallis and Tarleton. We rather suspect, however, that it was in consequence of the unfortunate issue of the pitched battle, as agreed upon between himself and Marion; a more probable cause of odium among his comrades, than any reluctance, which he might express, to violate the common laws of humanity.

CHAPTER XIII

WATSON AND DOYLE PURSUE MARION † HE BAFFLES AND HARASSES THEM † PURSUES DOYLE † HIS DESPONDENCY, AND FINAL RESOLUTION

The preparations of Col. Watson for pursuing and destroying our partisan in his stronghold, were at length complete. He sallied forth from Fort Watson about the first of March, and, with a British regiment and a large body of loyalists—a force quite sufficient, as was thought, for the desired object—marched down the Santee, shaping his course for Snow's Island. At the same time, Col. Doyle, at the head of another British regiment, intended for co-operation with Watson, was directed to proceed by way of M'Callum's Ferry, on Lynch and down Jeffers' Creek, to the Pedee. Here they were to form a junction.

Marion had no force to meet these enemies in open combat. His number did not much exceed three hundred, but he had other resources of his own which better served to equalize them. Doyle's approach was slow, and it seems partially unsuspected. In fact, in order to meet his enemies, and make the most of his strength, Marion had generally called in his scouting parties. Of Watson's movements he had ample information. His scouts, well provided with relays of horses, traversed the country between his camp and Camden. Advised correctly of Watson's progress, he made one of those rapid marches for which he was famous, and met him at Wiboo Swamp, about midway between Nelson's and Murray's ferries. At this place commenced a conflict as remarkable as it was protracted. The advance of Watson consisted of the Tory horse, under Col. Richboo. Col. Peter Horry led Marion's advance, consisting of about thirty men; the remainder of the brigade lay in reserve. The encounter of the two advanced parties produced a mutual panic, both recoiling upon their main bodies; but that of Horry was the first to recover; and the command to charge, given by Marion himself, produced the desired effect. Horry was at length driven back by Watson's regulars, and the field-pieces, which finally dislodged him.

They were pursued by the Tory horse of Harrison, which, pressing upon the main body, gained some advantages; and, in the uncertainty of the event, while there was some confusion, afforded an opportunity for several instances of great individual valour. As the column of Harrison pressed over the causeway, which was narrow, Gavin James, a private of great spirit and gigantic size, mounted on a strong grey horse, and armed with musket and bayonet, threw himself in advance of his comrades, and directly in the path of the enemy. Taking deliberate aim, he fired his piece, dropped his man, and drew a volley from those in front of him, not a shot of which took effect. His determined position and presence, in the centre of the narrow causeway, produced a pause in the advance. A dragoon rushed upon him, and was stricken down by the bayonet. A second, coming to the assistance of his comrade, shared the same fate, but, in falling, laid hold of the muzzle of James' musket, and was dragged by him in the retreat some forty or fifty paces. This heroism was not without its effect. If the men of Marion faltered for a moment, such examples, and the voice of their general, re-invigorated their courage. Capts. Macauley and Conyers, at the head of the cavalry, arrested the advance of the Tories; and Harrison himself fell, mortally wounded, by the hands of Conyers. The Tories were dispersed, and sought shelter from the infantry of Watson, before the advance of which Marion deemed it prudent for the time to retire.

Marion lost nothing by this meeting. Its effect upon the Tories was highly beneficial. They had suffered severely in killed and wounded, and were thus intimidated at the outset. Watson encamped that night on the field of battle, and Marion a few miles below. The next morning the pursuit was resumed. Watson marched down the river, Marion keeping just sufficiently ahead of him to be able to post an ambuscade for him at the first point that seemed suitable for such a purpose. At Mount Hope, Watson had to build up the bridges, and sustain a second conflict with a chosen party of Marion's, led by Col. Hugh Horry. By bringing forward his field-pieces, and drilling the swamp thickets with grape, he succeeded in expelling Horry, and clearing the way for his column. But the same game was to be renewed with every renewal of the opportunity.

When Watson drew near to Murray Ferry, he passed the Kingstree road; and, coming to that of Black river, which crosses at the lower bridge, he made a feint of still continuing along the Santee; but soon after wheeled about, and took the former route. This manoeuvre might have deceived a less wary antagonist than Marion. He was soon aware of the enemy's intention. Detaching Major James, at the head of seventy men, thirty of whom were M'Cottry's rifles, he ordered him to destroy the bridge, and so post himself as to command it. He himself kept his eye fixed upon Watson. This bridge was on the main pass to Williamsburg, and the men chosen for its defence were judiciously taken from that part of the country. It was naturally supposed that, in sight of their cottage smokes, they would struggle manfully against the enemy's forces.

James proceeded with great rapidity, and, avoiding the road, crossed the river by a shorter route. He reached the bridge in time to throw down two of the middle arches, and to fire the string pieces at the eastern extremity. As soon as the chasm was made, he placed M'Cottry's riflemen at the end of the bridge and on each side of the ford. The rest of his detachment were so stationed as to co-operate, when required, with their comrades. Marion arriving soon after, strengthened the force of James with the Pedee company under Captain Potts, and took post himself, with the main body, in the rear. These arrangements had scarcely been effected when Watson made his appearance. At this place the west bank of the river is considerably higher than the east. The latter is low and somewhat swampy. On the west, the road passes to the bridge through a ravine. The river was forty or fifty yards wide, and though deep, was fordable below the bridge. The ravine was commanded by M'Cottry's rifles. As soon as Watson approached the river, which he did from the west, his field-pieces opened upon the passage which conducted to the ford. But the position assigned to Marion's men, on the eastern side of the river, effectually protected them. To bring the field-pieces to bear upon the low grounds which they occupied, was to expose the artillerists, upon the elevated banks which they occupied, to the deliberate and fatal fire of the riflemen. Watson was soon made aware of the difficulties of the passage. Not a man approached within gun-shot that did not pay the penalty of his rashness; and those who drew nigh to succor or carry off the wounded, shared the same fate. It was determined to attempt the ford, and the advance was put forward, as a forlorn hope, with this desperate purpose. The officer leading it, came on very gallantly, waving his sword aloft and loudly encouraging his men. His progress was fatally arrested by M'Cottry's rifle. The signal drew the fire of the riflemen and musketeers, with whom the banks were lined, and the heavy and deliberate discharge drove back and dispersed the British advance, nor did the reserve move forward to its assistance. Four brave fellows attempted to carry off the officer who had fallen, but they remained with him.

Watson was terrified. He was heard to say that "he had never seen such shooting in his life." There was no effecting the passage in the face of such enemies, and stealing down to the banks of the river, on the side which they occupied, and wherever the woods afforded shelter, the British skirmished with Marion's flankers across the stream until night put an end to the conflict.

The next morning Watson sent that dispatch to Marion which, from its lugubrious tenor, has acquired a degree of notoriety much greater than the name of the officer from whom it emanated. He complained to Marion of his modes of fighting, objected to the ambuscades of the partisan, and particularly complained that his picquets and sentinels should be shot down when they had no suspicion of danger. He concluded by urging upon Marion to come out and fight him like a gentleman and Christian, according to the laws of civilized warfare. While the tone of the letter was thus lugubrious, its language was offensive. He applied to the partisans the epithets 'banditti and murderers.' Marion returned no answer to this precious document, but renewed his order to his nightly patrols, to shoot the sentinels and cut off the picquets as before. He thought the measure quite as legitimate in such a war, as the burning the house and hanging the son of the widow.

But though Marion returned no answer by the flag, to the letter of Watson, there was a dispatch by one of the brigade, of a somewhat curious character. There was a sergeant in the brigade by the name of McDonald, of whom something has been heard before. He was the same bold fellow who had so closely pursued Major Gainey into Georgetown, leaving his bayonet in the possession and person of the latter. He was distinguished by his great coolness and courage, an extraordinary degree of strength, and a corresponding share of agility. He was as notorious among the enemy for his audacity, as he was among his comrades for his great modesty and goodness of heart. It appears that, among some of Watson's captures, while pressing hard upon our partisans, had been the entire wardrobe of McDonald. The sergeant felt it as something more than a loss of property that his clothes should be taken by the enemy. It was a point of honor that he should recover them. His message to Watson was of this purport. He concluded with solemnly assuring the hearer of the flag, that if the clothes were not returned he would kill eight of his men. Watson was furious at a message which increased the irritation of his late discomfiture. Knowing nothing himself of McDonald, he was disposed to treat the message with contempt; but some of his officers, who knew better the person with whom they had to deal, begged that the clothes of the sergeant might be returned to him, for that he would most certainly keep his word if they were not. Watson complied with the suggestion. When the clothes appeared, McDonald said to the bearer, "Tell Col. Watson, I will now kill but four of his men." Two days after he shot Lieut. Torriano through the knee with a rifle, at a distance of three hundred yards.

Marion, the next day, took post on a ridge below the ford of the river, which is still popularly called "The General's Island." His rifles still effectually commanded the passage and baffled every attempt of Watson to cross. Pushing M'Cottry and Conyers over the river, they exercised themselves in cutting off his patroles and picquets. To save himself from these annoyances, Watson retreated a little higher up the river and pitched his camp at Blakeley's plantation, in the most open field that he could find. Here he remained for ten days almost environed by his adroit and active enemy. Night and day was he kept in a condition of alarm and apprehension. The cavalry beat up his quarters when he slept, while the riflemen picked off his men the moment they exposed themselves. It was while he was in this situation that the brave Capt. Conyers presented himself daily before the lines of the enemy, either as a single cavalier, or at the head of his troop, demanding an opponent. The anecdote has been already narrated in another chapter.

The temper of Watson was very much subdued by this sort of warfare. His next letter to Marion was of very different tone from that sent but a few days before. He now solicits a pass from his enemy for Lieut. Torriano and others wounded, whom he desired to send to Charleston. This was promptly granted. Meanwhile he employed a negro from Chevin's plantation to carry a letter to the commandant at Georgetown. In endeavouring to make his way, the negro was killed and the letter fell into the hands of Marion. It contained a woful complaint of the unfair mode of fighting pursued by the partisans, and implored a reinforcement.[70] In fact Watson was literally besieged. His supplies were cut off, his progress arrested, and so many of his men perished in the continual skirmishing, that he is reported by tradition to have sunk them in Black river in order to conceal their numbers. He was finally compelled to decamp. If his path was beset with dangers, it was death to remain in his present situation. Making a forced march down the Georgetown road, he paused when he reached Ox swamp, six miles below the lower bridge. His flight had been harassed by light parties of the Americans; but here he found them prepared for, and awaiting him. The road through which he was to pass, was skirted by a thick boggy swamp, and before him the causeway was covered with trees which had been felled to obstruct his passage. The bridges were destroyed, and Marion lay directly in his path, prepared for a final encounter. Watson shrunk from the prospect, and determined upon another route. Wheeling to the right he dashed through the open pinewoods, for the Santee road, about fifteen miles. When overtaken by Marion upon this road, his infantry were hurrying forward, like horses, at a full trot. But few natural obstacles attended his progress on this path, and the extraordinary rapidity of his flight had put him considerably ahead of his pursuers. But he was not yet to escape. The cavalry of Horry, and the riflemen of M'Cottry, galled him at every step in flank and rear. When he reached Sampit bridge a last skirmish took place, which might have terminated in the complete defeat of the enemy, but for the cowardice of a Lieut. Scott, of Horry's detachment. Watson was attacked fiercely in the flank and rear by the whole force of Marion. His horse was killed, and his own life endangered. The affair was equally short and sharp, and had it not been that the ambush placed by Horry failed to discharge its duty, Watson would, in all probability, never have reached Georgetown, or only reached it on parole. He gained it finally in safety, thoroughly harassed and discomfited by the subtle enemy who he had gone forth, with a superior force, and a confident hope, to destroy or capture.

But the success of our partisan against Watson did not necessarily dispose of his enemies. While he had been engaged in the events, as just given, Col. Doyle had succeeded in penetrating to his haunts on Snow's Island. That famous retreat had been entrusted to a small body of men under the command of Col. Ervin. Ervin was defeated, and Doyle obtained possession of all Marion's stores. Arms and ammunition were emptied into Lynch's Creek, and this at a period, when every ounce of powder, and pound of shot, were worth, to our partisans, their weight in gold. It was while moving from Sampit towards Snow's Island, that Marion was apprised of this mortifying intelligence. It was a matter to be deplored certainly, but it was one of those events that could not have been prevented. The force of Marion was too small to suffer him to play the admirable game, already described, with Watson, yet leave a sufficient body of men in camp for its protection. He had only to console himself by taking his revenge, and he turned the head of his columns in pursuit of Doyle. This officer made his way to Witherspoon's Ferry, on Lynch's Creek, where he lay in a good position on the north side of the Ferry. Marion approached him cautiously, with M'Cottry's mounted riflemen in advance. Arriving at the creek a detachment of the British was found on the opposite side, engaged in scuttling the ferry boat. The riflemen drew nigh unperceived, and poured in a well directed and deadly fire, which produced the utmost consternation. The fire was returned in volleys, but the limbs and branches of the trees suffered infinitely more than the riflemen who lay behind them. Marion now made his arrangements for crossing the stream. But this was not to be done in the face of the enemy, with the creek before him wide and swollen. Marion moved rapidly up the creek, which he swam at the first favourable point some five miles above Witherspoon's. This brought him nearer to Doyle's position, but the latter had not waited for him. Whether it was that he had little taste for the sort of annoyances to which Watson had been subjected, or that he had received instructions from Lord Rawdon to join him at Camden, in all haste, it is certain that he made the greatest speed in hurrying in that direction.

It was at this period that Marion held a consultation with Horry, in which he is represented by that officer as in an unusual state of despondency. His enemies were accumulating around him with unwonted rapidity, and in greater force than ever. Watson, furious at his late disasters, and mortified with the result of his confident anticipations, had sallied forth from Georgetown with a reinforcement. He had gone towards the Pedee, where he strengthened himself with the large body of Tories which Gainey had commanded. Horry tells us of a third body of men at the same time in the field, with Doyle and Watson, and all addressing themselves to the same object, his utter expulsion from the country. At that moment the expulsion of our Partizan would leave the conquest of the State complete.

In these emergencies, with these foes accumulating around him, the mind of Marion naturally addressed itself with more gravity than usual to the task of his extrication from his enemies. His countenance, as Horry describes it, was troubled. But, with his usual taciturnity, he said nothing on the subject of his anxieties. Seeing him walking alone, and in deep revery, Horry approached him, and said—

"General, our men are few, and, if what I hear be true, you never wanted them more."

Marion started, and replied—

"Go immediately to the field officers, and know from them, if, in the event of my being compelled to retire to the mountains, they will follow my fortunes, and with it carry on the war, until the enemy is forced out of the country. Go, and bring me their answer without delay."

It was a peculiarity in Marion's character, that he should have entrusted such a commission to a subordinate. But it accords with all that we have seen of the reserve and shyness of his moods. The simple remark to Horry indicates his admirable firmness, his calculations, even of possible necessities long in advance, and his instinctive mode of encountering them as he best might. His determination, on his own account, to carry on the war against the enemy in the mountains, till they or himself were expelled from the country, denotes the unsubmitting patriot. The reader must not forget that, at this moment, there was no force in the State but his own, arrayed against the British. Sumter was still *hors de combat* from his wound. The army of Greene, having with it Pickens, and other native partisans, together with a considerable force of native militia, was in North Carolina, watching the movements of Cornwallis. Lord Rawdon, with a strong British garrison, held Camden. Charleston and Georgetown, Ninety-Six and Granby, Forts Watson and Motte, were all held, with numerous other conspicuous points, by the British; and with Watson, whose force now numbered a thousand men, Doyle half that number, and several active and large bodies of Tories prepared to co-operate with these against our partisan, the danger of Marion's situation, and his patriotic resolve of character, are conspicuous at a glance.

Horry sought the officers, and promptly returned to his commander. To a man they had pledged themselves to follow his fortunes, however disastrous, while one of them survived, and until their country was freed from the enemy. Marion's countenance instantly brightened—we cannot forbear the use of Horry's own language, though it may provoke a smile—"he was tip-toed"—(i.e.)—he rose upon his toes—and said "I am satisfied—one of these parties shall soon feel us."[71]

CHAPTER XIV

MARION RENEWS HIS PURSUIT OF DOYLE † CONFRONTS WATSON † IS JOINED BY COL. LEE † INVESTS AND TAKES FORT WATSON † FORT MOTTE TAKEN † ANECDOTE OF HORRY AND MARION

Marion instantly put his men in motion in pursuit of Doyle. In crossing the swamp of Lynch's Creek, during the night, several of the soldiers lost their arms, in consequence of the freshet. The swamp was inundated, and it required all their dexterity and promptitude to save themselves. Snatching a hasty breakfast, the pursuit was continued all day, and resumed the next morning until ten o'clock, when they found such signs of the superior speed and haste of the enemy, as to preclude all possibility of overtaking him. They had been necessarily delayed by the passage of the swamp, and had not made sufficient allowance for the speed with which an enemy might run when there was occasion for it. Here they found that Doyle had destroyed all his heavy baggage, and had sped in such confusion towards Camden, that his encampment, and the road which he traversed, were strewn with canteens and knapsacks, and everything, not necessary to defence, which might retard his progress.

Marion, somewhat surprised at a flight for which he could not then account, for his own force was far inferior to that of Doyle, yet saw that the fugitive was beyond present pursuit. He wheeled about, accordingly, and set his men in motion for another meeting with Watson. That commander, now strengthened, and just doubling the numbers of our partisan, with fresh supplies of provisions and military stores, had once more pushed for the Pedee. He took the nearest route across Black river, at Wragg's Ferry, and, crossing the Pedee at Euhaney, and the Little Pedee at Potato Ferry, he halted at Catfish Creek, one mile from the present site of Marion Courthouse. Marion crossed the Pedee, and encamped at the Warhees, within five miles of the enemy. Here he planted himself, in vigilant watch of the force which he could not openly encounter. In addition to the want of men, he labored under a still greater want of ammunition. When asked by Capt. Gavin Witherspoon, whether he meant to fight Watson—a measure which Witherspoon thought particularly advisable—before he was joined by any more bodies of Tories, he answered, "That would be best, but we have not ammunition."

"Why, general,' said Witherspoon, "my powder-horn is full"

"Ah, my friend!" was the reply of Marion, "you are an extraordinary soldier; but for the others, there are not two rounds to a man."

Thus stood the two parties; and thus it but too frequently stood with our partisan—wanting the most simple resources by which to make his own genius and the valor of his men apparent. That the former was alive and equal to emergencies, even in such a condition of necessity, may be inferred from the fact, that he should dare take such a position, so immediately contiguous to an enemy double his own force, and abounding in all the requisite materials of war. The inactivity of Watson is only to be accounted for by his total ignorance of the resourceless state of Marion's rifles.

While Marion and Watson were thus relatively placed, the former was apprised of the return of Greene to South Carolina. This intelligence accounted for the hasty retreat of Doyle. He was summoned by Lord Rawdon to Camden, to strengthen that position against the American force, which was advancing in that direction. The reappearance of Greene was a source of heartfelt joy to those who, but a little while before, had anticipated the necessity of flying before the foe, and taking shelter in the mountains. It was because of the absence of the American army that Rawdon was enabled, as we have seen, to concentrate his chief force upon Marion. The presence of Greene, which had caused the recall of Doyle, must, as Marion well knew, effect that of Watson also. He was preparing himself accordingly, when further advices brought him news of the approach of Colonel Lee, with the Continental Legion, to his own assistance. He dispatched a guide to Lee, and by means of boats, which he always kept secreted, the Legion was transported over the Pedee, and a junction with Marion's force was effected on the fourteenth of April.

The tidings which had brought such gratification to the camp of Marion, had as inspiring, though not as grateful an effect in that of Watson. He lost no time in breaking up his encampment. The safety of Rawdon and Camden was paramount, and, wheeling his two field-pieces into Catfish Creek, and burning his baggage, as Doyle had done, he sped, with similar precipitation, in the same direction. The route taken in his flight declared his apprehensions of Marion. He trembled at the recollection of the recent race between them—the harassings and skirmishings night and day—the sleepless struggles, and unintermitting alarms. Recrossing the Little Pedee, and avoiding Euhaney, he passed the Waccamaw at Greene's Ferry, and, retreating through the Neck, between that river and the sea, crossed Winyaw Bay, three miles in width, and, in this manner, arrived in Georgetown. A slight glance at any map of the country, keeping in mind that Watson's object was really Camden, will show the reader the extent of his fears of that wily and indefatigable enemy from whom he had previously escaped with so much difficulty.

Marion was exceedingly anxious to pursue Watson, but Lee, though subordinate, succeeded in preventing this desire. Instructions which he brought from Greene, and which he earnestly dwelt upon, required their co-operation against the British posts below Camden. Lee urged, also, that such a pursuit would take them too far from Greene, with the movements of whose army it was important that Marion's force should act as intimately as possible. Marion yielded the point with great reluctance, and was heard repeatedly after to regret that his orders did not permit him to follow the dictates of his own judgment. Had he done so, with his force strengthened by the Continental bayonets, and new supplies of powder for his rifles, Watson's flight to Georgetown, which he could scarcely have reached, would have been far more uncomfortable than he found it on the previous occasion.

Lee led the way with his legion towards the Santee, while Marion, placing Witherspoon with a small party on the trail of Watson, pursued his line of march through Williamsburg. Having once resolved, Marion's movements were always rapid and energetic. On the fifteenth of April, only a day after the junction with Lee, he was before Fort Watson.

This was a stockade fort, raised on one of those remarkable elevations of an unknown antiquity which are usually recognized as Indian mounds. It stands near Scott's Lake on the Santee river, a few miles below the junction of the Congaree and Wateree. The mound is forty feet in height, and remote from any other elevation by which it might be commanded. The garrison at this post consisted of eighty regular troops, and forty loyalists. It was commanded by Lieut. McKay, a brave officer, of the regular service. To the summons of Marion he returned a manly defiance, and the place was regularly invested.

Besieged and besiegers were alike without artillery; with a single piece, the former might well have defied any force which Marion could bring against him. The place would have been impregnable to the Americans. As it was, its steep sides and strong palisades forbade any attempt to storm. To cut off the garrison from Scott's Lake, where it procured water, was the first step taken by the besiegers. But the besieged, by sinking a well within the stockade, below the level of the contiguous water, counteracted the attempt. For a moment, the assailants were at fault, and, without artillery, the prospect was sufficiently discouraging. But while doubting and hesitating, Col. Mayham, of the brigade, suggested a mode of overawing the garrison which was immediately adopted. At a short distance from the fort there grew a small wood, a number of the trees of which were hewn down, and transported upon the shoulders of the men within a proper distance of the mound. Here, during the night, all hands were actively employed in piling the wood thus brought, in massive and alternate layers, crosswise, until the work had reached a sufficient elevation. At dawn, the garrison were confounded to find themselves, at wakening, under a shower of rifle bullets. Thus overlooked, the fort was no longer tenable; and a party of volunteers from the militia, headed by Ensign Baker, and another of Continentals, from the legion, led by Mr. Lee, a volunteer, ascended the mound with great intrepidity, and gained the abbatis, which they proceeded to destroy. This movement brought the garrison to terms, and a capitulation immediately followed. But the leaguer had consumed eight days, the progress of which had been watched with equal anxiety by both parties. The Americans apprehended, and the garrison anticipated, the approach of Watson with an overwhelming force for the relief of the besieged. But Watson did not appear. He no longer had an overwhelming force. His flight to Georgetown was marked by loss and desertion. It appears that his panic, or his sense of duty, led him rather to avoid Marion and to reach Camden without interruption. He very prudently, therefore, after crossing the Santee, on the route from Georgetown, moved down by Monk's Corner, added to his force the garrison of that place, and then cautiously advanced to the Santee. He resolved rather to leave Fort Watson to its fate, than risk a force which might be necessary to the exigencies of Rawdon. Watson was considered by the British one of their best partisans, yet never had poor warrior been so worried and harassed, as, with a superior force, he had been by Marion. Yet, in his second expedition in pursuit of the latter, had he been able to co-operate with Doyle, with the Tories of Harrison and Gainey, all preparing for the same object, the escape of our partisan would have been miraculous. At no time, during their pursuit of him, was his force equal to the smallest one of theirs. He must have been expelled the country, as he himself seemed to apprehend, or he must have fallen in the conflict.

We have so little at the hands of Marion, in the shape of correspondence, that we are tempted to give his official letter to General Greene, apprising him of the fall of Fort Watson. It is dated—

Fort Watson (Scott's Lake), April 23, 1781.
Sir—

Lieut.-Col. Lee made a junction with me at Santee, the 14th inst., after a rapid march from Ramsay's mill, on Deep River, which he performed in eight days. The 15th we marched to this place and invested it. Our hope was to cut off their water. Some riflemen and Continentals immediately took post between the fort and the lake. The fort is situated on a small hill, forty feet high, stockaded, and with three rows of abbatis round it. No trees near enough to cover our men from their fire. The third day after we had invested it, we found the enemy had sunk a well near the stockade which we could not prevent them from [doing]; as we had no entrenching tools to make our approach, we immediately determined to erect a work equal in height to the fort. This arduous work was completed this morning by Major Maham, who undertook it. We then made a lodgment on the side of the mound, near the stockade. This was performed with great spirit and address by Ensign Johnson, and Mr. Lee, a volunteer in Col. Lee's legion, who with difficulty ascended the hill and pulled away the abbatis, which induced the commandant to hoist a flag. Col. Lee and myself agreed to the enclosed capitulation, which I hope may be approved by you. Our loss on this occasion is two killed, and three Continentals and three militia wounded. I am particularly indebted to Col. Lee for his advice and indefatigable diligence in every part of these tedious operations, against as strong a little post as could well be made, and on the most advantageous spot that could be wished for. The officers and men of the legion and militia performed everything that could be expected; and Major Maham of my brigade, had, in a particular manner, a great share of this success by his unwearied diligence in erecting the tower which principally occasioned the reduction of the fort. In short, sir, I have had the greatest assistance from every one under my command. Enclosed is a list of the prisoners and stores taken, and I shall, without loss of time, proceed to demolish the fort; after which I shall march to the high hills of Santee, encamp at Capt. Richardson's, and await your orders.

(Signed) Francis Marion.

In taking post at the Santee Hills, the object of Marion was to take such a position as would enable him to watch all the several roads by which Watson could make his way to Camden. It was important, if possible, to prevent his junction with Lord Rawdon, thus increasing the ability of that commander to cope with Greene's army, which now lay before that place. But Marion was not able to encounter Watson without assistance. Lee, with his legion, had been withdrawn by Greene soon after the capture of Fort Watson, and our partisan's force in camp, from concurring circumstances, was now reduced to about eighty men. Eighty of his brigade were detached under Col. Irvine to Rafting Creek, in order to cut off supplies from Camden. Another party was engaged in watching a rising of the Tories on the Pedee, who, in the absence of Marion himself, had manifested a disposition to resume the offensive; Col. Harden, with another detachment, was on the Salkehatchie, having first succeeded in the capture of Fort Balfour at Pocotaligo, in which he made nearly a hundred prisoners. Other small detachments had thinned the little army of our partisan to such a degree that it was of small efficiency where it was; and, just at this juncture, numerous desertions took place from two concurring circumstances. The approach of Marion to the hills had brought on the battle of Camden. Unwilling that Greene's force should be increased by the militia of the former, Rawdon had resolved not to wait for Watson, but to march out and give battle before the coming of either. He did so. The affair was not decisive, but Greene was compelled to yield the field to his enemy. He lost nothing, whether of honor or position, by this result. But, as the news spread, the defeat was exaggerated. It was supposed to be another affair such as that of Gates, and Marion's small body of men was still farther lessened by desertion. There was still another reason for its present feebleness. The time of the year was the very height of the planting season, and the farmer-soldiers, in numbers, left the camp in order to hurry to their homes and set their crops. This, though not allowed by the regular disciplinarian, was, in the mind of the militiaman, a duty quite as imperative as any that he owed to his family. Indeed, it was inseparable from his necessities that, where the Government did not give him bread, he must make it for himself. His family could not starve, and if he could fight without pay, it was not possible that he should do so without food. In the sort of warfare which Marion had hitherto carried on, he had been willing to recognize these necessities on the part of his followers. Co-operating with an army differently constituted, it was scarcely possible to do so, with any hope of their permanent usefulness. Just at this juncture, in particular, he felt the peculiarly mortifying character of his situation.

To enable Marion to contend with Watson, Greene dispatched Major Eaton, with a body of Continentals, to his assistance, with instructions to throw himself across the path of Watson. But Eaton, by an unhappy misunderstanding of his duty, failed to reach him in season for this object.

When he did join him, which was on the evening of the 2d of May, it was too late. Marion, writing to Greene, says, 'Major Eaton's not coming up sooner has made me lose a great deal of precious time. I shall cross the Santee at Wright's Bluff to-morrow.' He did so, but Watson had already passed, and succeeded in eluding Greene also, and in reaching Camden in safety.

We have spoken of Col. Harden's proceedings against Fort Balfour, and the capture of that post. This officer was a very brave and active gentleman, rapid in his movements, and resolute in his objects. As soon as Marion had received intelligence of Greene's approach to South Carolina, he had dispatched Harden with seventy select men, well mounted, to penetrate through the country, and crossing the enemy lines of communication, to stir up the people in all that region which lies southwest of Charleston. So rapid and unexpected were his movements, that he took the enemy everywhere by surprise, and rendered himself for the time, the very terror of the loyalists upon the route. His force increased with its progress. The inhabitants yearned for an escape from British authority, and joined his troop. His seventy men soon became two hundred, and while he baffled the pursuit of the superior, he visited with sudden and severe chastisement the disaffected, along and on both sides of the Savannah river. Ascending this, he soon communicated with Pickens, then operating against Augusta and Ninety-Six. Nothing now was wanting but the fall of the enemy's chain of posts, to complete the recovery of the whole country within thirty miles of the sea. In contributing to this desirable object Marion, now strengthened by the Continentals of Lee and Eaton, invested Fort Motte on the river Congaree.

This post was the principal depot of the convoys from Charleston to Camden, and sometimes of those destined for Forts Granby and Ninety-Six. A large new mansion-house belonging to Mrs. Motte, situated on a high and commanding hill, had been chosen for this establishment. It was surrounded with a deep trench, along the inner margin of which a strong and lofty parapet was raised. To this post had been assigned a sufficient garrison of one hundred and fifty men. This force was increased by a small detachment of dragoons from Charleston, which had been thrown into it a few hours before the appearance of the Americans. The garrison was commanded by Capt. McPherson, a firm and gallant officer.

Opposite to Fort Motte, to the north, stood another hill where Mrs. Motte, who had been expelled from her dwelling, resided in an old farm-house. On this, Lee took position with his corps: Marion's men occupied the eastern declivity of the same ridge on which stood the fort.

The place was very soon invested. The six-pounder with which Greene had furnished Marion, was mounted on a battery raised in the quarter which he occupied, for the purpose of raking the northern face of the enemy parapet. McPherson was in the possession of a wall-piece, but he had not been able to adapt it for use before the investment took place. It does not seem to have been even used during the siege. His chief hopes lay in being relieved by a detachment from Camden, not doubting its arrival before his assailant could push his preparations to maturity. The works of the latter advanced rapidly, and the place was summoned on the 20th of May. The reply declared the determination of the besieged to try the strength and patience of the besiegers. These had now every motive for perseverance. They were advised of the approach of Rawdon, with all his force, to the relief of the fort. That stern commander, finding Camden was no longer tenable against the increasing forces of the Americans, and unable to maintain his several posts with his diminished strength, was aiming to contract his scattered bodies into narrower limits. Having made a second, but unsatisfactory, demonstration upon Greene, he destroyed his unnecessary baggage, and, leaving Camden in flames, he once more abandoned it to the Americans. Greene advised Marion of his retreat, and urged him to expedition. On the next night he reached the country opposite Fort Motte, and his numerous fires on the highest grounds on his route, encouraged the garrison with hopes of success, which were not to be realized.

What was to be done, was to be done quickly, on the part of the besiegers. The process of battering by cannon would be too slow. Some shorter mode was to be adopted, to anticipate the approach of Rawdon. The ready thought of our partisan suggested this process. It was known that the large mansion of Mrs. Motte occupied the greater part of the area of the fort; but a few yards of ground within the works remained uncovered by it. To burn the house by fire would compel the surrender of the garrison.

The necessity was very reluctantly communicated to the widow by whom the property was owned. But she was one of those glorious dames of the Revolution, to whom the nation is so largely indebted for the glory of that event. She had received the American officers with a hospitality which made them almost shrink from suggesting their purposes; but as soon as they were made known, she put them perfectly at ease upon the subject. With something more than cheerfulness—with pride—that any sacrifice on her part should contribute to the success of her countrymen, in so dear an object, she herself produced a bow, with all the necessary apparatus, which had been brought from India, and which she had preserved. By the arrows from this bow the fire was to be communicated to her dwelling.

Everything being in readiness, the lines were manned and an additional force stationed at the batteries, lest the enemy, in the moment

Mrs. Motte presenting the American Officers with the Bow and Arrows.

of desperation, might prefer risking an assault, rather than endure the mortification of a surrender. A flag was again sent to McPherson, but the sight of Rawdon's fires on the other side of the river encouraged him with the belief that he might still resist successfully.

The bow was put into the hands of Nathan Savage, a private in Marion's brigade. It was noon when the attempt was made. The scorching rays of the noonday sun had prepared the roof for the conflagration. Balls of blazing rosin and brimstone were attached to the arrows, and three several shafts were sent by the vigorous arm of the militia-man against the roof. They took effect, in three different quarters, and the shingles were soon in a blaze. McPherson immediately ordered a party to the roof, but this had been prepared for, and the fire of the six-pounder soon drove the soldiers down. The flames began to rage, the besiegers were on the alert, guarding every passage, and no longer hopeful of Rawdon, McPherson hung out the white flag imploring mercy. The gentle nature of Marion readily yielded to his prayer, though, as Lee tells us, "policy commanded death."

In this siege Marion lost two brave fellows, one of whom has been more than once conspicuous in this narrative—the daring Sergeant McDonald, and Lieutenant Cruger. McDonald had reached a lieutenancy before he fell. The prisoners were paroled, but their officers before leaving partook of a sumptuous dinner given by Mrs. Motte to the victors. This noble lady, whose grace of demeanor is represented as quite equal to her patriotism, presided at her table, in such a manner as to render all parties at home. Col. P. Horry tells us of some of the incidents which took place at the dinner. A captain of the British army, taken among the prisoners, on finding himself near Horry, said to him:

"You are Col. Horry, I presume, sir." Horry answered in the affirmative. "Well," said the other, "I was with Col. Watson when he on Sampit fought your General Marion. I think I saw you there with a party of horse. I think you were also at Nelson's Ferry, when Marion surprised our party at the house? But," added the officer, "I was hid in high grass and escaped. Were you not there also?" Horry answered, "No! It was my brother Hugh." "Well," said the captain, "*you* were fortunate in your escape [at Sampit] for Watson and Small had 1200 men." "If so," said Horry, "I certainly was fortunate, for I did not suppose they had more than half that number." The captain then added—"I consider myself equally fortunate in escaping at Nelson's old field." "Truly, you were," answered Horry dryly; "for Marion had but 30 militia on that occasion." "At this," says our worthy Colonel, "the captain's countenance fell, and he retired, and avoided me the rest of the day. General Greene, the next day

(Greene had reached Marion's camp that night) said to me, "Col. Horry, how came you to affront Capt. Ferguson?" I answered, he affronted himself by telling his own story. It militated so greatly against himself as to compel the officers who were near to laugh. "The captain and I, sir, agreed that we were both equally fortunate in war." Greene replied, "Capt. Ferguson's memory was only too good."[72]

While at the hospitable table of Mrs. Moultrie, it was whispered in Marion's ears, that Col. Lee's men were even then engaged in hanging certain of the Tory prisoners. Marion instantly hurried from the table, seized his sword, and running with all haste, reached the place of execution in time to rescue one poor wretch from the gallows. Two were already beyond rescue or recovery. With drawn sword and a degree of indignation in his countenance that spoke more than words, Marion threatened to kill the first man that made any further attempt in such diabolical proceedings.

CHAPTER XV

CORRESPONDENCE OF MARION AND GREENE
† ANECDOTE OF COL. SNIPES † MARION TAKES
GEORGETOWN † ATTEMPT OF SUMTER AND MARION
ON COL. COATES † BATTLE OF QUINBY BRIDGE

I t was while Marion was most actively engaged in the investment of Fort Motte, that a correspondence took place between himself and General Greene, which had nearly resulted in the loss of his invaluable services to the country. A pure and noble spirit, Marion was particularly sensitive to reproach, and felt deeply its injustice. From the moment that Greene took command of the southern army, he had yielded the most profound deference to his wishes, had seconded his slightest suggestions, timed his own movements with a studied regard to those contemplated by the commander, and, whenever the service would allow, had devoted his little band to such duties as would lead to the promotion of all those larger plans which were contemplated for the execution of the grand army. His scouts had served for pioneers, his cavalry procured provisions for the camp, and it was to Marion alone that Greene looked for all his intelligence. But there was one favorite object which Greene had in view, to which our partisan could contribute little. The want of a cavalry force had been particularly felt by the former, and he had been sedulous in the endeavor to supply this want, from the very first of his southern campaigns. He had been pressingly calling upon Sumter, Marion, and every officer, who might be thought able to procure him a supply of horses; and active agents of his own had been scouring every quarter of the country in search of this indispensable agent of all great military operations. His quest had been comparatively vain. The British had been before him throughout the country. The dragoons of Tarleton had swept the stables; and, where this was not the case, the horses were held by militia men, to whom they were quite as indispensable as to the grand army. Marion's troopers could only be of service while in possession of their horses—they had large and extensive tracts of country to traverse—could procure no intelligence without—and, any attempt to dismount a soldier from his favorite steed, would be to produce a degree of discontent in his mind which would most certainly deprive the country of his services. To expect that the partisan militia under Marion and Sumter, who had been constantly on horseback, in the face of the enemy, should deliver their horses up to others who possessed no higher claim upon the country than themselves, as to expect more largely than was altogether reasonable, from the liberality or the patriotism of any set of men. A few, such as could be spared, had been supplied by Marion. He never, for an instant, contemplated the dismounting of his troopers—those hardy fellows who had been constant in all vicissitudes—who had murmured at no tasks—shrunk from no adventures—and spared neither themselves nor their property, when the necessities of the country required, at periods when there was no grand army to divide with themselves the honors and the dangers of the war. Nay, to dismount them was, in fact, to disarm himself. It appears, however, that this was expected of him. An unfortunate letter of Col. Lee, dated the 23d May, and addressed to Greene, contained this paragraph.

"General Marion," says the letter, "can supply you, if he will, with one hundred and fifty good dragoon horses, most of them impressed horses. He might, in my opinion, spare sixty, which would be a happy supply."

The effect of this communication upon Greene was immediate and painful. Believing that he had been ill-used, and vexed that Marion, knowing his necessities, and with the power to relieve them, should yet have forborne to do so, though urgently exhorted, he frankly declared his feelings in the very next letter to our partisan. Marion did not dissemble his indignation in his reply. He repels the charge that he had ever withheld supplies which he might have furnished, and concludes his letter by requesting permission to resign—firmly, but respectfully, intimating his resolution to retire from service as soon as Fort Motte should be reduced. Greene, in an instant, from this reply, perceived the mischief that he had done. He wrote instantly to Marion, and succeeded, though with difficulty, in overcoming his resolution. He says: "My reason for writing so pressingly for the dragoon horses, was from the distress we were in. It is not my wish to take the horses from the militia, if it will injure the public service. The effects and consequences you can better judge of than I can. You have rendered important services to the public with the militia under your command, and have done great honor to yourself, and I would not wish to render your situation less agreeable with them, unless it is to answer some very great purpose; and this, I persuade myself, you would agree to, from a desire to promote the common good…"

From the same letter, we make another extract: "I shall always be happy to see you at head-quarters, but cannot think you seriously mean to solicit leave to go to Philadelphia. It is true, your task has been disagreeable, but not more so than others, it is now going on seven years since the commencement of this war. I have never had leave of absence one hour, nor paid the least attention to my own private affairs. Your State is invaded—your all is at stake. What has been done will signify nothing, unless we persevere to the end. I left a family in distress, and everything dear and valuable, to come and afford you all the assistance in my power, to promote the Service. It must throw a damp upon the spirits of the army, to find that the first men in the State are retiring from the busy scene, to indulge themselves in more agreeable amusements. However, your reasons for wishing to decline the command of the militia, and go to Philadelphia, may be more pressing than I imagine, I will, therefore, add nothing more on this subject till I see you."

The adroit mixture of reproach with commendation, was not done without reflection. Greene seems to have understood the character of Marion. But there was some oblique injustice in his letter. A man's patriotism is not to be reproached, because he wishes to escape injustice and indignity. The best of patriots will be apt to become disgusted with a service in which their claims are neglected, their performances slurred over, and their motives impeached; and this, too, at a period, and after long periods, of service, in which they have watched, toiled, and fought, without hope or prospect of reward. When General Greene compared the disagreeableness of Marion's toils with those of others, he certainly overlooked, not only the peculiar character of those toils, but the peculiar privations which distinguished the career of Marion's men, and the particularly painful duties which so frequently belonged to it. His own previously expressed opinions with regard to the warfare, as carried on between Whig and Tory in the south, will be found to furnish a sufficient commentary upon the comparison which he thus makes. Greene himself, by the way, is not without blame in some respects, in relation to the southern commanders of militia. The slighting manner in which he spoke of them, and of their services, in letters not intended to be public, was such, that some of them, Sumter for example, never forgave him. His prejudices were those of the regular service, the policy of which is always to disparage the militia. To Marion himself, his language was of a different character. Take the following extract of a letter, written to the latter only one month before the correspondence above referred to. This letter is dated, from the camp before Camden, April 24, 1781, and will give a faint idea of the true claims of Marion upon the regard of his country. "When I consider," writes Greene, "how much you have done and suffered, and under what disadvantage you have maintained your ground, I am at a loss which to admire most, your courage and fortitude, or your address and management. Certain it is, no man has a better claim to the public thanks than you. History affords no instance wherein an officer has kept possession of a country under so many disadvantages as you have. Surrounded on every side with a superior force, hunted from every quarter with veteran troops, you have found means to elude their attempts, and to keep alive the expiring hopes of an oppressed militia, when all succor seemed to be cut off. *To fight the enemy bravely with the prospect of victory, is nothing; but to fight with intrepidity under the constant impression of defeat, and inspire irregular troops to do it, is a talent peculiar to yourself.* Nothing will give me greater pleasure than to do justice to your merit, and I shall miss no opportunity of declaring to Congress, to the commander-in-chief of the American army, and to the world, the great sense I have of your merit and your services."

The correspondence of Greene with Marion, on the subject of the horses, closed with a letter on the part of the latter, in which he turned off the affair on grounds that proved his feelings tranquillized. A present of a fine horse, for Greene's own use, accompanied this letter. It has been shown that, on the day of the capture of Fort Motte, Greene rode into the camp of Marion, at that place. We can conceive of no other motive for his presence here, than a desire to make his reconciliation perfect. He brought no force with him to promote the object of the besiegers, and his stay was limited to a brief interview.

But the evil effect of this affair did not end here. The militia, alarmed at the idea of having their horses taken from them, soon began to scatter, and, pleading the planting season upon which they had entered—some, indeed, without any plea,—they left the camp in numbers, and before the leaguer was well over, the force of Marion was reduced to something less than two hundred men. With this remnant of his brigade, as soon as Fort Motte was yielded, Marion detached himself from the regular troops and struck down towards Monk's Corner, hanging upon the skirts of Lord Rawdon's army, then in full retreat from Camden.

Perhaps the most interesting portions of our traditionary history in the South, will be found to have occurred to the scattered bodies of the partisan cavalry, while on their return movements to and from the army, after such a dispersion as that from which the brigade of Marion was now suffering. It was no easy matter for the small group, or the single trooper, to regain the family homestead, or the friendly neighborhood in which their wives and little ones were harbored. Every settlement through which they passed had its disaffected population. It might be small or large, but its numbers did not affect its activity, and, with the main body of the Whigs in camp, or on the road, the Tories, in remote sections of the country, were generally equally strong and daring. These waylaid the customary pathways, and aware of all the material movements of the regular troops, made their arrangements to cut off stragglers or small detached bodies. When we consider the active malignity by which the civil war in Carolina was marked; the wild forests in which it took place; the peculiar ferocity which it stimulated, and the various characteristics of the local modes of warfare, the chase and the surprise, we shall have no occasion for wonder at the strange and sometimes terrible events by which it was distinguished. One of these, which occurred to Captain, afterwards Colonel Snipes, of Marion's brigade, is a remarkable instance; and, as it has been told elsewhere, in connection with the life of Marion, it may well claim a place in this narrative.

Snipes was a Carolinian, of remarkable strength and courage. He was equally distinguished for his vindictive hatred of the Tories. He had suffered some domestic injuries at their hands, and he was one who never permitted himself to forgive. His temper was sanguinary in the extreme, and led him, in his treatment of the loyalists, to such ferocities as subjected him, on more than one occasion, to the harshest rebuke of his commander. It is not certain at what period in the war the following occurrence took place, but it was on one of those occasions when the partisan militia claimed a sort of periodical privilege of abandoning their general to look after their families and domestic interests. Availing himself of this privilege, Snipes pursued his way to his plantation. His route was a circuitous one, but it is probable that he pursued it with little caution. He was more distinguished for audacity than prudence. The Tories fell upon his trail, which they followed with the keen avidity of the sleuth-hound. Snipes reached his plantation in safety, unconscious of pursuit. Having examined the homestead and received an account of all things done in his absence, from a faithful driver, and lulled into security by the seeming quiet and silence of the neighborhood, retired to rest, and, after the fatigues of the day, soon fell into a profound sleep. From this he was awakened by the abrupt entrance and cries of his driver. The faithful negro apprised him, in terror, of the approach of the Tories. They were already on the plantation. His vigilance prevented them from taking his master in bed. Snipes, starting up, proposed to take shelter in the barn, but the driver pointed to the flames already bursting from the building. He had barely time to leave the house, covered only by his night shirt, and, by the counsel of the negro, to fly to the cover of a thick copse of briars and brambles, within fifty yards of the dwelling, when the Tories surrounded it. The very task of penetrating this copse, so as to screen himself from sight, effectually removed the thin garment which concealed his nakedness. The shirt was torn from his back by the briars, and the skin shared in its injuries. But, once there, he lay effectually concealed from sight. Ordinary conjecture would scarcely have supposed that any animal larger than a rabbit would have sought or found shelter in such a region. The Tories immediately seized upon the negro and demanded his master, at the peril of his life. Knowing and fearing the courage and the arm of Snipes, they did not enter the dwelling, but adopted the less valorous mode of setting it on fire, and, with pointed muskets, surrounded it, in waiting for the moment when their victim should emerge. He, within a few steps of them, heard their threats and expectations, and beheld all their proceedings. The house was consumed, and the intense heat of the fire subjected our partisan, in his place of retreat, to such torture, as none but the most dogged hardihood could have endured without complaint. The skin was peeled from his body in many places, and the blisters were shown long after, to persons who are still living.[73] But Snipes too well knew his enemies, and what he had to expect at their hands, to make any confession. He bore patiently the torture, which was terribly increased, when, finding themselves at fault, the Tories brought forward the faithful negro who had thus far saved his master, and determined to extort from him, in the halter, the secret of his hiding-place. But the courage and fidelity of the negro proved superior to the terrors of death. Thrice was he run up the tree, and choked nearly to strangulation, but in vain. His capability to endure proved superior to the will of the Tories to inflict, and he was at length let down, half dead,—as, in truth, ignorant of the secret which they desired to extort. What were the terrors of Snipes in all this trial? What his feelings of equal gratitude and apprehension? How noble was the fidelity of the slave—based upon what gentle and affectionate relationship between himself and master—probably from boyhood! Yet this is but one of a thousand such attachments, all equally pure and elevated, and maintained through not dissimilar perils.

While Marion was operating against Forts Watson and Motte, Sumter, with like success, had besieged the British posts at Orangeburg and Granby. It was the loss of these posts, and the dread of the subsequent concentration of the whole American force against Camden, that had prompted the destruction and abandonment of that place by Lord Rawdon. This was the plan and object of Greene. The precipitate movements of Rawdon, who anticipated the purpose of the former, necessarily defeated it. Pickens was operating against Augusta; while Sumter, leaving the investment of Granby,

Col. Snipes saved by his faithful negro.

the conquest of which was considered sure, to Col. Taylor, proceeded down the country, with the two-fold object of harassing the descent of the British army, and to prevent them from carrying off the cattle of the inhabitants. In the former object, neither Marion nor himself had much success. They did not succeed in effecting a junction, and the sanguine desire of Sumter, with united forces, to operate boldly upon the retreating army of Rawdon, was not encouraged by Greene, who preferred a safe and sure, though slow progress, to any attainment of his end by a hazardous attempt, however glorious. The task of holding Rawdon in check, was confided to Marion and Sumter, while Greene proceeded with his whole army, to the investment of the post of Ninety-Six, at the village of Cambridge. In the execution of their duties, the two partisans closed in upon the British commander until he established a line of fortified posts, extending from Georgetown, by Monk's Corner, Dorchester, &c., to Coosawhatchee. Within this line our partisans continually made incursions, keeping the enemy in constant check and apprehension. They were not in force to do more. Georgetown, however, separated by water courses and swamps of great magnitude, from the other posts, was left with a garrison so feeble, as to tempt Marion to proceed against it. The parishes that lie along the Santee, on both sides, towards its mouth, had turned out with so much zeal on his return into their neighborhood, that he soon found himself in sufficient force to cover the country with a strong detachment under Col. Mayham, while, with his main body, he went against Georgetown. He appeared before this place on the 6th of June, and instantly began his approaches. But his simple demonstration was sufficient. The enemy made but a show of resistance. As the attempt was pressed, the garrison fled to their galleys, and took a position in the bay beyond the reach of the Americans. They finally abandoned the harbor altogether. It was not in the power of Marion to man the post efficiently, and his policy forbade that he should do it inadequately. Accordingly, he deliberately removed the military stores and public property, up the Pedee, then, demolishing the works, returned to join his detachment in St. Stephens. While at Georgetown, however, it is recorded that he replenished his wardrobe, and fitted himself out with a becoming suit of regimentals. This was an event, in the career of our partisan, to be remembered by his followers. He indulged, it seems, for the first time, in some other of the luxuries of the campaigner. A couple of mules were employed for the transportation of his baggage, and his usual beverage of vinegar and water was occasionally diversified by a bowl of coffee at breakfast. A little before this,—perhaps soon after General Greene had penetrated the State,—he had appointed himself a couple of secretaries for the purpose of greater dispatch in letter writing—his correspondence necessarily increasing, in consequence of his connection with the more expanded operations of the army. State, he did not affect, and the simplicity and modesty of his character may be easily inferred from this petty enumeration of the aids and comforts which he thought proper to draw from his successes.

While Marion, in person, proceeded against Georgetown, Col. Peter Horry was dispatched with a strong body of men against the loyalists on the Pedee, a wild and blood thirsty band of borderers, under the conduct of Major Gainey, of whom we have had occasion to speak already. Horry succeeded in awing Gainey into submission, and in extorting from him a treaty by which he consented, with his officers and men, to maintain a condition of neutrality. This submission, though complete, was but temporary. It required subsequently the decisive proceedings of Marion, and his personal presence, to enforce its provisions. But of this hereafter.

While Greene, with the main American army, was proceeding against Ninety-Six, preparations were made by the British in Charleston, for ravaging the country on the south side of the Santee. The people of St. John and St. Stephen's parishes, had shown too active a zeal in the cause of liberty, to escape punishment, and it was resolved that their country should be laid waste. The loyalists of Charleston, and that vicinity, had been embodied in a regiment, and, under Col. Ball, prepared to carry this design into execution. But Marion, apprised by his scouts and spies of every movement in the city, and unable with his present force to meet with that of Ball, determined, however painful the necessity, to anticipate his proceedings; and with his usual celerity, he laid waste the country himself; removing, across the Santee to places of safety, not only all the stock and cattle, but all the provisions, that could be collected. They were thus saved, as well for the subsistence of his men, as for the proprietor. Anxious to oppose himself more actively to the enemy, he sent pressing dispatches to Greene for assistance in covering the country. Col. Washington, with his admirable corps of cavalry, was accordingly dispatched to his assistance. We have seen that the commander-in-chief had proceeded in person against the British post at Ninety-Six. To Sumter and Marion had been entrusted the care of Rawdon. They were required to check and prevent his progress in the event of any attempt which he might make to relieve the post. They were unsuccessful in doing so. The arrival of a British fleet with reinforcements, comprising three fresh regiments from Ireland, enabled Rawdon to despise any attempts, which, with their inferior force, our partisans might make. Some idea of the diligence of Marion and the excellence of his plans for procuring intelligence, may be gathered from the fact that the Charleston paper of the

2d of June, announcing the arrival of these regiments, was in his possession the very day on which it was printed, and transmitted instantly, through Sumter's command, to Greene.[74] Greene was unsuccessful in his attempts on Ninety-Six. The place was relieved, after an obstinate defence, by Rawdon, who, with his new troops, by forced marches, arrived in time for its deliverance. Greene was compelled to retreat after much sanguinary fighting. He was pursued by Rawdon for a small distance but the latter, contenting himself with having rescued, withdrew the garrison, and abandoned the place to the Americans. He was in no condition to pursue his enemy or to maintain his position. His Irish regiments were not to be trusted, and the maintenance of the city and the seaboard were paramount considerations. With such active and enterprising foes as Marion and Sumter, between his army and his garrison, he felt the insecurity of his hold upon the country. His posts in the interior had now everywhere fallen into the hands of the Americans. Augusta, with the three posts, Cornwallis, Grierson and Galphin, had just been yielded to the arms of Pickens and Lee. There were no longer any intermediate posts of defence, from Orangeburg to Ninety-Six, and the latter was now so thoroughly isolated, that prudence led to its abandonment. This necessity brought with it another, which was much more painful and humiliating to the unfortunate loyalists of that country, who had so long sided with the British arms against their countrymen. They were compelled to abandon their homes and share the fortunes of the retreating army. They were without refuge, and the spirit of the warfare had been such as to leave them hopeless of mercy in any encounter with the Whigs. A mournful cavalcade followed in the train of the British army, and retarded its progress. Greene, as he discovered Rawdon's movements to be retrograde, turned upon his retreating footsteps. His cavalry harassed the enemy and hastened his flight. At Ancrum's ferry on the Congaree, Greene, in advance of his army, joined Marion and Washington, the latter with his cavalry, the former with four hundred mounted militia; and, at the head of these two corps, pressing down the Orangeburg road, on the 6th of July, he succeeded in passing Lord Rawdon. Retaining command of Washington's cavalry, he dispatched Marion with his mounted militia to intercept a valuable convoy, freighted not only for relief of Rawdon's army, but it with all the various supplies and material necessary for the establishment of the British post at Granby. Marion was unsuccessful. The convoy under Lieut.-Col. Stewart escaped without being conscious of its danger. He had taken one of two roads, while Marion watched for him upon the other. On the morning of the 8th, Stewart and Rawdon effected a junction in Orangeburg. The condition of the British army on that day is thus described in a letter of Marion to Greene:

"Their troops are so fatigued they cannot possibly move. Three regiments were going to lay down their arms, and it is believed they will to-day, if they are ordered to march. They have no idea of any force being near them."

At Orangeburg, Rawdon was too strongly posted for any attempts of Greene. Here, with his own force and that of Stewart, numbering fifteen hundred men, he was joined by Col. Cruger from Ninety-Six, with thirteen hundred more. Orangeburg is situated on the east bank of the North Edisto, which half encircles it. North and south are swamps and ravines, which so nearly approach each other as to leave but a narrow and broken passage on the east side. The gaol, a strong brick building of two stories, not inferior to a strong redoubt, with some other buildings, commanded the approach. "The crown of the hill on which it stood, was sufficiently spacious for manoeuvering the whole British army, and the houses and fences afforded shelter against all attempts of the American cavalry or mounted militia," while, in case of defeat, the bridge in their rear afforded as secure means of retreat. An attempt upon such a position, with a force consisting chiefly of mounted infantry, would have been folly, and Greene, after a brief demonstration, determined to withdraw one half of his army towards the Congaree, while the other was sent forward upon that memorable incursion into the lower country, by which the enemy, from all quarters, were driven into Charleston; and, with the exception of the force at Orangeburg, for a brief period, every vestige of British power was swept away, down to the very gates of the former place. The command of this detachment was given to Sumter. Acting under him, were Marion, Lee, the Hamptons, Taylor, Horry, Mayham, and others of those active partisans who had kept alive the war from the beginning. The command consisted of all the State troops, Lee's legion, and a detachment of artillery, with one field piece; in all about a thousand men. The object of this movement was not only to strike at the British line of posts, but to divert the attention of Rawdon from the Congaree, where it was his policy to re-establish himself in force.

The force under Sumter, as it approached the scene of operations, was broken into separate detachments. Dorchester was yielded without resistance to the corps under Lee, while Col. Wade Hampton, pressing to the very lines of Charleston, captured the guard and patrol at the Quarter House, and spread terror through the city. Sumter and Marion then proceeded against the post at Biggin, held by Col. Coates of the British army, a spirited officer, with a garrison of five hundred infantry, one hundred and fifty horse, and one piece of artillery. The post at Biggin consisted of a redoubt at Monk's Corner, and the church, about a mile distant, near Biggin Bridge. This church was a strong brick building, which covered the bridge and secured the retreat at that point, by way of Monk's Corner. Biggin Creek is one of many streams which empty into Cooper river. Of these, it is the most northwardly. On the east of this creek, the road to Charleston crosses Watboo and Quinby Creeks. The destruction of Watboo bridge rendered impracticable the retreat by the eastern route, and this bridge, accordingly, became an important object to both the British and Americans. A detachment of Marion's men, under Col. Mayham, was sent forward to destroy the Watboo bridge, and thus cut off the retreat of the enemy. But the position and force of Col. Coates prevented the approach of Mayham, and he waited the advance of the main body. On the 16th July, he was reinforced by a detachment under Col. Peter Horry, who, assuming the command, proceeded to the attempt upon the bridge. The enemy's cavalry opposed themselves to the attempt; a short action ensued; they were defeated and driven back with loss. The mounted riflemen broke through them, and a number of prisoners were taken. Horry then dispatched a party to destroy the bridge, and remained to cover the men engaged in the work. But the enemy soon re-appeared in force, and Horry, with his working party, was compelled to retire, in turn, upon the main body. Sumter, believing that Coates had marched out to give him battle, took post in a defile, and awaited him; but the purpose of the enemy was only to gain time—to wear out the day, amusing him, while they made secret preparations for flight. Their stores were accumulated in the church, which had been their fortress, and, at midnight, the flames bursting through the roof of the devoted building announced to the Americans the retreat of the foe. The pursuit was immediately commenced, and, in order that it might not be impeded, the only piece of artillery which Sumter had, was unfortunately left behind, under Lieut. Singleton. Lee and Hampton led the pursuit until, having passed the Watboo, they discovered that the cavalry of the enemy had separated from the infantry, taking the right hand route. Hampton then struck off in pursuit of the former, in hope to overtake them before they could reach the river; but he urged his panting horses in vain. They had completed their escape, and secured the boats on the opposite side, before he could come up with them.

Marion's cavalry, meanwhile, under Col. Mayham, had joined the Legion cavalry in pursuit of the infantry. About a mile to the north of Quinby Creek, the rear-guard of the retreating army was overtaken. With this body, which consisted of one hundred men, under Capt. Campbell, was nearly all the baggage of the British army. Terrified by the furious charge of the Americans, they threw down their arms without firing a gun. Favored by this circumstance, the cavalry of Mayham, and the Legion, pressed forward. Coates had passed Quinby Bridge, and made dispositions for its demolition, as soon as the rear-guard and baggage should have passed. The planks which covered the bridge had been loosened from the sleepers, and a howitzer, at the opposite extremity, was placed to check the pursuit. But, as the rear-guard had been captured without firing a shot, their commander was unapprised of their fate, and unprepared for immediate defence. Fortunately for his command, he was present at the bridge when the American cavalry came in view. His main body, at this moment, was partly on the causeway, on the south side of the bridge, and partly pressed into a lane beyond it—in situations so crowded as to be almost wholly incapable of immediate action. Coates, however, coolly took measures for his safety. Orders were dispatched to them to halt, form, and march up, whilst the artillerists were summoned to the howitzer, and the fatigue party to the destruction of the bridge.

The legion cavalry were in advance of Mayham's command. Captain Armstrong led the first section. Their approach to the bridge was marked by all the circumstances of danger. They were pressing upon each other into a narrow causeway, the planks of the bridge were fast sliding the water, and the blazing port-fire hung over the howitzer. The disappearance of the fatigue party from the ridge would be the signal for it to vomit death upon the ranks of the approaching Americans. There was no time for deliberation. Armstrong, followed close by his section, dashed over the bridge and drove the artillerists from the gun. Lieutenant Carrington followed, but the third section faltered. Mayham, of Marion's cavalry, feeling the halt, charged by them; but the death of his horse arrested his career. Captain Macauley, who led his front section, pressed on and passed the bridge. The causeway was now crowded; the conflict was hand to hand. Some of the working party, snatching up their guns, delivered a single fire and fled. Two of the legion dragoons were slain at the mouth of the howitzer, several wounded. But the officers remained unhurt. Coates, with several of the British, covered by a wagon, opposed them with their swords, while their troops were hurrying forward to where they could display. Meanwhile, Lee, with the rest of the legion, had reached the bridge, which they proceeded to repair. A momentary pause for reflection, a glance before and around them, revealed to Armstrong and Macauley, the fact that they were almost alone, unsupported by their party, and with the British recovering themselves in front. They reflected that, only while the British officers were in their rear, should they be secure from the fire of the enemy in front; and, urging their way through the flying soldiers on the causeway, they wheeled into the woods on their left, and escaped by heading the stream. Had they been followed by the whole party, boldly charging across the bridge, the entire force of the enemy must have laid down their arms. The British were so crowded in the lane and causeway, in such inextricable confusion, without room to display or to defend themselves, that they must have yielded by spontaneous movement to avoid being cut to pieces. The reproach lies heavily against the halting cavalry, that could leave to their fate the brave fellows who had crossed the bridge.

Colonel Coates dared not longer trust himself in the open country in the face of a cavalry so active and powerful. Retiring to Shubrick's plantation, after destroying the bridge, he resolved to defend himself under cover of the buildings. These were situated on a rising ground, and consisted of a dwelling-house of two stories, with outhouses and fences. They afforded security against cavalry, and a good covering from the American marksmen.

It was not till 3 o'clock, P.M., that Sumter, with the main body of the Americans, reached the ground. He found the British drawn up in a square in front of the house, and ready to receive him. As he had very few bayonets, to march directly up to the attack would have been out of the question. He divided his force into three bodies. His own brigade, led by Cols. Middleton and Polk, Taylor and Lacy, advanced in front, under shelter of a line of negro houses, which they were ordered to occupy. Marion's brigade, thrown into two divisions, was ordered to advance on the right of the British, where there was no shelter but that of fences, and those within forty or fifty yards of the houses held by the enemy. The cavalry constituted a reserve, to cover the infantry from pursuit.

Sumter's brigade soon gained the negro houses, from whence they delivered their rifles with great effect. Col. Taylor with about forty-five men of his regiment, pressing forward to the fences on the enemy left, drew upon him the bayonets of the British, before which they yielded. Marion's men, in the meantime, seeing the danger of Taylor's party, with a degree of firmness and gallantry which would have done honor to any soldiers, rushed through a galling fire and extricated them; and, notwithstanding the imperfect covering afforded them by the rail fence along which they ranged themselves, they continued to fight and fire as long as a single charge of ammunition remained with the corps. The brunt of the battle fell upon them, and they maintained in this, the reputation acquired in many a border struggle. More than fifty men, all of Marion's, were killed or wounded in this affair, but the loss did not dispirit the survivors. They were drawn off in perfect order, only when their ammunition was expended.

The fight lasted three hours, from four o'clock until dark. Seventy of the British fell. But the want of the field-piece left behind with Singleton, and the failure of their ammunition, not a charge of which remained with the Americans, at close of the fight, saved the enemy, whose infantry alone, according to Sumter, was superior to his whole force. The Americans attacked them with half their number. But Coates held his position, and tidings of the approach of Rawdon, who had left Orangeburg, prompted Sumter to retreat across the Santee. His expedition had not been successful. It does not concern us to inquire by whose errors or defects it failed. Enough, that, in all things, where Marion and his men were concerned, they acquitted themselves in a manner calculated to sustain their former reputation. The attack upon Coates at the house, we are told, was made against Marion's opinion, who blamed Sumter for wasting the lives of his men. Without a field-piece, it was scarcely possible that an inferior should have succeeded against a superior force, in a strong position. Sumter was courageous to rashness. His spirit could not be restrained in sight of the enemy. With a brave force at his command, he was not satisfied to be idle, and his courage was frequently exercised at the expense of his judgment. The men of Marion complained that they had been exposed unnecessarily in the conflict. It is certain that they were the only sufferers. Had Sumter but waited for his artillery, and simply held the enemy in check, the victory must have been complete, and this victory was of the last importance to the Americans. It would have involved the loss of one entire British regiment, at a moment when, two others having been required at New York from South Carolina, the force remaining with Rawdon would have been barely adequate to the retention of Charleston. This necessity would have withdrawn the latter general at once from Orangeburg, and the subsequent bloody battle of Eutaw would have been averted accordingly. Greene, speaking of this combat, writes:—"The affair was clever, but by no means equal to what it ought to have been. The whole regiment of six hundred men would have been captured, if General Sumter had not detailed too much, and had not mistaken a covering party for an attack." It may be added, that the party actually engaged in the attack on Coates, were almost exclusively South Carolina militia. Under favorite leaders they had betrayed no such apprehension as are natural enough to men who lack confidence in themselves and captains. They had shown the courage of veterans, though they may have failed of that entire success which is usually supposed to follow from a veteran experience.

CHAPTER XVI

MARION MOVES SECRETLY TO PON-PON †
RESCUES COL. HARDEN † DEFEATS MAJOR
FRAZIER AT PARKER'S FERRY † JOINS THE MAIN
ARMY UNDER GREENE † BATTLE OF EUTAW

After the battle of Quinby the joint forces of Sumter and Marion were separated. The former retired up the Congaree; the latter took charge of the country on the Santee; while Greene placed himself in a camp of rest at the High Hills in the district which has since taken the name of Sumter. His troops were in a wretched state of incapacity, in consequence of sickness. The region to which he retired was famous for its salubrity, and the intense heat of the season effectually forbade much military activity. The opposing generals were content to watch each other. It was while he held this position that Col. Hayne, of the militia, was executed as a traitor by the British. The case of this gentleman was that of many in the State. He had taken parole at a time when the country was overrun by the enemy. This parole was subsequently withdrawn by the conquerors, when they supposed the people to have been subdued, and desired their services as militia. But the British were in turn driven from the field. The Americans acquired the ascendant. The section of the country in which Hayne resided was overrun by a detachment of Marion, under Col. Harden, and Hayne availed himself of the occasion to take up arms for his country. He was a popular gentleman, and soon gathered a strong party of militia. His career was distinguished by some small successes, and, with a party of Col. Harden's horse, by a sudden dash in the vicinity of Charleston, he succeeded in taking prisoner General Williamson, formerly of the Americans, whose life was forfeited to the country. The capture of Williamson put all the available cavalry of the British into activity, and by an unfortunate indiscretion, Hayne suffered himself to be overtaken. His execution soon followed his capture. This was a proceeding equally barbarous and unjustifiable—neither sanctioned by policy nor propriety. It took place after a brief examination, and without any trial. The proceeding was equally unauthorized by civil and martial law. It was not long before this, as the reader will remember, that Marion, in consequence of the execution of some of men by the British, had threatened them with retaliation. Greene, who knew the decisive character of Marion, and was apprehensive that this wanton crime would render him as prompt as he was fearless, in avenging it, thus writes to prevent him: "Do not take any measures in the matter towards retaliation, for I do not intend to retaliate upon the *Tory* officers, but the *British*. It is my intention to demand the reasons of the Colonel's being put to death; and if they are unsatisfactory, as I am sure they will be, and if they refuse to make satisfaction, as I expect they will, to publish my intention of giving no quarter to British officers, of any rank, that fall into our hands. Should we attempt to retaliate upon their militia officers, I am sure they would persevere in the measure, in order to increase the animosity between the Whigs and Tories, that they might stand idle spectators, and see them butcher each other. As I do not wish my intentions known to the enemy but through an official channel, and as this *will be delayed for some few days to give our friends in St. Augustine time to get off*, I wish you not to mention the matter to any mortal out of your family."

Weems represents Marion as being greatly averse to this measure of retaliation, and as having censured those officers of the regular army who demanded of Greene the adoption of this remedy. But the biographer wrote rather from his own benevolent nature than from the record. Marion had no scruples about the necessity of such a measure in particular cases; and, however much he might wish to avoid its execution, he was yet fully prepared to adopt it whenever the policy of the proceeding was unquestionable. Fortunately, the decisive resolutions which were expressed by the Americans, their increasing successes, the fact that they had several British officers of reputation in their hands,—all conspired to produce, in the minds of the enemy, a greater regard to the rights of justice and humanity. As retaliation in such cases is justifiable only as a preventive and remedial measure, it now ceased to be necessary; and, with proper views of the affair, the resolves of Greene and Marion were suffered to remain unexpunged, in proof of their indignation, rather than their purpose. But a few days had elapsed after the execution of Hayne when a party of Marion's men, under Captain Ervine, fell in with and captured a favorite British officer, Captain Campbell, with two subalterns, in charge of a convoying detachment. They were at once committed to the provost guard, and soon communicated their apprehensions to Charleston. A meeting of British officers was held, and their dissatisfaction at this new feature, introduced into the warfare of the country, was expressed in such terms, as contributed, along with the prompt proceedings of the Americans, to bring Balfour, the commandant of Charleston, under whose authority the execution of Hayne had taken place, to a better sense of mercy and prudence. We shall have no farther occasion to refer to these proceedings. It is enough that the threat of retaliation, followed up by such decided movements as left no doubt of the resolution of the Americans, produced all the beneficial effects which could have accrued from its execution.

The incursion of Sumter and Marion into the low country drew Lord Rawdon from Orangeburg, with five hundred men, to Charleston, from which place, after lingering just long enough to witness the death of Hayne, he sailed for New York. He left Lieut.-Col. Stewart in command of Orangeburg. From this post, Stewart moved to McCord's ferry, on the Congaree, on the south side of which he took post, amidst the hills near the confluence of the Wateree and Congaree. Greene's camp lay directly opposite, and the fires of the mutual armies were distinctly seen by each other. The heat of the weather suspended all regular military operations. Two large rivers intervening secured each from sudden attack, and their toils were confined to operating in small detachments, for foraging or convoy. In this service, on the American side, Col. Washington was detached—as soon as the course of Stewart was ascertained—down the country across the Santee; Lee was sent upward, along the north bank of the Congaree; the latter to operate with Col. Henderson, then in command of Sumter's brigade, at Fridig's ferry, and the former to strike at the communication between the enemy and Charleston, and to co-operate with Marion and Mayham, in covering the lower Santee. Col. Harden, at the same time, with a body of mounted militia, had it in charge to straiten the enemy upon the Edisto.

The activity of these several parties and their frequent successes were such that Stewart was compelled to look for his supplies to the country below him. This necessity caused him to re-establish and strengthen the post at Dorchester, in order to cover the communication by Orangeburg; and to place a force at Fairlawn, near the head of the navigation of Cooper river, from which supplies from Charleston were transported to head-quarters over land. As this route was watched by Marion, Washington and Mayham, the British commander was compelled, in order to secure the means of communication with the opposite bank of the Congaree and to draw supplies from thence, to transport boats adapted to the purpose, on wagon-wheels, from Fairlawn to the Congaree.

Such were the relative positions of the two armies until the 22d of August, when Greene, calling in all his detachments except those under

Marion, Mayham and Harden, broke up his camp at the High Hills and proceeded to Howell's ferry, on the Congaree, with the intention immediately to cross it and advance upon Stewart. That officer, on hearing of the movement of the Americans, fell back upon his reinforcements and convoys, and took up a strong position at the Eutaw Springs.

Meanwhile, Marion disappeared from the Santee on one of those secret expeditions in which his wonderful celerity and adroit management conducted his men so frequently to success. His present aim was the Pon-Pon. Col. Harden was at this time in that quarter, and closely pressed by a superior British force of five hundred men. Detaching a party of mounted militia to the neighborhood of Dorchester and Monk's Corner, as much to divert the enemy from his own movements as with any other object, he proceeded with two hundred picked men on his secret expedition.

By a forced march, he crossed the country from St. Stephen's to the Edisto—passing through both lines of the enemy communication with Charleston, and reached Harden—a distance of one hundred miles—in season for his relief. His approach and arrival were totally unsuspected by the enemy, for whom he prepared an ambush in a swamp near Parker's ferry. A small body of his swiftest horse were sent out to decoy the British into the snare. A white feather, rather too conspicuously worn by one of his men in ambush, had nearly defeated his design. Some Tories passing, discovered this unnecessary plumage, and one of them fired upon the wearer. This led to an exchange of shots; but Major Frazier, by whom the British were commanded, assuming the party thus concealed to be that of Harden, whom it was his aim to find, pursued the horsemen whom Marion had sent out to entice him to the ambuscade. His cavalry was led at full charge within forty yards of the concealed riflemen. A deadly fire was poured in, under which the British recoiled; attempting to wheel and charge the swamp, they received a second; and, closely wedged as their men were upon the narrow causeway over which they came, every shot bore its warrant. There was no retreating, no penetrating the ambush, and the British cavalry had but to go forward, along the road to the ferry, thus passing the entire line of the ambuscade. The corps was most effectually thinned by the time it got beyond rifle reach; and still more fatal would have been the affray to the advancing infantry of Frazier—a large body, with a field-piece—but for one of those lamentable deficiencies of materiel, which so frequently plucked complete success from the grasp of the Americans. The ammunition of our partisan failed him, and he was compelled to yield the ground to the enemy, who was otherwise wholly in his power. The British loss was unknown. Twenty-seven dead horses were counted on the

Marion defeating Major Frazier at Parker's Ferry.

field the day after; the men had all been buried. As Marion's men fired with either a ball or heavy buck-shot, and as none would aim at horses, the loss of the British must have been very great. Nine days after, at the battle of Eutaw, they had few cavalry in the field.

But, though the victory was incomplete, Marion had attained his object. He had rescued Harden, without loss to himself. He had traversed more than two hundred miles of country, through a region held by the enemy; returned by the same route,—delivered his prisoners to the care of Mayham,—returned twenty miles below the Eutaw, in order to watch the communication between that place and Fairlawn—then, at the call of Greene, made a circuit and passed the British army, so as to reach a position on the south side of the Santee, in the track of Greene's advance; and all this in the brief compass of six days. Yet, of these movements, which merited and received the particular thanks of Congress, we are without any data in our records. The complimentary resolution of Congress fixes the battle at Parker's ferry on the 31st August.

Seventeen miles from Eutaw Springs, at Laurens' plantation, Marion effected a junction with the commander-in-chief. Greene was pressing forward to a meeting with Stewart. Of this object the latter seemed to have been profoundly ignorant up to this moment. But the day before, he knew that Marion was twenty miles below him, and did not conjecture that, by marching the whole night, he had thrown himself above him to join with Greene. Without this junction he had no apprehension that the latter, with an inferior force, would venture an attack upon him, in the strong position which he held. On the afternoon of the 7th September, the army reached Burdell's tavern on the Congaree road, seven miles from the Eutaws. The force under Greene amounted to two thousand men, all told. That under General Stewart was probably about the same. It is estimated to have been two thousand three hundred. These were all disciplined troops, and a large proportion of the old regiments consisted of native marksmen from the ranks of the loyalists. In cavalry, Greene had the advantage, but a great portion of his men were militia. In artillery the two armies were equal. The British had five and the Americans four pieces.

The memorable battle of the Eutaw Springs was fought on the 8th September. At four o'clock in the morning the Americans moved from their bivouac down to the attack. The day was fair, but intensely hot; but the combatants at the commencement of the battle were relieved by the shade of the woods. The South Carolina State troops and Lee's legion formed the advance under Colonel Henderson. The militia, both of South and North Carolina moved next, under Marion. Then followed the regulars under Gen.

Sumner; and the rear was closed by Washington's cavalry, and Kirkwood's Delawares, under Col. Washington. The artillery moved between the columns. The troops were thus arranged in reference to their order of battle.

Of the approach of the Americans Stewart was wholly ignorant on the evening of the 7th. The only patrol which had been sent up the Congaree road had been captured during the night, and Stewart himself says, in excuse, that "the Americans had waylaid the swamps and passes in such a manner as to cut off every avenue of intelligence." So entirely secure had he felt himself in his position, which was a strong one, that he had sent out an unarmed party of one hundred men, in the very direction of Greene's advance, to gather sweet potatoes. This party, called a rooting party, after advancing about three miles, had pursued a road to the right, which led to the river plantations. Advised, by two deserters from the North Carolina militia, of Greene's approach, Stewart dispatched Captain Coffin, with his cavalry, to recall the rooting party, and to reconnoitre the Americans. Before Coffin could effect either object, he encountered the American advance, and, in total ignorance of its strength, charged it with a degree of confidence, which led Greene to imagine that Stewart with his whole army was at hand. Coffin was easily repulsed; the rooting party, alarmed by the firing, hurried from the woods, and were all made prisoners. Meanwhile, Stewart, now thoroughly aware of the proximity of his enemy, pushed forward a detachment of infantry, a mile distant from the Eutaw, with orders to engage and detain the American troops while he formed his men and prepared for battle. But Greene, whom the audacity of Coffin had deceived, halted his columns where they stood, and proceeded to display them. The column of militia formed the first line; the South Carolina militia in equal divisions on the right and left, and the North Carolinians in the centre. General Marion commanded the right, General Pickens the left, and Col. Malmedy the centre. Col. Henderson, with the State troops, including Sumter's brigade, covered the left of this line, and Col. Lee, with his legion, the right. The column of regulars also displayed in one line. The North Carolinians, under Gen. Sumner, occupied the right; the Marylanders, under Col. Williams, the left; the Virginians, under Col. Campbell, the centre. Two pieces of artillery were assigned to each line. Col. Washington moved in column in the rear, keeping himself in reserve. In this order, the troops pressed forward slowly, as the country on both sides of the road was in wood, and prevented much expedition. Moving thus, the first line encountered the advance parties of Stewart, and drove them before it, until the entire line of the British army, displayed in order of battle, received, and gave shelter to, the fugitives.

The troops of Stewart were drawn up in one line at about two hundred yards west of the Eutaw Springs; the Buffs on the right, Cruger's corps in the centre, and the 63d and 64th on the left. Major Marjoribanks, with three hundred of his best troops, was strongly posted, so as to flank the Buffs, under shelter of a thick wood on the Eutaw creek, which covered the right of the whole line; the left was, in military *parlance*, 'in air'—resting in the wood, and supported by Coffin's cavalry—reduced to a very small number—and a respectable detachment of infantry. His ground was altogether in wood, but, at a small distance, in the rear of his line, was an open field, on the edge of which, stood a strong brick dwelling, with offices, out-houses, and a palisadoed garden, in all of which a stout resistance might be made. On this brick house, Stewart had already cast his eyes, as the means of saving his army in any *dernier* necessity. The house was of two stories, and abundantly strong to resist small arms. Its windows commanded all the open space around. Major Sheridan was ordered to throw himself into it, with his command, in case of an unfavorable issue to the fight; and in this position to overawe the Americans, and cover the army. Feeble in cavalry, in which the Americans were strong, there was no other means for retreat and support in the event of a capital misfortune.

The American approach was from the west. The first line, consisting wholly of militia, went into action, and continued in it with a coolness and stubbornness which, says Greene, "would have graced the veterans of the great king of Prussia." Such conduct was almost invariable on their part, wherever Marion or Pickens commanded. Steadily and without faltering, they advanced into the hot test of the enemy fire, with shouts and exhortations, which were not lessened by the continual fall of their comrades around them. Their line was all the while receiving the fire of double their number—they were opposed to the entire line of the British. The carnage was severe and very equal on both sides. The two pieces of artillery were at length disabled, and after exchanging seventeen rounds with the enemy, the militia began to falter. Gen. Sumner was ordered up to their support, with the North Carolina Continentals. With the advance of Sumner, Stewart brought into line on his left, the infantry of his reserve, and the battle, between fresh troops on both sides, raged with renewed fury. From the commencement of the action, the infantry of the American covering parties, right and left, had been steadily engaged. The State troops, under Henderson, had suffered greatly. The American left, which they flanked, falling far short of the British right in length, they were exposed to the oblique fire of a large proportion of the British left, and particularly of the battalion commanded by Marjoribanks. Henderson himself was disabled, and his men, denied to charge the enemy under whose fire they were suffering—for they were necessary to the safety of the artillery and militia—were subjected to a trial of their constancy, which very few soldiers, whatever may have been their training, would have borne so well.

Meanwhile, the brigade of Sumner recoiled from the fire of the greater numbers opposed to them in front. At this sight, the exultation of the British Left hurried them forward, assured of certain victory. Their line became deranged, and the American general, promptly availing himself of the opportunity, issued his command to Col. Williams, who had in charge the remaining portion of his second line, to "advance, and sweep the field with his bayonets." The two battalions obeyed the order with a shout. The Virginians, when within forty yards of the enemy, poured in a destructive fire, and the whole second line with trailed arms pressed on to the charge. The advanced left of the British recoiled, and, just at this juncture, the legion infantry delivered an enfilading fire, which threw them into irretrievable disorder. The British centre, pressed upon by the fugitives, began to give way from left to right, and the fire of the Marylanders, poured in at the proper moment, completed their disaster. Their whole front yielded, and the shouts of the Americans declared their exultation, as at a victory already won. Unquestionably, the day was theirs. The enemy had fled from the battle. But a new one was to begin, in which victory, at present so secure, was taken from their grasp. In the effort to prevent the enemy from rallying, and to cut him off from the brick dwelling, into which Sheridan, obeying the commands of Stewart, had thrown himself as soon as the necessity became apparent, the greatest loss of Americans was sustained. Marjoribanks still held his ground, with his entire battalion, in the thick woods which skirted Eutaw Creek, and so well covered was he that, in an attempt to penetrate with his cavalry, Col. Washington became entangled in the thicket, and fell into the hands of the enemy, while his men suffered severely from their fire, and his troop was routed. A second time were they brought to the charge, but with no better success than before. Marjoribanks still maintained his position, watching the moment when to emerge from the thicket with the best prospect of safety to himself, and hurt to the Americans. He was soon to have an opportunity.

The British line had yielded and broken before the American bayonet. The latter pressed closely upon their heels, made many prisoners, and might have cut them off, and, by isolating Marjoribanks, forced him to surrender, but for one of those occurrences which so frequently in battle change the fortunes of the day. The course of the fugitives led them directly through the British encampment. There everything was given up for lost. The tents were all standing, the commissaries had abandoned their stores, and the numerous retainers of the army were already in full flight for Charleston. When the pursuing Americans penetrated the encampment, they lost sight of the fugitives in the contemplation of various objects of temptation which, to a half-naked and half-starved soldiery, were irresistible. The pursuit was forborne; the Americans fastened upon the liquors and refreshments scattered among the tents; and the whole army, with the exception of one or two corps, then fell into confusion. Yet, so closely had the British been pursued to the shelter of the house, and so narrow was their escape, that some of the Americans had nearly obtained entrance with them. It was only by shutting the door against some of their own officers, that they made it secure against the enemy; and in retiring from the house, now a citadel, the Americans only found safety by interposing the bodies of the officers, thus made captive at the entrance, between themselves and the fire from the windows. One ludicrous incident is told of Major Barry, who was taken in this manner, and made use of as a shield by Lieut. Manning, as he retreated from before the house, which otherwise he could not have left in safety. Without struggling or making the slightest effort for his extrication, Barry only enumerated his own titles with a profound solemnity. "Sir, I am Henry Barry, Deputy Adjutant General of the British army, Secretary to the Commandant of Charleston, Captain in the 52d regiment" &c. "Enough, enough, sir," answered Manning. "You are just the man I was looking for. Fear nothing: you shall *screen me* from danger, and I shall take special care of you." Manning escaped in safety with his prisoner. But there were many brave officers far less fortunate. Many were destined to perish in the miserable after struggle, who had gone gloriously through the greater dangers of the fight. The British tents had done what the British arms had failed to do. Victory was lost to the Americans. Scattered throughout the encampment, the soldiers became utterly unmanageable. The enemy, meanwhile, had partially recovered from their panic. The party of Sheridan were in possession of the house. Another party held possession of the palisaded garden. Coffin was active with his remnant of cavalry, and Marjoribanks still held a formidable position in the thicket on Eutaw Creek. From the upper windows of the house, the musketry of Sheridan traversed the encampment, which the Americans now trembled to leave, lest they should suffer from their fire. Every head that emerged from a tent was a mark for their bullets. Aware, by this time, of the extent of his misfortune, Greene ordered a retreat, which Hampton's cavalry was commanded to cover. In the execution of this duty Hampton encountered the British cavalry. A sharp action ensued; the latter fled, and in the ardor of pursuit, the American horse approached so near to the position of Marjoribanks as to receive a murderous fire, which prostrated one-third of their number and scattered the rest. Before they could again be brought together, Marjoribanks, seizing upon the chance afforded by a temporary clearing of the field, emerged from the wood, at a moment which enabled him to put a successful finish to the labors of the day. Two six-pounders, which had been abandoned by the British, had been turned upon the house the Americans; but in their eagerness they had brought the pieces within the range of fire from the windows of the house. The artillerists had been shot down; and, in the absence of the American cavalry, Marjoribanks was enabled to recover them. Wheeling them under the walls of the house, he took a contiguous position, his own being almost the only portion of the British army still in a condition to renew the action. The Americans yielded the ground about the house, but were promptly rallied in the skirts of the wood. The British were too much crippled to pursue; and the respite was gladly seized upon by the Americans to plunge headlong into the neighboring ponds, to cool the heat and satisfy the intense thirst occasioned by such efforts under the burning sun of a Carolina September. Both sides claimed the victory, and with equal reason. In the first part of the day it was clearly with the Americans. They had driven the enemy from the field, in panic and with great loss. They were in possession of five hundred prisoners, nearly all of whom they retained. They had taken two out of the five pieces of artillery which the British had brought into the action and, something more to boast, considering the proverbial renown of the British with this weapon, it was at the point of the bayonet that they had swept the enemy from the ground. The British took shelter in a fortress from which the Americans were repulsed. It is of no consequence to assert that the latter might have taken it. They might—it was in their power to have done so,—but they did not; and the promptitude with which the British availed themselves of this security, entitles them to the merit which they claim. We are constrained to think that the business of the field was strangely blundered by the Americans at the sequel. This may have arisen from the carnage made at this period among their officers, particularly in their persevering, but futile endeavors, to extricate the soldiers from their tents. Under cover of a contiguous barn, the artillery presented the means of forcing the building and reducing the garrison to submission. The attempts made at this object, by this arm of the Americans, were rash, badly counselled, and exposed to danger without adequate protection. The British were saved by this error, by the luxuries contained within their tents, by the spirited behavior of Coffin, and the cool and steady valor of Marjoribanks.

CHAPTER XVII

RETREAT OF THE BRITISH FROM EUTAW †
PURSUIT OF THEM BY MARION AND LEE †
CLOSE OF THE YEAR

That the results of victory lay with the Americans, was shown by the events of the ensuing day. Leaving his dead unburied, seventy of his wounded to the enemy, breaking up a thousand stand of arms, and destroying his stores, General Stewart commenced a precipitate retreat towards Fairlawn. The British power in Carolina was completely prostrated by this battle. Five hundred prisoners fell into the hands of the Americans, and it was Greene's purpose to have renewed the fight on the next day; but the flight of Stewart anticipated and baffled his intentions. He commenced pursuit, and detached Marion and Lee, by a circuitous route, to gain the enemy's front, and interpose themselves between him and the post at Fairlawn from which Major M'Arthur had been summoned, with five hundred men, to cover the retreat. But this plan was unsuccessful. So precipitate was the march of Stewart, and so happily concerted the movements of the two British officers, that they effected a junction before Marion and Lee could reach Ferguson Swamp, their place of destination. The cavalry of the enemy's rear guard fell into the hands of the Americans, but Stewart was beyond pursuit. In this flight, amongst others, the British lost the brave Major Marjoribanks, who died of fever, and was buried on the road. While they admitted a loss, in killed, wounded, and missing, of half the number brought into the field, that of the Americans was nearly equally severe, and fell with particular severity upon the officers. Sixty-one of these were killed or wounded; twenty-one died upon the field. The returns exhibit a loss of one hundred and fourteen rank and file killed, three hundred wounded, and forty missing—an aggregate exceeding a fourth of all who marched into battle. Many of Marion's men were killed, though not so many as he lost in the affair of Quinby. Among his officers, Capt. John Simons, of Pedee, was slain, and Col. Hugh Horry wounded.

Greene retired to the high hills of Santee, while Marion proceeded to encamp at Payne's plantation, on Santee river swamp. This was one of his favorite places of retreat. Here, in the depths of a cane-brake, within a quarter of a mile from the Santee, he made himself a clearing, "much," says Judge James "to his liking," and, with the canes, thatched the rude huts of his men. The high land was skirted by lakes, which rendered the approach difficult; and here, as in perfect security, he found forage for his horses, and provisions in abundance for his men. Such a place of encampment, at such a season, would hardly commend itself now to the citizen of Carolina. The modes and objects of culture, and probably the climate, have undergone a change. The time was autumn, the most sickly period of our year; and, to sleep in such a region now, even for a single night, would be considered certain death to the white man. It does not seem, at that period, that much apprehension of malaria was felt.

But Marion did not linger long in any one situation. Hearing that the British were about to send their wounded from Fairlawn to Charleston, his restless enterprise prompted him to aim at the capture of the detachment. Moving rapidly by night, he threw himself below the former place, on the opposite bank of the river, and would certainly have intercepted them, but for a slave of one of the plantations, who, hastening to the British camp, reported his proximity. The arrival of a superior force compelled him to steal away with a caution like that which marked his approach.

The command of the British army, in consequence of a wound received by General Stewart at Eutaw, had devolved on Major Doyle. This army, recruited by the force of M'Arthur, was still, after all its losses, fully two thousand men. That of Greene, reduced by wounds and sickness, could not muster one thousand fit for duty. His cavalry had been greatly thinned by the late battle, and it was not until the cavalry of Sumter's brigade could be brought together, with Marion's mounted infantry, and the horse of Horry and Mayham, that the superiority of the American general could be restored. Doyle had taken post at Fludd's plantation, three miles above Nelson's Ferry, on the Santee, with the main body of the British; M'Arthur held the post at Fairlawn, with a detachment of three hundred. Doyle, with some instinctive notion that his time was short, busied himself in a career of plunder which threatened to strip the plantations south of the Santee and Congaree, and westward to the Edisto, not only of every negro which they contained, but of all other kinds of property. Over this region, the feebleness of the American forces, and their present deficiency in cavalry, gave him almost entire control. The opposite banks were guarded by Marion and Hampton, who afforded protection to everything that could be moved across, and presented themselves at every point to the enemy, whenever he attempted the passage of the river. Marion was at this time an invalid, but, however much he might need, he asked for no repose or exemption from service when the enemy was in the field. His force was also reduced by sickness. Col. Mayham alone had no less than one hundred men unfit for duty. Other circumstances kept the militia from coming to the summons of Marion. Those on the borders of North Carolina were detained to meet and suppress a rising of the loyalists of that State under Hector M'Neil, and even those in his camp were unprovided with ammunition. Early in October, we find him writing pressingly to General Greene and Governor Rutledge for a supply. Rutledge answers, on the 10th of that month, "I wish to God it was in my power to send you ammunition instantly, but it is not." Col. Otho Williams, in the temporary absence of Greene, writes, in answer "Our stock of ammunition is quite exhausted— we have not an ounce of powder, or a cartridge, in store." And yet, it was under similar deficiencies that the men of Marion had labored from the beginning; and half the time had they gone into battle with less than three rounds of powder to a man. Williams further writes: "His Excellency, Governor Rutledge, has intimated that you meditate an expedition over the Santee. In making your determination, if it is not settled, permit me to recommend to your consideration, that *the General depends upon you entirely for intelligence of the enemy's motions.*" The activity of our partisan, his elasticity of character, his independence of resources, and usefulness to others, are all to be gathered from these two extracts.

Late in September of this year, Governor Rutledge issued a proclamation, requiring that the disaffected should come in within thirty days, and perform a six months tour of duty. The condition of pardon for all previous offences was attached to this requisition. The idea of this proclamation was borrowed from similar ones of the British generals, when they first overran the country. The object was to secure those persons, of whom there were numbers, who in the declining fortunes of the British, were not unwilling to turn upon and rend their old friends, no longer capable of protecting or providing for them. The measure was of doubtful policy, since it appealed to the basest feelings of humanity. Its effects were considerable, however; numbers presented themselves in the ranks of Marion, showing finely in contrast with his ancient and half-naked veterans. "Their new white feathers" says James, "fine coats, new saddles and bridles, and *famished* horses, showed that they had lately been in the British garrison." Their appearance, not to speak of their previous career, naturally inspired distrust in the minds of those whose scars and nakedness were the proofs of their virtue; and another measure, which was adopted about this time, had the farther effect of impairing the value of that efficient brigade upon which Marion had been accustomed to rely. In order to promote the growth of the new regiments, it was permitted to all such persons as could hire a substitute to claim exemption from military duty. This was a temptation too great to be resisted by those old soldiers who had served from the first, who had left their families in wretched lodgings, in poverty and distress, and from whose immediate neighborhood the presence of the war was withdrawn. The six months men were easily bought up to fill their places. The result was very injurious to the *morale* of the brigade, and the evil effects of the measure were soon felt in the imperfect subordination, the deficient firmness, and the unprincipled character of the new recruits. It was productive also of differences between two of Marion's best officers, Horry and Mayham, which wrought evil consequences to the country. Being commissioned on the same days as colonels of the new regiments, they quarrelled about precedency. The fruits of this difference will be seen hereafter.

As the winter set in, the army began to recruit, and the militia to embody under their several commanders. Greene was joined by Cols. Shelby and Sevier, with five hundred mountaineers, and these, with Horry and Mayham, were ordered to place themselves under Marion, to operate in the country between the Santee and Charleston. Sumter, at the same time, with a brigade of State troops and some companies of militia, was ordered to take post at Orangeburg, to cover the country from the inroads of the loyalists from Charleston. Pickens, in the meantime, with his regiments, traversed the border country, keeping in awe the Indians, and suppressing the predatory movements of the Tories. About the 1st November, the separate commands of Marion and Sumter crossed the rivers, and advanced in the direction of the enemy. The latter soon fell in with Cunningham's loyalists in force, and found it prudent to fall back. But he kept Cunningham in check with a body of men fully equal to his own. Marion, also, was compelled to come to a halt, by encountering General Stewart, posted at Wantoot, with nearly two thousand men. Stewart was at this time following up the peculiar labors which had been undertaken by Major Doyle when in temporary charge of the army. He was collecting slaves and laying in provisions, preparing for siege in, and subsequent flight from, Charleston. The fall of Cornwallis, at Yorktown, was known in the American camp on the 9th of November. It had been anticipated in the British some time before. With the fate of that commander, virtually terminated the British hope of re-conquering the country, and the proceedings of their officers in the south, as elsewhere, looked forward to the approaching necessity of flight. It was only becoming that they should spoil the Egyptians previous to their departure.

The capture of Cornwallis produced a jubilee in the American camp. In that of Marion the ladies of Santee were permitted to partake. He gave them a fete—we are not told what were the refreshments—at the house of Mr. John Cantey. "The General," says James, "was not very susceptible of the gentler emotions; he had his friends, and was kind to his inferiors, but his mind was principally absorbed by the love of country;" and the Judge rather insinuates that the pleasure he felt on this occasion arose from the fall of Cornwallis more than from the presence of the ladies.

On the same day, the 9th October, he received the thanks of Congress for "his wise, decided, and gallant conduct, in defending the liberties of his country, and particularly for his prudent and intrepid attack on a body of British troops, on the 31st August last; and for the distinguished part he took in the battle of the 8th September."

On the 18th November, the camp of the Hills was broken up, and General Greene advanced with his army, to the Four Holes, on the Edisto, in full confidence that the force under Marion would be adequate to keep General Stewart in check. But, by the 25th of the same month, our partisan was abandoned by all the mountaineers under Shelby and Sevier, a force of five hundred men. This was after a three weeks' service. This miserable defection was ascribed to the withdrawal of Shelby from the army on leave of absence. But, in all probability, it was due to their impatience of the wary sort of warfare which it was found necessary to pursue. The service was not sufficiently active for their habits. Marion had been warned that he must keep them actively employed, but all his efforts to do so had been unsuccessful. He had approached Stewart at Wantoot, but, though the force of the latter was nominally far superior to that of the partisan, he could not be drawn out of his encampment. This was a subject of equal surprise and chagrin to Marion. Subsequently, the reason of this timidity on the part of the British general was discovered. A return, found on an orderly-sergeant who fell into Marion's hands, showed that, out of two thousand two hundred and seventy-two men, Stewart had nine hundred and twenty-eight on the sick list. The only services in which the mountaineers were employed, while with Marion, were in attacks on the post at Fairlawn, and the redoubts at Wappetaw; and these required detachments only. The movement against the latter was instantly successful—the enemy abandoned it on the approach of the Americans. But the post at Fairlawn was of more value, in better

condition of defence, a convenient depot, and, being in the rear of the
British army, then stationed at Wantoot, promised a stout resistance. The
American detachment against this place was led by Mayham. In passing
the post at Wantoot, he was ordered to show himself, and, if possible, to
decoy the British cavalry into the field. The manoeuvre did not succeed,
but it brought out a strong detachment, which followed close upon
his heels, and required that what he should undertake should be done
quickly. On approaching Fairlawn, he found everything prepared for
defence. He lost no time in making his advances. A part of his riflemen
were dismounted, and, acting as infantry, approached the abbatis, while
his cavalry advanced boldly and demanded a surrender. The place, with
all its sick, three hundred stand of arms, and eighty convalescents, was
yielded at discretion.

With these small affairs ended the service of the mountaineers in
Marion's army. They retired to their native hills, leaving Marion and
Greene enmeshed in difficulties. It was on the strength of this force, chiefly,
that the latter had descended from the hills, and he was now unable to
recede. Marion, too, relying upon their support, had crossed the Santee
and placed himself in close proximity on the right of the enemy. But the
feebleness and timidity of Stewart, and his ignorance of the state of affairs
in Marion's camp, saved these generals from the necessity of a retreat which
would have been equally full of danger and humiliation. The movement
of Greene across the Congaree induced him to draw towards Charleston,
and Marion was left in safety. The timidity shown by the enemy encouraged
Greene, and, dispatching a select party of horse under Wade Hampton, he
followed hard upon their steps with as many chosen infantry. His purpose
was the surprise of Dorchester. Stewart was descending to the city by
another route. Hampton's advance fell in with a reconnoitering party of
fifty men, and suffered few to escape and though Greene did not succeed in
surprising the post at Dorchester, his approach had the effect of producing
its abandonment. During the night, the garrison destroyed everything,
threw their cannon into the river, and retreated to Charleston. Greene did
not venture to pursue, as the enemy's infantry exceeded five hundred men.
Meanwhile, Stewart had hurried on by Goose-creek Bridge, and, joining
the fugitives from Dorchester, halted at the Quarter House, and prepared to
encounter the whole army of Greene, which, in their panic, was supposed
to be upon their heels. Such was the alarm in Charleston that General
Leslie, who now succeeded Stewart, proceeded to embody the slaves, in
arms, for the defence of that place,—a measure which was soon repented
of and almost as soon abandoned.

Greene fell back upon his main army, which had now advanced to
Saunders' plantation on the Round O., while Marion, pressing nearer
to Charleston, kept the right of the enemy in check. The movements of
our partisan were left to his own discretion. Greene, in all cases, not only
suffers the judgment of the former to determine for himself his course,
giving him a thoroughly independent command, but he betrays the most
respectful desire on frequent occasions to have his opinion. Thus, on the
5th of November, he writes to him: "Gen. Sumter has orders to take post
at Orangeburgh, to prevent the Tories in that quarter from conveying
supplies to town, and his advanced parties will penetrate as low as
Dorchester; therefore, you may act in conjunction with him, or employ
your troops on the enemy left, as you may find from in formation they can
be best employed. Please to give me your opinion on which side they can
be most useful." On the 15th of the same month, he writes again: "You
are at liberty to act as you think advisedly. I have no particular instructions
to give you, and only wish you to avoid surprise." The latter caution to
a soldier of Marion's character and prudence was scarcely necessary,
but he was so near the enemy, and the latter in such superior force, that
the suggestion, on the part of Greene, was only natural. Where Greene
himself lay, two rivers ran between his army and that of the British.
Without ammunition himself, and informed of reinforcements which the
enemy had received, to preserve a respectful distance between them, was,
on the part of the American commander, only a becoming caution. It
was now December, and the troops, both of Greene and Marion, were
without the necessary clothing. They had neither cloaks nor blankets. On
the 14th of that month, Greene received a supply of ammunition, *all* of
which he sent to Marion—no small proof of the confidence which he felt
that, in such hands, it would not be thrown away.

Thus closed the campaign of 1781. By manoeuvre, and a successful
combination of events, the British troops had been driven down the
country and restrained within the narrow neck of land contiguous to
Charleston. The encampment of the main army continued at the Round
O. Marion was at Watboo on Cooper river, watching the enemy's right;
Sumter held Orangeburg and the bridge at Four Holes; Hampton with
fifty State cavalry kept open the communication between Marion and the
commander-in-chief; Cols. Harden and Wilkinson watched the enemy's
movements on the south between Charleston and Savannah: and Col.
Lee, posted in advance, with a light detachment, kept him from prying into
the real weakness of the American army. In the ignorance of the British
general, lay the security of the American; for, at this particular time,

there were not eight hundred men at Greene's headquarters. A glance at any map of South Carolina will show the judgment with which these several posts were taken, at once for easy co-operation of the Americans, as for the control of all the country above the positions actually held by the British. The territory of the State, with the exception of that neck of land which lies twelve or fifteen miles up from Charleston, between the approaching rivers Ashley and Cooper, had all been recovered from the enemy. But the necessities of the Americans, the want of military *materiel*, the thinness of the regiments, and the increasing strength of the British, derived from foreign troops and accessions from other posts in America, left it doubtful, under existing circumstances, whether it could be long retained. But this misgiving was not allowed to prejudice or impair the popular hope, resulting from the apparent successes of their arms; and one of the modes adopted for contributing to this conviction was the formal restoration of the native civil authority. The members of the State Assembly, of whom Marion was one, were accordingly required by the proclamation of Governor Rutledge—who had held almost dictatorial powers from the beginning of the war—to convene at Jacksonborough at an early day of the ensuing year.

CHAPTER XVIII

MARION SUMMONED TO THE CAMP OF GREENE
† DEFEATS THE BRITISH HORSE AT ST. THOMAS †
LEAVES HIS COMMAND TO HORRY, AND TAKES HIS
SEAT IN THE ASSEMBLY AT JACKSONBOROUGH, AS
SENATOR FROM ST. JOHN'S, BERKELY † PROCEEDINGS
OF THE ASSEMBLY † CONFISCATION ACT † DISPUTE
BETWEEN COLS. MAYHAM AND HORRY † THE
BRIGADE OF MARION SURPRISED, DURING HIS
ABSENCE, BY A DETACHMENT FROM CHARLESTON †
MARION'S ENCOUNTER WITH THE BRITISH HORSE †
CONSPIRACY IN THE CAMP OF GREENE

While the army of Greene lay at Round O., considerable alarm was
excited in the American camp by tidings of large reinforcements
made to the British strength in Charleston. General Leslie was now in
command of the latter. The contraction of the American military cordon
had very greatly straitened the resources and comforts of the British general.
The numerous refugees who had taken shelter in the city with their families,
the great accumulation of horses within the lines, and the vigilant watch
which was maintained over the islands and the neck by the American
light detachments, soon contributed to lessen the stock of provisions in
the capital, and to cut off its supplies. One consequence of this condition
was to compel Leslie to put two hundred of his horses to death; while, by
all other possible means, he collected his provisions from the surrounding
country. Considerable parties were kept upon the alert for this object, and,
to facilitate the movements of these parties, strong posts were established at
Haddrel's Point and Hobcaw. The situation of these posts, on the extremities
of tongues of land, to which assistance might easily be conveyed by water,
and from which retreat, to an attacking enemy, was difficult, rendered them
comparatively safe, for the present, against the Americans. But the situation

of Leslie was one of uncomfortable constraint, and it was natural that he should avail himself of any prospect which might promise him relief. It was readily believed, therefore, in the American camp, that, with the acquisition of new strength, by the arrival of reinforcements from abroad, Leslie would seek break through the cordon put around him. The rumor of his approach, in strength, caused Greene to issue his orders to Marion to repair to headquarters with all the force he could draw after him. Our partisan promptly obeyed the summons; but, on his way to join with Greene he left a detachment of mounted infantry in the neighborhood of Monk's Corner, to watch the motions of the enemy.

But Leslie's purpose was mistaken. His strength had been exaggerated. He had no designs upon the camp of Greene, being no doubt quite as ignorant of his weakness as the latter was of the British strength. But the detachment left by Marion near Monk's Corner caught the attention of the enemy, and, in the absence of the partisan, it was thought accessible to a proper attempt from Charleston. In all the movements of the British, it is very evident that they attached no small importance to the presence of this chief. A detachment of three hundred men, cavalry and infantry, was transported by water to the north bank of the Wando river. This body moved with equal secrecy and celerity. But they were disappointed in their aim. Marion had returned from the Continental camp to his own. The storm which threatened the former was overblown, and he was in season to avert that by which the latter was threatened. His force was scarcely equal to that of the enemy. He nevertheless resolved upon attacking them. In order to keep them in play, while he advanced with his main body, Cols. Richardson and Scriven, with a part of Mayham's horse, were dispatched with orders to throw themselves in front of the British, and engage them until he could come up. This order was gallantly executed. They encountered the enemy's advance near the muster-house of St. Thomas, charged them vigorously, and succeeded in putting them to flight, with some slaughter. Capt. Campbell, of the British, and several others, were killed. But the pursuit was urged too far. The cavalry of Mayham, by which this success had been obtained, was of new organization. Their training had been partial only. It was seen that, though they drove the British horse before them, their own charge was marked by disorder. Hurried forward by success, they rushed into the jaws of danger, and were only brought to their senses by an encounter with the whole of the British infantry. A volley from this body drove them back in confusion, while the cavalry, which had been flying before them, encouraged by the presence of the infantry, rallied upon the steps of the pursuers, and drove them in turn. They suffered severely, wedged upon a narrow causeway, which gave them as little room for escape as evolution. Twenty-two fell upon the spot, by the fire of the infantry. The rest were rallied when sufficiently far from the more formidable enemy, and, turning upon the British cavalry, once more put them to flight. But the event left Marion too weak to press the encounter. He contented himself with watching the motions of the British, and they were sufficiently respectful not to press him to any less pacific performance. They were satisfied to pursue their march, and, gathering a few head of cattle, to retire to foregoing the more important object of their incursion. The field clear, Marion left his brigade in charge of Horry, and repaired to Jacksonborough, to attend the Assembly, to which he had been elected a member from St. John, Berkely, the same parish which he represented in the Provincial Congress at the beginning of the war. This was early in the year 1782. The Legislature met at Jacksonborough, a little village on the Edisto or Pon-Pon river, on the 18th January of this year. This position, almost within striking distance of the British army at Charleston, was chosen with particular reference to the moral influence which the boldness of such a choice would be likely to have upon the people, and the confidence which it seemed to declare in the ability of the American army to render the place secure. To make it so, Greene moved his troops across the Edisto, and took post at Skirving's plantation, six miles in advance of Jacksonborough, and on the road which leads to Charleston. There was yet another step necessary to this object. The British, in addition to Charleston and the "Neck" held possession of two islands, James and John, which belong to that inner chain of isles which stretches along the coast from Charleston to Savannah, separated from the main by creeks and marshes, and from one another by the estuaries of rivers, sounds, or inlets. On John's Island, which is fertile, extensive, and secure, the enemy held a very respectable force under Col. Craig. Jacksonborough was within striking distance of this force. It could be approached by boats or galleys, in a single tide. It was equally assailable from this point by land. As a matter of precaution, it was considered necessary to disperse this force, and it was soon ascertained, not only that the island was accessible, but that the enemy, relying upon the protection of his armed galleys, was unapprehensive of attack. The attempt was entrusted to Cols. Lee and Laurens, who, with separate parties, were to reach the point of destination by different routes. One of the parties lost the road, and failed to co-operate with the other. The movement was only partially successful. A second was designed, and succeeded. The galleys were driven from their station by the artillery, and Laurens penetrated to Craig's encampment. But the latter had already abandoned it. A few stragglers fell into the hands of the Americans, but nothing more. The preceding attempt had just sufficed to convince Craig of the insecurity of the place, and he had taken timely precautions against suffering from a repetition of the attempt.

The Legislature assembled according to appointment. The proclamation of the Governor, to whom, from the beginning of the war, had been accorded almost dictatorial powers, precluded from election and suffrage all persons who had taken British protections; and, as those who were true to the State had been very generally active in the ranks of her military, it followed, as a matter of course, that a great proportion of the members were military men. Among these were Sumter and Marion. The former, about this time, yielded his commission to the authorities, on account of some slight or injustice to which he had been subjected, and left the army when he took his seat in the Assembly. General Henderson succeeded to his command. The Jacksonborough Assembly was highly distinguished, as well for its talent as for its worth and patriotism. Its character was, perhaps, rather military than civil. Constituting as they did, in a slave community, a sort of feudal aristocracy, and accustomed, as, for so long a time they had been, to the use of the weapons of war, its members wore the deportment of so many armed barons, gathered together quite as much for action as resolve. It was not only unavoidable, but highly important at this juncture, that such should be the character of this body. Who could so well determine what were the necessities of the country—what the exigencies of the people—what the local resources and remedies—as those who had fought its battles, traversed every acre of its soil, and represented its interests and maintained its rights when there was no civil authority? What legislators so likely to yield the popular will, as men who, like Marion and Sumter, had become its rallying leaders—whom the people had been accustomed to obey and follow, and by whom had been protected. It was equally important that the legislation should come from such sources, when we consider the effect upon the enemy, still having a foothold in the State. They might reasonably apprehend that the laws springing from such a body would be marked by a stern directness and decision of purpose which would leave nothing to be hoped by disaffection or hostility; and their proceedings did not disappoint the expectations of friend or foe.

The measures of this Assembly were marked by equal prudence and resolve. They passed a new act respecting the militia, and one for raising the State quota of Continental troops. One of their measures has been questioned as unwise and impolitic—that, namely, for amercing and confiscating the estates of certain of the loyalists, and for banishing the most obnoxious among them. Something, certainly, is to be said in favor of this act. If vindictive, it seems to have been necessary. It must be remembered that, in consequence of a previous proclamation of the Governor, none but the most implacable and virulent of the Tories were liable to its operation—none but those who rejected very liberal offers of indulgence and conciliation. This proclamation had opened the door to reconciliation with the State, on very easy terms to the offenders. It gave them timely warning to come in, enrol themselves in the American ranks, and thus assure themselves of that protection and safety which they had well forfeited. Their neglect or refusal to accept this proffer of mercy, properly incurred the penalties of contumacy. These penalties could be no other than confiscation of property and banishment of person. Reasons of policy, if not of absolute necessity, seemed to enforce these penalties. How was the war to be carried on? Marion's men, for example, received no pay, no food, no clothing. They had borne the dangers and the toils of war, not only without pay, but without the hope of it. They had done more—they had yielded up their private fortunes to the cause. They had seen their plantations stripped by the enemy, of negroes, horses, cattle, provisions, plate—everything, in short, which could tempt the appetite of cupidity; and this, too, with the knowledge, not only that numerous loyalists had been secured in their own possessions, but had been rewarded out of theirs. The proposed measure seemed but a natural and necessary compliance with popular requisition. Besides, the war was yet to be carried on. How was this to be done? How long was it yet to last? What was to be its limit? Who could predict? Congress was without money—the State without means. For a space of three years, South Carolina had not only supported the war within, but beyond her own borders. Georgia was utterly destitute, and was indebted to South Carolina for eighteen months for her subsistence; and North Carolina, in the portions contiguous to South Carolina, was equally poor and disaffected. The Whigs were utterly impoverished by their own wants and the ravages of the enemy. They had nothing more to give. Patriotism could now bestow little but its blood. It was with an obvious propriety resolved, by the Jacksonborough Assembly, that those who had proved false to the country should be made to suffer in like degree with those who had been true, and who were still suffering in her defense. As a measure of prolonged policy—contemplated beyond the emergency—there may be objections to the Confiscation Act; but the necessities of the time seemed to demand it, and it will be difficult for any judgment, having before it all the particulars of the cruel civil war through which the country had gone—not to speak of the army, and the present and pressing necessity for maintaining it—to arrive at any other conclusion, or to censure the brave man who urged and advocated the measure. The proceeding seems perfectly defensible on general principles, though in particular instances—as in the application of all general principles—it may have been productive of injury. The estates of the loyalists, by this measure, were seized upon as a means for building up the credit of the State, supplying it with the necessary funds for maintaining order as well as war, and for requiting and supporting that army which was still required to bleed in its defense.

What part was taken in this act by Marion, is not known. Though kind and indulgent in his nature, he was stern and resolute in war. We have no reason to suppose that he entertained any scruples about a proceeding, the necessity of which, at the time, seems to have been beyond all dispute.

The absence of our partisan from his brigade, was almost fatal to it. He left it with reluctance, and only with the conviction that his presence in the Senate was important to the interests equally of the army and the country. Indeed, without him there would not have been a quorum. There were only thirteen Senators present. He was interested, besides, in the passage of the new Militia Act, and in one designed to raise the State quota of Continental troops. These were sufficient to compel his presence. But he remained with reluctance. His letters from Jacksonborough betray the most constant anxiety about his brigade. He had yielded it to Horry with the most earnest exhortations to caution. By his orders, the latter, the more completely to ensure its safety, removed to a position on the north side of Wambaw, a creek emptying into the Santee. Here, in an angle formed by the two roads which pass from Lenud's Ferry road to Horry's plantation, about a quarter of a mile from the bridge, Horry occupied a post which caution might have rendered safe. In his rear was a wood. His newly raised regiment, not half complete, lay at Durant's plantation, about a mile above, under the command of Major Benson. Horry does not seem to have been remiss in his duties, but about this time he fell sick, and, for some time before, he had been, and still was, somewhat wilful. There was an unhappy dispute between himself and Col. Mayham, touching rank and precedence. The latter refused to be commanded by the former, claiming to be equal in commission, and, when Marion went to Jacksonborough, separated his corps from the brigade, posted them higher up the river, and, being a member of the Legislature, proceeded to Jacksonborough also. Greene was not unwilling, in the present juncture of affairs, that the native officers should be present at the deliberations of this body. The civil objects were just then even more important than the military.

The contumacy of Mayham was a subject of the most earnest discussion. Both Marion and Greene decided against him; yet both were reluctant to offend him, as they knew his value as a cavalry officer. Mayham seems to have acted under some erroneous impressions of the independence of a legionary brigade, as he claimed his to be. He also complained of the free use which Marion made of his cavalry, and the severe duties he was required to perform. To this, Greene replies: "You are to consider how extensive the country he has to guard, and how much he depends upon your corps. This will account for the hard service you have been put to. The general is a good man, and when you consider his difficulties, and make just allowances, perhaps you will have little to complain of but the hard necessity of the service."

But this reply did not produce its effect, and Mayham certainly erred, as a soldier, in complaining of the severity of his tasks. In the old chivalrous periods, the peculiar severity of the duties assigned to knighthood was recognized gratefully, as matter of compliment and trust. He still held off; and Marion promptly demanded, that, if Mayham had any independent right of command, while nominated under him, he might be at once withdrawn from the brigade. Mayham's manner and tone were quite respectful but tenacious; and while the discussion was in progress, and he holding off from Horry, events were brewing which were destined to terminate the unfortunate dispute by a capital misfortune.

Again taking advantage of the absence of Marion, an expedition was set on foot in Charleston, against Horry. A detachment of two hundred horse, five hundred infantry, and two pieces of artillery, under Col. Thomson (better known in after-times as Count Rumford), prepared to ascend Cooper river. Its preparations were not conducted with such caution, however, but that they became known to the vigilant friends of the Americans in and about the city. The army was warned of their preparations. Greene hinted to Marion the necessity of returning to his command. The latter replies, by declaring his great anxiety to do so, but urges the impossibility of leaving the Senate, lest the Assembly should be broken up—an event which might be of fatal importance to the cause, unless the great business of the session were first disposed of. He promises to move as soon as this should be the case. The actual movement of the British detachment made it impossible that Marion should longer delay to rejoin his brigade, and, accompanied by Col. Mayham, he reached the ground on which the regiment of the latter was encamped, by a circuitous route and rapid riding, on the 24th February. Here they were unhappily told that the enemy was retiring. Marion, accordingly, remained to rest and refresh himself, while Mayham paid a visit to his own plantation. In a few hours after Mayham's departure, an express arrived with the mortifying intelligence that the brigade had been surprised and dispersed. Marion, instantly putting himself at the head of Mayham's regiment, hurried on toward Wambaw, the scene of the event, to check pursuit and collect and save the fugitives.

We have seen the position of Horry. He had sent out his scouts on all the roads by which the approach of an enemy might be apprehended. Feeling himself secure, and being sick, he went over the river on the 24th, the day of the catastrophe, to his plantation, leaving the brigade under the command of Col. M'Donald. Major Benson, as will be remembered, held a position, with the incomplete regiment of Horry, at Durant's plantation, about a mile above that of the brigade. By some unaccountable remissness of patrols or videttes, the British cavalry, under Coffin, surprised the latter post. Benson, it is said, had been told by Capt. Bennett, who commanded the scouts in St. Thomas's, that the enemy was approaching; but the information was brought to him while at dinner, and a keen appetite made him slow to believe tidings which might have lessened the enjoyment of the meal. Bennett proceeded to Horry's head-quarters, where Col. M'Donald happened to be at dinner also. He proved equally incredulous, but desired Major James, who had just arrived in camp, to take command of his regiment. The surprise of Benson's was complete, and he paid for his remissness or indifference with his life. The firing at Durant's convinced M'Donald of his error; but, in all probability, the surprise was quite as complete in the one command as in the other. There were two regiments of "six-months' men" that is to say, "reformed Tories" who had come in under the proclamation issued by Governor Rutledge. These broke at the first encounter with the enemy. In their flight, and to prevent pursuit, they threw off the planks from Wambaw bridge. Fortunately, a strong body, under Major James, checked the pursuit for a space, and gave an opportunity for the fugitives to save themselves. Many of them crossed the river by swimming, but some were drowned in the attempt. The thickets saved the infantry. No prisoners were taken. The British gave no quarter. Successful against Benson and M'Donald, the enemy pressed forward in the direction of Marion's approach, but without having any knowledge of his proximity. He had halted with the cavalry of Mayham, at the house of Mrs. Tydiman, about four miles from the scene of the disaster, to refresh his men and horses. The latter were unbitted and feeding, when the whole of the enemy's cavalry made their appearance. It would seem, from the indecision of their commander, that he was no less surprised at falling in with this body of Marion's men, than was our partisan at his sudden appearance. His hesitation under this surprise gave the Americans an opportunity to recover themselves. It was the opinion of Mayham, that, had the charge been sounded the moment that he came in view, the whole regiment must have been lost. There was no retreat, save by the river, and by the lane through which they had entered the plantation, and of this the enemy had full command. The halt and hesitation of the British—their seeming alarm—at once afforded Marion the means of extrication from his predicament. To bit and mount their horses, was, for his cavalry, the work of a moment. Though not counting half the numbers of the enemy, Marion's instant resolution was to issue forth by the lane, and attack them. They had displayed themselves in front of it. Just before the lane was an old field, and a little to the right a pond of water. Marion, placing a small body of infantry to great advantage along the fence, ordered his column of cavalry to advance through the lane to the attack. His men were well mounted; in this respect, if inferior in numbers, they had a manifest advantage over the British. The latter had been too long cooped up in the walls of Charleston, on short commons, to be very serviceable; and the cavalry of Mayham, though somewhat too much crowded with the "new-made Whigs," were yet confident, from long experience, in their ability to contend with the enemy. Marion himself was confident, but was destined, in this instance, to lose, what he himself, in his dispatches, has styled, "a glorious opportunity of cutting up the British cavalry." His men moved to the extremity of the lane, before which the enemy had halted, with a firm and promising countenance. The front section was led by Capt. Smith, an officer of approved courage, who, in a very recent affair at St. Thomas' muster-house, had signally distinguished himself. Yet, seized with a sudden panic, the moment that he reached the end of the lane, he dashed into the woods on the right, and drew after him the whole regiment. Marion himself, who was near the head of the column, was borne away by the torrent, which he in vain struggled to withstand. The rush was irresistible—the confusion irretrievable. All efforts to restrain or recover the fugitives were idle, until they had reached the woods. There Marion succeeded in rallying a party, and at this point the pursuit of the enemy was checked, and the fugitives partly rallied. They had sustained but little loss in lives; but the shame, the disgrace of such a panic, was immeasurably humiliating. The British showed no eagerness in the pursuit. They seemed to doubt the bloodless victory which they had won, and content with their own escape, were not unreasonably urgent with fortune to make their victory complete. They subsequently, after they had fully recovered from their panic, contrived greatly to exaggerate the importance of the event. One of the newspapers of the day has the following:—"Things bear a better prospect than they did. Colonel Thomson has defeated General Marion in South Carolina, killed one hundred men, and Marion was drowned, attempting to escape." The only officer drowned in the flight, was Lieut. Smyzer of Horry's cavalry.

The loss of the brigade in horses and accoutrements was greater than in men. Their greater loss, however, was of that confidence in themselves and one another, which it was one of the greatest objects of Marion's training to inspire. The true secret of the superiority of regulars over militia-men lies in the habit of mutual reliance. They feel each other's elbows, in military parlance—they are assured by the custom of mutually depending one upon the other. This habit impresses them with a conviction, which the terrors of conflict do not often impair, that they will not be deserted; and, thus assured, they hurry into the battle, and remain in it so long as the body with which they move can act together. Once broken, however, the cry is "*sauve qui peut.*" Not so with militia-men. They never forget their individuality. The very feeling of personal independence is apt to impair their confidence in one another. Their habit is to obey the individual impulse. They do not wait to take their temper from their neighbor right and left. Hence their irregularity—the difficulty of restraining them—of making them act in routine, and with entire reference to the action of other bodies. So far from deriving strength from feeling another's elbow, they much prefer elbow room. Could they be assured of one another, they were the greatest troops in the world. They *are* the greatest troops in the world—capable of the most daring and heroic achievements—wherever the skill of the commander can inspire this feeling of mutual reliance. Frequent co-operation of the same persons under the same leader produces it, and makes them veterans. The old soldiers of the brigade had it in perfection. It was one of the excellences of Marion that it followed so certainly and rapidly from his peculiar training. That it should be lost or impaired, was a most serious evil. That it would not have been endangered, we are sure, had it not been that the brigade no longer consisted of the brave fellows who had clung to him through the campaigns of the last two years. The new recruits were, in all probability, to blame for the mischance and something, perhaps, is due to the unhappy quarrel between Mayham and Horry. The former was terribly mortified by the affair—mortified that Marion should have hurried to the scene of action without apprising him, and vexed that his own regiment should have behaved so badly. He complains that others should "expend the strength of the regiment without giving *him* the satisfaction of being present." Captain John Caraway Smith, the officer who led the column thus disastrously aside, resigned the day after the affair. His conduct had been habitually brave. But a short time before, as already shown, he had behaved with the most determined and audacious gallantry at the head of the same troop. That their training was defective is beyond question, but no imputation rested upon their courage or his own. Nevertheless, we have Napoleon's authority for the opinion that every man has his *moment de peur.* No man is equally firm on all occasions. There are moods of weakness and irresolution in every mind, which is not exactly a machine, which impair its energies and make its course erratic and uncertain. The truth was known in earlier ages. The old poets ascribed it to supernatural influence. Envious deities interposed between valor and its victim, paralysing the soul of the one and strengthening that of the other. Thus we find even Hector, upon occasion, the slave of panic, and Paris, on the other hand, almost emulating the spirit of his brother.

The conduct of Captain Smith, in this affair, has been excused by Mayham. He ascribes it to an error of Marion himself. He says that, "Marion (who was an infantry officer) gave the order to *file off from the house to the right,* instead of ordering to *charge*! This induced his officers to believe that they were to retreat and not to fight." This may be true; but it is scarcely probable. Retreat from the house, except into the river, seems to have been cut off. The only other avenue was the lane. At the end of this was the enemy, drawn out in order of battle. Upon these the advance was ordered. We have seen that Marion himself exulted in the conviction that the enemy was in power. His exultation could not have been entirely concealed from his officers. It must have declared itself in some way. The halt and hesitation of the British were perceptible to all. They were in superior numbers, and when they reached the head of the lane, the horses of the American cavalry were unbitted and feeding. A sudden and resolute charge, according to Mayham, on the part of the British, would have resulted in the entire defeat of the regiment. That they did not order this charge betrayed their apprehensions, and should have encouraged, in similar degree, the Americans—*did* encourage them, and hence the resolve of Marion to advance upon them. That it should be supposed he would hurry forward, in the very teeth of the enemy, only to dash aside in confusion from the struggle, is scarcely reasonable. But Mayham was offended with Marion. The latter had decided against him in the controversy with Horry; and the subsequent movement against the British, without stopping to require his presence, was another mortifying circumstance which he was not likely to forget. Biassed by his feelings, he was not willing to believe that the seeming slight was in reality due to the emergency of the case, which would not allow a moment's hesitation in movement at such a juncture.

As soon as the presence of Marion was known, the fugitives gathered around him. But for his absence they had never been dispersed. Horry's regiment was very much crippled; Mayham's in equally bad condition. Of M'Donald's, and the brigade, a few hundred were soon brought together; and with his deranged and dispirited band, our partisan retired beyond the Santee to repair and recruit his strength, and revive the confidence of his men in their leaders and themselves. In the meanwhile, the country which he had so recently covered and protected was harried by the British. They improved the interval of his absence by successful incursions. The cattle had been already put beyond their power, on the other side the Santee; but they stripped the plantations within their reach, as well of slaves as of provisions. Greene could do nothing to prevent them. His own army was in a state of convulsion and commotion; suffering from distress and discontent, and threatened with dissolution. Recent occurrences had awakened his fears for his own security.

One result of Marion's recent disaster was to put an end to the dispute between Horry and Mayham. Their respective regiments were so reduced, after the affair at Wambaw, that it was deemed advisable to amalgamate them. Having resolved upon this measure, Gov. Mathews, who had succeeded Rutledge, applied to Marion to know who of the two was the best cavalry officer—an opinion which Marion yielded with great reluctance. His personal preferences went with Horry, but he could not hesitate in declaring for Mayham. Horry, with the ambition of a spirited soldier, eagerly desired a command of cavalry,—was a good infantry officer, and had all the requirements of skill and bravery. But he was no horseman, and it is said that, in several of the charges, he was indebted to some one or other of his men for his own safety, being commonly unhorsed. His gallantry and patriotism were equally unquestionable. They had been displayed from the beginning of the war. The preference shown Mayham caused Horry's resignation from the service; but to console him for the mortification Marion made him commandant of Georgetown, a post which united the responsibilities and duties of a military and civil service.

With the adjournment of the Assembly at Jacksonborough, the army of Greene moved down from Skirving's plantation to Bacon's bridge, at the head of Ashley river. Here, within twenty miles of the enemy, a dangerous conspiracy ripened almost to maturity among the Pennsylvania troops, composed in part of the very mutineers who had triumphed over government in the insurrection in Jersey, and who, as Lafayette observed,[75] "had been well paid and well clothed in consequence of it." This, we believe, was the only body of troops furnished to the Southern army, during the Revolution, from any of the States north of Maryland and Delaware. We make this remark with the view to the correction of a very general error, arising from the vague manner in which it is customary for our historians to speak of the sources of the *personnel* of the Southern army. The armies led by Gates and Greene, to the defence of Carolina, were truly from States north of her, but they were not Northern States. Two fine bodies of troops came from Maryland and Delaware, but the rest were from Virginia and North Carolina,—with the exception of the Pennsylvania line, of which we have now to speak. These, as we have seen, had been refractory in Jersey, and instead of being punished, were paid for their sedition. It was natural that they should endeavor to renew an experiment which had already proved so profitable. The mutineers were directed by one Sergeant Gornell. Their number is unknown. They were solely of the Pennsylvania line, and might have been successful but for an attempt which they made upon the fidelity of the Marylanders. Their purpose was to deliver Greene to the enemy, and otherwise facilitate the objects of the latter, who were to make a concerted movement, in force, upon the American army, at a prescribed moment. The integrity of the Marylanders, whom Gornell approached, was not to be shaken; and to their fidelity and the quick ears of one of the camp-women, the army was indebted for its safety. The circumstances were all in favor of the success of the conspirators. There was a general discontent in the army. The troops were badly fed and clothed—were unpaid, doubtful of pay, and suffering present distresses. They were inactive. Many of them were new recruits. Greene was no longer surrounded by the tried and true men and officers, who had borne the brunt of the contest. The term of service of the former had in great part expired, some of his best officers were on furlough, and he had offended others. Sumter had left the army in disgust; Pickens was operating against the Indians; Marion was recruiting his brigade on the Santee; Williams had gone home; Howard was in Maryland, scarcely recovered from his wounds; Wayne was in Georgia, doing good service in that quarter; St. Clair was absent on leave; Lee had gone to Virginia to get married, and his legion was almost shorn of officers; Eggleston had gone with him to Virginia, and the brave fellows, Armstrong and Carrington, had fallen into the hands of the enemy. The time was well chosen for mutiny, and as the hour drew near for the consummation of the purpose of the conspirators, the British army was a set in motion from below,—not so secretly, however, but that their movements were made known to the Americans. Symptoms of mutiny became apparent in the camp, and it was necessary to proceed with vigor. Doubtful of a large number of those around him, Greene summoned Marion with all his force from the Santee, while his own army was kept in order of battle. The arrest of Gornell, with that of four others, all sergeants of the Pennsylvania line, took place the night before the conspiracy was to take effect; Gornell was tried and executed; the others were sent under guard into the interior. This proceeding was the signal for the flight of at least a dozen more, who, having been committed, broke away on the night of Gornell's seizure, and found protection with the enemy, who advanced in force to receive them. This prompt proceeding suppressed the mutiny. The development of the conspiracy, the state of preparedness in the camp of Greene, and the movement of Marion, had the effect of discouraging the farther advance of the British army; and Marion, while yet in motion for the camp of Greene, from which he was but eight miles distant, was summoned in haste to the protection of Georgetown, against which the enemy was reported to have sailed from Charleston. A forced march of four days brought him to White's Bridge, when it was discovered that the alarm was unfounded. The enemy had not shown himself, and was not nigh. In this march of one hundred and sixty miles, Marion's men had but a single ration of rice. Their sole food, with this exception, was lean beef. The march took place in April, when there is no forage for cattle, and when such as survive the winter, are compelled to wander far in the swamps and thickets in search of the scanty herbage which sustains them. The march of our partisan in these two expeditions was conducted solely on foot. The country south of the Santee had been so completely foraged by the British, daring his vacation of it, that he was compelled to dismount his infantry in his movements until the spring herbage should enable him to feed his horses. His force was reduced to two hundred militia and one hundred and twenty horse. It was the wish of General Greene that he should take post as near the enemy as possible, in order both to shorten his limits beyond Cooper river, and to enable Col. Laurens, who now commanded the legion of Lee, to pass the Ashley, and close upon the British between the latter river and Goose Creek. But with his infantry dismounted, he dared not venture so completely within the reach of an enemy so superior; and with the double purpose of securing a retreat, if necessary, and of forming a junction with any party when desirable, either at Huger's Bridge, over the west branch of Cooper river, or at Strawberry Ferry, he took post at Sinkler's plantation on the Santee. This left him within twenty-five miles of each of these designated routes. His cavalry meanwhile patrolled the country as low as Haddrell and Hobcaw, and in sight of the British posts at those places. They thus procured the earliest news of the enemy movements, and checked his incursions in that quarter. The effect of Marion's presence with his brigade was soon felt, as well by his people as by the British. By the latter it was deemed important to relieve themselves from a neighbor at once so vigilant and inconvenient. A messenger, feigning to be a deserter, was dispatched by General Leslie, whose plan was to make his way through the scouts of Marion to the Scotch and loyal settlements on the borders of North Carolina. These were to be stirred up to insurrection, and Marion was to be diverted from a quarter in which his presence was particularly annoying. The messenger succeeded in his object, but was less fortunate in his return. He had done the mischief required at his hands, fomented the insurrection, and set the loyalists in motion. The proofs were conclusive against him, and he perished by military execution. The timely notice which Marion obtained of his labors enabled him to prepare against the event.

CHAPTER XIX

MARION SUMMONED WITH HIS FORCE TO THAT OF GREENE † INSURRECTION OF THE LOYALISTS ON THE PEDEE † MARCHES AGAINST THEM † SUBDUES THEM † TREATS WITH GAINEY † FANNING † PROTECTS THE TORY, BUTLER, FROM HIS MEN † RETURNS TO THE COUNTRY BETWEEN THE SANTEE AND THE COOPER † MOVES TO PROTECT GEORGETOWN FROM THE BRITISH FLEET † TAKES POST AT WATBOO, ON COOPER RIVER † DEFEATS THE BRITISH CAVALRY UNDER MAJOR FRASIER

Meanwhile, the main body of the army under Greene continued to suffer diminution. On the first of May a large proportion of the North Carolina troops were entitled to and claimed their discharge. No recruits were expected from the North, and it became necessary to draw together all the force that South Carolina could afford. The Government of this State, from its first re-organization, had faithfully endeavored to re-establish the South Carolina line, but without money or means, with very little corresponding success. A few recruits were obtained from among those who had recently received their discharge, but the service had been of a kind to baffle all the temptations and arguments of the recruiting officers. In the emergency of the case, it became indispensable to look to the militia under Marion, Pickens and Henderson; and these leaders were accordingly required to repair to head-quarters.

The withdrawal of the former, with his troops, from the region of country which they had so lately covered, was the signal for that rising of the loyalists upon the Pedee, to instigate which the unfortunate emissary of General Leslie had been dispatched from Charleston. The absence of Marion was considered auspicious to the new movement. He had scarcely reached Dorchester when his ancient enemy, Major Gainey, appeared in arms at the head of a considerable body of troops, both cavalry and infantry. A small command under Col. Baxter, which had been left by Marion to observe their movements, was too feeble to make head against them, and it became necessary for Marion himself to retrace his steps, and arrest the progress of the insurrection. Placing himself at the head of Mayham's cavalry, he promptly advanced in the direction of the enemy. So rapid were his movements, so vigilant his watch, so well devised his plans, that he reached the Pedee country long before his approach was suspected. His presence, on the present occasion, was a surprise. It had long been a terror; so much so that but for his remoteness at the camp of Greene, they had, in all probability, never ventured to resume their arms. Three separate bodies of men, by a judicious arrangement of our partisan, prepared to enter their country at the same moment. These were so placed, that, though operating separately, they might yet be made to co-operate if desired. The effect was such as to paralyse the incipient resolution of the loyalists. They showed no disposition for fight; and feeling their temper, conscious of his difficulties, and now no longer hopeful of help from the British, Gainey dispatched a flag to Marion with proposals to treat for a pacification. He was not unwilling to renew the treaty which, just one year before, he had entered into with Horry, who then acted as the lieutenant of our partisan. This treaty, influenced by British emissaries, the Tories had very imperfectly kept. In small squads they had been perpetually rising, and committing trespasses upon their neighbors whenever the withdrawal of Marion's men afforded them opportunity. They had now everything to fear from his anger; but they also knew his willingness to forgive. Relying upon this, and making a merit of necessity, the communication of Gainey expressed the warmest solicitude for peace. To this Marion was prepared to listen. Commissioners were appointed on both sides. They met, but, unhappily, they recognized in each other well known personal opponents. They had often met in strife, and could not forbear alluding to their encounters. The conversation grew warm, the parties excited, and instead of coming to terms, the commissioners almost came to blows. They separated with increased resentment. A fierce skirmish followed, and the attempt to adjust their differences was renewed between the respective commanders. Marion was anxious to effect a pacification. His services were required below on the Santee and Cooper, to check the incursions of the British, and he consented to meet and confer with Gainey in person. This determination was censured by some of his officers. They denounced Gainey as a leader of banditti; and, certainly, his conduct, on many occasions, deserved the reproach. They reproached Marion for committing his dignity in treating with such a person. But this suggestion did not affect him. He was governed by views and principles very far superior to those which influence the ordinary soldier. His pride did not suffer from such censures. His reply was equally prompt and conclusive. He told them that he "aimed at no higher dignity than that of essentially serving his country."

The result was satisfactory to our partisan. Making a merit of necessity, Gainey yielded without requiring any farther resort to blows. At the Bowling Green, between the Great and Little Pedee, more than five hundred men laid down their arms, submitting to conditions which were rather strict than severe. Marion and Gainey met at Birch's mill on the 8th June, when a treaty was drawn up having for its basis the articles of the preceding arrangement with Horry. By this treaty, Gainey and his men were to lay down their arms and not to resume them unless ordered to do so by the authorities of the State; they bound themselves to deliver up all negroes, horses, cattle and other property of which they had dispossessed the people of this or any other State—to demean themselves as peaceable citizens, and submit to the laws of the State—to deliver up all contumacious and rebellious persons within their district—to deliver up all deserters from the regular service—to sign a declaration of allegiance to the United States, and to South Carolina in particular, and to abjure the British crown, and to surrender all British property. Compliance with these conditions, was to ensure them full pardon for their treasons to the State, and the enjoyment of their property as citizens within it; while individuals not choosing to comply, were to be permitted, with their wives and children, a safe progress to the British lines. From the benefits of this treaty, some few atrocious offenders were excepted. Major Gainey removed with those who preferred to adhere to the fortunes of the British. He did not side with their determination, but he deemed it a duty to see that those who had followed his arms, should be put in safety beyond the reach of their enemies: an honorable resolve certainly. Before his departure he waited upon Marion and said: "Honor, sir, requires that I should yield my commission to Col. Balfour, from whom I received it; but this done, I shall immediately return to the country and seek your protection." This was frankly promised him, and with every confidence in the assurance of Marion, as soon as he had concluded his affairs in Charleston he promptly returned and enrolled himself in the American ranks. One of the loyalist specially exempted from the privileges of the treaty with Gainey, was a notorious marauder by the name of Fanning. He was a sanguinary ruffian, with considerable talents, but brutal, reckless, and most inveterate in his hostility to the American cause. Shortly after the treaty with Gainey, this person appeared in the truce ground at the head of a small party. It was feared that he would stir up the revolt anew.

He came for that purpose. Marion was at once upon the alert. His force, divided into three bodies, occupied various parts of the lately disaffected districts, and overawed the spirit of revolt, if it yet existed. Finding the cause hopeless in that quarter, Fanning sent a flag to Marion with a request that he would grant a safe-conduct to his wife, and some property, to the British garrison in Charleston. Against any such concession the officers of Marion expostulated. They were unwilling that so cruel a ruffian should receive any indulgence. But Marion looked more deeply into the matter, and yielded a prompt compliance with the request. "Let but his wife and property reach the British lines, and Fanning will follow. Force them to remain, and we only keep a serpent in our bosom." Such was his reasoning, and the truth of it was very soon apparent. Finding the hope of insurrection fruitless, Fanning fled the country, and was as soon in Charleston as his wife.

The disaffected district was now covered by his troops, busied in securing all persons who, declining to retire to the British, still withheld their submission from the American authorities. In the execution of this duty, some licentiousness followed—such irregularities as are apt to occur where soldiers traverse a subdued territory. Intimations of these irregularities reached the ears of the partisan. No individual was charged with offence, and no particulars were given; but Marion took occasion to declare his indignation in the presence of officers and men. "I have heard insinuations," said he, "which, if true, would disgrace my command; no accusation has been made; but I wish you clearly to know that let officer or soldier he proved guilty of crime, and he shall hang on the next tree." His firmness and sincerity were known; and he heard of no more license. While engaged in the irksome duty of arresting the recusant, he was equally busy in granting written protections to those who subscribed frankly to the conditions of the treaty. The judicious disposition and immediate presence of his force—the terror inspired by his successes—the knowledge which they had of his mercy, and their evident abandonment by the British—had the effect of bringing crowds to his camp, trebling the number of his own troops, seeking the proffered securities. Such was the consumption of paper on this occasion, or rather such the poverty at head-quarters, that old letters were torn up, the backs of which were put in requisition for this object. While at Birch's mills, on the Pedee, among others who sought the protection of Marion was one Capt. Butler, who had made himself particularly odious by his crimes and ferocity. He had been conspicuous as the oppressor of the Whig inhabitants of the Pedee. He was not ignorant of the detestation in which he was held, and it was with some misgivings that he sought the required protection. His appearance in the American camp was the signal for a commotion. There were among the

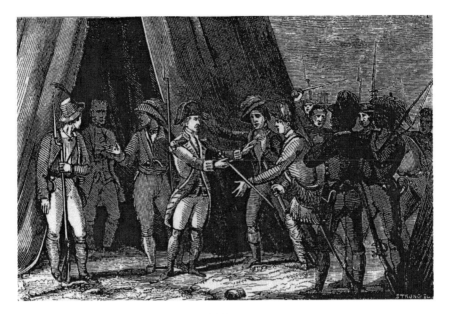

Marion protects the Tory, Butler, from his Men.

men of Marion some who were connected with persons who had suffered by the atrocities of Butler. They determined to avenge their friends. They resolved that no protection should save him, and an intemperate message to that effect was sent to Marion. Marion instantly took Butler to his own tent, and firmly answered those by whom the message was brought: "Relying on the pardon offered, the man whom you would destroy has submitted. Both law and honor sanction my resolution to protect him with my life." A still more intemperate message reached him, declaring that "Butler should be dragged to death from his tent—that to defend such a wretch was an insult to humanity." To this Marion made no reply, but calling around him the members of his family, and some of his most trusty followers, he gave them to understand that he should expect their co-operation at all hazards in protecting the culprit from violence. "Prepare to give me your assistance, for though I consider the villany of Butler unparalleled, yet, acting under orders as I am, I am bound to defend him. I will do so or perish." The mutiny threatened to be formidable, and that night, Marion succeeded with a strong guard in conveying the prisoner to a place of safety. The treaty with Gainey put an end to the domestic feuds upon the Pedee, and anxious to regain the local confidence which they had forfeited, numbers of the loyalists of this quarter, following the example of their leader, entered the ranks of the Americans, and though too late to be of effectual service in the war, yet furnished sufficient proofs of their fidelity.

No farther necessity appearing for the longer stay of Marion on the Pedee, he prepared to return to his former range along the rivers Cooper and Santee. His absence from this region afforded an opportunity for the enemy to renew their depredations from Charleston. Marion had left Colonel Ashby in command of his infantry, when, at the head of Mayham's horse, he hurried to encounter Gainey, and quell his insurrection. Ashby, pressed by a superior British force, had been compelled to yield before it, and this intelligence left our partisan no moment of respite after quelling the commotions on the Pedee, before he was required to return and cover the country which had so long been indebted to his vigilance for protection. In leaving the Pedee, with still some doubts of the newly converted loyalists of that quarter, he left Col. Baxter with one hundred and fifty trusty men, to maintain the ascendency which he had just acquired. This object was of the last importance, not only with reference to the doubtful *personnel* of the country, but the valuable *materiel*, cattle and provisions, which might have been carried off to the enemy. Suspicious of the fidelity of the loyalists, there was every reason to fear that it might be too strongly tested. The British were known to be preparing a fleet of small vessels for some enterprises directed northwardly, and no object of importance seemed more obvious than that of renewing the disturbances on the Pedee and possessing themselves of the immense plunder which that region of country might still afford.

All precautions taken, our partisan hurried his return. But had he not been joined by a newly raised corps under Major Conyers, he must have marched alone. So rapid had been his movements, so unremitting his duties, that the cavalry of Mayham which he led, were completely broken down. He was compelled to leave them behind him to recruit. At Murray's Ferry, on the Santee, he halted to collect his militia, and await the arrival of Mayham's corps. Here he consolidated the commands of Mayham and Conyers into one regiment; and about the middle of July was enabled once more to cross the Santee with a force of three hundred dismounted infantry, and a respectable body of horse. With these he took post on the Wassamasaw, in a position which, while it was secure, enabled him to co-operate with the detachments of the main army in covering the country. Here his vigilance was again conspicuous. His parties were constantly busy. His own movements to and fro, wherever an enemy could approach, or was suspected, were continual, from the Cooper to the Santee. His objects were threefold—to check the irruptions of the enemy, to cut off their supplies, and to provide for his own people. His scouting parties penetrated in every hostile direction—sometimes as low as Daniel's Island and Clement's Ferry—points almost within the ken of the British garrison. But the, enemy was no longer enterprising. They were not often met. Their cavalry was few and inferior, and their exigencies may be inferred from their uniforming and converting some of their captured negroes into troopers. One corps of these black dragoons, consisting of twenty-six men, was cut to pieces by one of Marion's scouting parties of twelve, commanded by Capt. Capers.

The British, tired of the war, were preparing to evacuate the country. Preparatory to this, it was necessary that they should lay in sufficient store of provisions. General Leslie had been preparing for this necessity and, late in July, a numerous fleet of small vessels, conveying eight hundred men, and convoyed by galleys and armed brigs, left Charleston to proceed, as it was conjectured, against Georgetown. This compelled Marion to hasten in that direction. Here he made every arrangement for moving the public stores to a place of safety. Black Mingo was preferred as the depot, for the honorable reason, as given in own words, that it was "a settlement of good citizens and at my earliest and most faithful followers." But the enterprise of the enemy was less hazardous. The collection of rice was their object. This was to be found in the greatest quantity on the Santee, from the banks of which river they carried off about six hundred barrels. Marion's force was thrown over the Sampit so as to intercept their march to Georgetown, but he could not impede their progress up the South Santee, protected as they were under the guns of their galleys.

With the departure of the enemy from the river, the completion of his arrangements for the removal of the stores at Georgetown, and the defense of that place, Marion again re-crossed the Santee and hurried to Watboo, on the Cooper. This river, leading to Charleston, to which the fleet of the enemy had returned, was naturally thought to be the next which they would attempt to penetrate. He had left a small body of infantry at this place, but this was deemed inadequate to the required duties. But they were sufficient at least to attract the attention of the British. Ignorant of Marion's return, believing him to be still at Georgetown, whither, it was known, he had taken all his cavalry,—a detach of dragoons, more than one hundred strong, was sent from Charleston, under Major Frasier against the post at Watboo. The rapidity of Marion's movements brought him back in season for its safety. It happened unfortunately, that, when he heard of the approach of this detachment, his cavalry were absent, patrolling down the river, maintaining their watch for the British fleet, which was the chief subject of apprehension. This fleet, meanwhile, had gone southwardly, pursuing the object of its former quest up the waters of the Combahee.

With the approach of Frasier, Marion dispatched his messengers in search of his cavalry, and to call in his pickets. Some of the latter had joined him before the enemy appeared. Frasier exhibited considerable conduct in making his approaches. He had taken an unfrequented route, and had succeeded in capturing some of the out-sentinels of our partisan. He advanced upon him in the fullest confidence of effecting a surprise—not of Marion, but of the smaller force under Col. Ashby, which he still believed to be the only force opposed to him. He was soon undeceived and found his enemy rather stronger than he expected, and drawn up in readiness for his reception. It was about the 25th of August. Marion lay at the plantation of Sir John Colleton, on the south side of Watboo Creek, and a little above the bridge. The situation pleased him, and it was one of his frequent places of encampment when he happened to be operating in the vicinity. The owner was a loyalist and had left the country. The mansion and his extensive range of negro houses afforded ample shelter for such a force as that which Marion commanded. With the gradual advance of Frasier, Marion seems to have been acquainted, but in the absence of his cavalry his only mode of obtaining intelligence was through his officers. These alone, of all the party in camp, were provided with horses. Of these, he ordered out a party under Capt. Gavin Witherspoon to reconnoitre. While they were absent, Marion put his infantry in order of battle. The main body occupied an avenue of venerable cedars, which, neglected during the war, in their untrimmed state, stood overgrown with branches, their long boughs trailing almost to the ground. His left, by which the enemy was compelled to advance, were placed under cover of some of the outbuildings. Thus prepared, he waited the approach of the British, though not without sundry misgivings. It must be confessed that, at this juncture, he had not the most perfect confidence in the force under his command. They consisted, in great proportion, of those who, in that day, were known as new-made Whigs—men who had deserted the enemy and been cleansed of their previous treasons by the proclamation of Governor Rutledge, which, not long before, had promised immunity to all who came in promptly with their adhesion and joined the American ranks. There were also present some of those who, under Gainey, had recently received the protection of Marion, on the truce ground of Pedee. Major Gainey himself was among them, and with forty of his people, was placed conspicuously in the column in preparation for the British approach. Well might Marion feel some uneasiness at his situation, particularly in the absence of the cavalry on which he could rely. But our partisan had the art of securing the fidelity of those around him, in quite as great a degree as he possessed that other great military art, of extracting good service out of the most doubtful materials. He concealed his apprehensions, while he endeavored to dissipate those of his men.

Meanwhile, Witherspoon, with the reconnoitering party, advanced but a little distance in the woods, when they were met by the enemy's cavalry and instantly charged. A long chase followed, which soon brought the pursuers into view of the partisan. His men were half concealed behind the thick boughs of the cedars beneath which they were drawn up. The interest of the chase, as they drew more near, was increased by a little incident which was greatly calculated to encourage the militia. When in full view, the horse of Witherspoon failed him, or his rider purposely fell behind to bring up the rear of his little escort. At this sight a British dragoon darted forward to cut him down. Witherspoon coolly suffered him to advance until he was almost within striking distance. With sword uplifted, the assailant had already risen in his stirrups to smite, when, quick as lightning, Witherspoon, who had watched him narrowly, poured the contents of carbine into his breast. This was followed by a shout from the Americans, and, with furious yells, the British dashed forward upon Marion's left. The reconnoitering partly melted before them, and the infantry delivered their fire with fatal effect. A dozen saddles were instantly emptied, Capt. Gillies of the British, who led the charge, being one of the first victims. The enemy soon rallied, and attempted first his right and then his left flank; but the evolutions of Marion were quite as ready, and, by changing his front promptly, and availing himself of the cover afforded by the houses and the fences, he showed the hazard of attempting a second charge to he too great for such a force as that of Frasier. For an hour after, the British manoeuvred around them, but without discovering any opportunity of retrieving or revenging their disaster. A single fire terminated this affair, and seldom has a single fire, where so small a front has been engaged, done such considerable execution. One officer and eight men were instantly killed; three officers and eight men wounded; five horses fell dead upon the field, a few were taken and many wounded. The discharge took place at thirty paces, and Marion's men usually fired with heavy buck-shot. His new-made Whigs stood the test bravely, showing a steadiness and courage, whilst opposed to their old allies, which soon set the heart of our partisan at ease. They had very good reasons for steadiness and valor. They fought with halters about their necks. Not a man of them, if taken, would have escaped the cord and tree. Marion did not lose a man, but he suffered a very serious loss of another sort. In the midst of the confusion of the fight, the driver of his ammunition wagon took fright, and made off with his charge in a direction which betrayed its flight to the enemy, who immediately sent a small detachment, by which it was taken. Marion had no cavalry to recover it; but five of his men, armed with the broad-swords of the British whom they had just slain, and mounted on their captured horses, volunteered to recover it. They actually succeeded in rescuing it from the detachment by which it was taken, but could retain it only till the fugitives could reach their main body and return with a force to which our volunteers could oppose no resistance. They were compelled to abandon the prize, which, had fortune seconded their endeavors, was certainly due to their merits. This little affair is a sample of that generous service which it was the happy faculty of our partisan to extract from his followers. It is to tradition that we owe the vague memory of numerous like advantages, of which history preserves no records. Under his guidance, his men seldom suffered panic. They fancied themselves invincible when he led. In the present instance he declared that not a man faltered—that he even had to restrain their eagerness, and prevent them rushing out into the open field, to meet the charge of the cavalry. His own coolness never deserted him. He never lost sight of the whole field, in the vehement action of a part. His keenness of vision, his vigilance of watch, his promptness in opposing his best resources to the press of danger, of covering his weak points, and converting into means and modes of defence and extrication, all that was available in his situation—were remarkable endowments, which soon fixed the regards of his followers, and upon which they unhesitatingly relied. In the absence of his cavalry, a defeat would have been a route; his infantry would have been cut to pieces, and his cavalry subsequently exposed to similar disaster. Had the latter been present, the safety of the British must have depended solely on the fleetness of their steeds. With this affair ended the actual conflicts of our partisan. His men were not yet disbanded. He himself did not yet retire from the field which he had so often traversed in triumph. But the occasion for bloodshed was over. The great struggle for ascendancy between the British crown and her colonies was understood to be at an end. She was prepared to acknowledge the independence for which they had fought, when she discovered that it was no longer in her power to deprive them of it. She will not require any eulogium of her magnanimity for her reluctant concession.

CHAPTER XX

THE BRITISH PROPOSE TERMS OF PACIFICATION
† REJECTED BY THE CIVIL AUTHORITIES † THEY PENETRATE THE COMBAHEE WITH THEIR FLEET † DEATH OF COL. LAURENS † ANECDOTE OF MARION † DEATH OF WILMOT † BRITISH EVACUATE CHARLESTON † MARION SEPARATES FROM HIS BRIGADE AT WATBOO † HIS MILITARY GENIUS

Though the war in Carolina was understood to be nearly at an end, and the toils and dangers of the conflict well nigh over, yet motives for vigilance still continued. There was ample room for vicissitudes. The British still held possession of Charleston and its harbor, but they were confined to these narrow limits. Here, watched on all sides by the impatient Americans, they made their preparations for a reluctant departure. The sole remaining contest between the opposing armies lay, in the desire of the one to bear with them as much of the spoils of war as possible, and of the other to prevent them. The greater motives for the war on both sides were at an end. The mother country had declared her willingness to forego the exercise of her ancient authority, and the Colonies were admitted to the freedom which they sought. In this state of things neither army attempted enterprises, the result of which could not affect the objects of either nation. Thus was spared the unnecessary shedding of blood. The forces under Greene continued gradually to contract their limits; while those of General Leslie remained comparatively quiescent. The British officer was governed by a proper wisdom. As the evacuation of Charleston was determined on, there was little use in keeping up the appearances of a struggle which had virtually ceased to exist. He suggested accordingly to Greene, that an intercourse should be established between town and country, by which the troops in the former might procure their necessary supplies in barter with the people. To provision his fleet and army was his object. For this he proposed a cessation of hostilities. It is to be regretted that this pacific proposition was not entertained. Some valuable lives might have been saved to the country—we may instance that of Col. Laurens. General Greene was not adverse to the proposition, but the civil authorities objected. Their reasons for opposing this humane suggestion are scarcely satisfactory. They believed that Leslie only aimed to accumulate provisions for the support of the British forces in the West Indies, and thus enable them to prosecute the war more vigorously against our French allies. This was an objection rather urged than felt. There was probably some feeling, some impatience of temper at the bottom, which prompted them to dispute, at the point of the sword, rather than yield to any suggestions of an enemy at whose hands they had suffered such protracted injuries. A little more coolness and reflection might have shown them, that, by refusing the application of Leslie, they only rendered it necessary that the British should pay in blood for those supplies for which they were not unwilling to pay in money. And blood usually calls for blood. The combat is never wholly on one side. It was virtually saying we can spare a few more citizens. The concession might have been made to the wishes of the British commander not only without any detriment to the service, but with absolute benefit to the people and the army. The provisions which the enemy required would have found a good market in Charleston, and the clothing, in lack of which the army was suffering severely, might have been procured for them at the same place on the most reasonable terms. Besides, the rejection of the overture was not necessarily a prevention of the purpose of the British. The American army was quite too feeble either to expel them from the country, or to arrest their foraging parties. The only effect of the rejection of the humane and pacific proposition of the British commander, was to compel the preparation of that fleet of small craft, which, under the guns of his galleys, was now penetrating the rivers, and rifling the grain from the wealthy plantations. We have seen Marion opposing himself to this fleet at Georgetown, and have witnessed their success upon the South Santee. The prompt return of our partisan to the head waters of Cooper river, in all probability, preserved that neighborhood from the foragers. With the tidings of their progress up the Combahee, the American light brigade, under General Gist, was ordered to oppose them. It was here that one of those events took place which furnished a conclusive commentary upon the ill—judged resolution by which the cessation of hostilities was rejected, and the British denied the privilege of procuring supplies in a pacific manner. Hearing of the movement of Gist, Col. Laurens, who was attached to his brigade, and was always eager for occasions of distinction, rose from a sick bed to resume the command of his division. He overtook the brigade on the north bank of the Combahee river, near the ferry. Twelve miles below, the extreme end of Chehaw neck protrudes into the bed of the river, which, between these points, is bounded by extensive swamps and rice fields. At this point a redoubt had been thrown up by General Gist. The enemy was already above, on the opposite side of the stream. Laurens solicited the command of this post for the purpose of annoying them in their retreat. Meanwhile, the American cavalry under Major Call, had been ordered round by Salkehatchie bridge, to join with the militia collected in that quarter for the purpose of striking at the enemy. With a howitzer, some matrosses and fifty infantry, Laurens moved down the river, and on the evening of the 26th reached the place of Mrs. Stock, sufficiently near to Chehaw Point to take post there by daylight the next morning. But the British were there before him. Baffled by the light brigade of Gist, in procuring provisions on the south side of the river, they had crossed it, and, apprised of the movements of Laurens, placed an ambush for him on his road to the Point. That night was spent by Laurens among the ladies of the place where he lingered. It is recorded that the company did not separate until a couple of hours before the time when the detachment was set in motion. The prospect of his encounter was the topic of conversation, and with the cheery, elastic spirit of youth, he gaily offered the ladies a conspicuous place from which they might enjoy a sight of the action without incurring its dangers. Before sunrise his voice was hushed forever. Unsuspicious of an enemy, he rode at the head of his command. The British were posted in a place thickly covered with fennel and high grass. With the advance guard when they were discovered, he promptly ordered a charge, gallantly leading which, he fell at the first fire. Laurens was one of those brave and ardent spirits, generous, high-souled, and immaculate, which, in times of sordid calculation and drilled soldiership, recall to our minds the better days of chivalry. He was the Bayard of the southern youth in the war of the revolution, uniting all the qualities of the famous chevalier, *sans peur et sans reproche.* That he should have fallen, unnecessarily, at the close of the war, when nothing was to be gained, and nothing to be saved, by valor,—and in an obscure encounter on a field of mere predatory warfare, doubles the mortification of such a close to a noble and admirable career. A lesson from the pure and correct code of Marion's military morals would have saved this precious blood, and preserved this gallant youth for nobler fortunes. The following anecdote will illustrate the admirable character of his mode of thinking on such subjects. While he held his position at Watboo, after he had beaten Frasier, he was advised that a British party, which had been dispatched to procure water at Lempriere's Point, could be cut off with little difficulty. The British were then preparing for embarkation. A parting blow was recommended, as calculated to hurry their movements, as well as to add something to the measure of patriot revenge for the wrongs and resentments of the past. But Marion resolutely refused to sanction the enterprise. His answer proves equally the excellence of his judgment and the benevolence of his heart. "My brigade," said he, "is composed of citizens, enough of whose blood has been shed already. If ordered to attack the enemy, I shall obey; but with my consent, not another life shall be lost, though the event should procure me the highest honors of the soldier. Knowing, as we do, that the enemy are on the eve of departure, so far from offering to molest, I would rather send a party to protect them."

This noble feeling would have saved the lives of Laurens, Wilmot, Moore, and other gallant young men, who were sacrificed at the last hour when all provocations to strife had ceased—when the battle was already won—when the great object of the war had been attained by the one party, and yielded, however reluctantly, by the other. Capt. Wilmot, with a small command, was stationed to cover Johns' Island, and to watch the passage by Stono. Fond of enterprise he was tempted occasionally to cross the river and harass the enemy on James' Island. In one of these adventures, undertaken in conjunction with the celebrated Kosciusko, against an armed party of the enemy's wood—cutters, he fell into an ambuscade, was himself slain, while his second in command, Lieut. Moore, severely wounded, fell into the hands of the British. This was the last blood shed in the American revolution. It need not to have been shed. The denouement of the protracted drama had already taken place. The conquest of the Indians by Pickens was complete; the Tories no longer appeared in bodies, though, for some time after, individuals of the scattered bands occasionally continued the habits of outlawry which the war had taught them, and dealt in deeds of midnight robbery and crime—and the British armies were simply preparing to depart. On the 14th of December, while the American columns entered the city from the neck, those of the British retired to their ships; the movements of which, as their white sails distended to the breeze, presented, in the language of Moultrie, "a grand and pleasing sight." It was a sight, however which the militia, always undervalued, always misunderstood and misrepresented, were not permitted to behold. They had fought the battle, it was true, "but the civil authority" conceived their uses to be over, and "they were excluded as dangerous spectators;" an unworthy and most ungrateful decision, in which, we are pleased to learn from a self-exculpatory letter of General Greene, he had no participation, and which he did not approve.

The forces of the British withdrawn from the shores of Carolina, the country, exhausted of resources, and filled with malcontents and mourners, was left to recover slowly from the hurts and losses of foreign and intestine strife. Wounds were to be healed which required the assuasive hand of time, which were destined to rankle even in the bosoms of another generation, and the painful memory of which is keenly treasured even now. But the civil authority takes the place of the military, and with the disappearance of the invader, the warrior lays aside his sword,—satisfied if he may still retain the laurels which his valor has won. Our partisan, yielding himself at the call of his country, was not the man to linger unnecessarily long upon the stage. The duties which had called him into the field were faithfully performed; how faithfully it has been the effort of this humble narrative to show. The time was come when he was to part with his brigade forever—when he was to take leave of those brave fellows, whom he had so frequently led to victory, never to dishonor. The separation was touching, but without parade. On this occasion his deportment was as modest as it had been through the whole period of their connection. Gathered around him among the cedars at his Watboo encampment, his followers were assembled to receive his last fare well. The simplicity which had marked his whole career, distinguished its conclusion. His address was brief but not without its eloquence—such eloquence as belongs to the language of unaffected and unadulterated truth. He acknowledged, with thanks, the services of the officers and men; dwelt passingly upon particular events of which they had reason to be proud, and bade them a friendly and affectionate farewell. The brief review which he made of their campaigns was well calculated to awaken the most touching recollections. He had been their father and protector. No commander had ever been more solicitous of the safety and comfort of his men. It was this which had rendered him so sure of their fidelity, which had enabled him to extract from them such admirable service. His simple entreaty stayed their quarrels and the confidence which they yielded to his love of justice, made them always willing to abide the decisions of his judgment. Officers and men equally yielded to the authority of his opinion, as they did to that which he exercised in the capacity of their commander. No duel took place among his officers during the whole of his command.

The province which was assigned to his control by Governor Rutledge, was the constant theatre of war. He was required to cover an immense extent of country. With a force constantly unequal and constantly fluctuating, he contrived to supply its deficiencies by the resources of his own vigilance and skill. His personal bravery was frequently shown, and the fact that he himself conducted an enterprise, was enough to convince his men that they were certain to be led to victory. In due degree with their conviction of his care and consideration for themselves, was their readiness to follow where he commanded. He had no lives to waste, and the game he played was that which enabled him to secure the greatest results, with the smallest amount of hazard. Yet, when the occasion seemed to require it, he could advance and strike with an audacity, which in the ordinary relations of the leader with the soldier, might well be thought inexcusable rashness. We have, already, in the opening of this biography, adverted to the melancholy baldness of the memorials upon which the historian is compelled to rely for the materials of his narrative. The reader will perceive a singular discrepancy between the actual events detailed in the life of every popular hero, and the peculiar fame which he holds in the minds of his countrymen. Thus, while Marion is everywhere regarded as the peculiar representative in the southern States, of the genius of partisan warfare, we are surprised, when we would trace, in the pages of the annalist, the sources of this fame, to find the details so meagre and so unsatisfactory. Tradition mumbles over his broken memories, which we vainly strive to pluck from his lips and bind together in coherent and satisfactory records. The spirited surprise, the happy ambush, the daring onslaught, the fortunate escape—these, as they involve no monstrous slaughter—no murderous strife of masses,—no rending of walled towns and sack of cities, the ordinary historian disdains. The military reputation of Marion consists in the frequent performance of deeds, unexpectedly, with inferior means, by which the enemy was annoyed and dispirited, and the hearts and courage of his countrymen warmed into corresponding exertions with his own. To him we owe that the fires of patriotism were never extinguished, even in the most disastrous hours, in the low country of South Carolina. He made our swamps and forests sacred, as well because of the refuge which they gave to the fugitive patriot, as for the frequent sacrifices which they enabled him to make, on the altars of liberty and a becoming vengeance. We are in possession of but few of the numerous enterprises in which he was engaged; imperfect memories of the aged give us glimpses of deeds for the particulars of which we turn in vain to the dusty pages of the chronicler. But we need not generalize farther upon the traits of his military character. We have endeavored to make these speak for themselves, page by page, in the narration of the events, so far as we know them, by which his reputation was acquired. It is enough that his fame has entered largely into that of his country, forming a valuable portion of its sectional stock of character. His memory is in the very hearts of our people. Of the estimation in which he was held by contemporaries more might be said, but these pages bear ample testimony of the consideration which he commanded from friend and foe. The testimonials of Moultrie, Greene, Lee and others, are conclusive of that rare worth and excellence— that combination of military and civil virtues—which biography cannot easily be found to excel.

CHAPTER XXI

MARION RETIRES TO HIS FARM, WHICH HE FINDS IN RUINS † IS RETURNED TO THE SENATE FROM ST. JOHN † HIS COURSE ON THE CONFISCATION ACT † ANECDOTES † IS MADE COMMANDANT AT FORT JOHNSON † HIS MARRIAGE † A MEMBER OF THE STATE CONVENTION IN 1794 † WITHDRAWS FROM PUBLIC LIFE † HIS DEATH

It was with no reluctance but with the cheerful preference which Marion had always given, since manhood, to the life of the farmer, that he returned to its simple but attractive avocations. But the world with him was, as it were, to be begun anew; no easy matter to one whose habits had been necessarily rendered irregular by the capricious and desultory influences of a military career; still more difficult in the case of one who has entered upon the last period of life. The close of the Revolution found him destitute of means, almost in poverty, and more than fifty years old. His health was good, however; his frame elastic; his capacity for endurance, seemingly, as great as ever. But his little fortune had suffered irretrievably. His interests had shared the fate of most other Southern patriots, in the long and cruel struggle through which the country had gone. His plantation in St. John's, Berkley, lay within a mile of one of the ordinary routes of the British army, and his career was not calculated to move them to forbearance in the case of one, whose perpetual activity and skill so constantly baffled their designs. His estate was ravaged, and subjected to constant waste and depredation. One—half of his negroes were taken away, and the rest only saved to him by their fidelity. The refuge in swamp and forest was as natural to the faithful negro, on the approach of the British uniforms, as to the fugitive patriot. Ten workers returned to him, when he was prepared to resume his farm, but he was destitute of everything beside. The implements of culture, plantation utensils, household furniture, stock, cattle and horses, clothes and provisions for his people, were all wanting, and all to be purchased, and he penniless. He received no compensation for his losses, no reward for his sacrifices and services. The hope of half pay was held out to him by his more sanguine friends, but this promise was never realized. But, with that cheerful spirit which hopes all things from time, and a meek compliance with what it brings, Marion proceeded to work out his deliverance by manly industry, and a devotion to his interests as true as that which he had yielded to the interests of his country. He had become fond of rural life, and the temporary estrangement of war seemed only to increase his desire for that repose in action, which the agricultural life in the South so certainly secures. But he was not permitted to retire from public service. The value of his services was too well known, and there was too much yet to be done, towards the repose and security of the country, to suffer them to be dispensed with. He was again returned to the Senate of the State by the people of St. John's. In this situation, he still maintained those noble and disinterested characteristics which had made him equally beloved and venerated. Two anecdotes are preserved of him in his official character, which deserve mention. Both of these grew out of the events of the war. The importance of the Confiscation Act, passed at the session of January 1782, at Jacksonborough, arose chiefly from the necessity of providing for the emergencies of the State and military, during the continuance of the war. Under existing circumstances, the measure was sustained by our partisan. But the case was altered when the British ministry abandoned their pretensions to the country, and when it was left by their armies. It was then that numerous offenders—those who had been least conspicuous for their Tory predilections—applied for the indulgence and forbearance of the State. Petitions were poured into the Legislature, sustained by such pleas and friends as the circumstances of the suppliants could procure—excusing their conduct, asserting their repentance, and imploring the restoration of their possessions. Marion's course in regard to these suppliants may be inferred from his previous character. There was nothing vindictive in his nature. He was superior to the baser cravings of a dogged vengeance, and his vote and voice declared his magnanimity. It so happened that the first of these petitions upon which he was called to act, came from one of that class of timid, time-serving persons, who, with no predilections for virtue, no sympathy for principles or country, simply shape their course with regard to safety. He was a man of wealth, and the effect of wealth in perilous times is but too frequently to render selfishness equally cowardly and dishonest. The amount of his offence consisted in trimming, while the strife was doubtful, between Whig and Tory, and siding with the latter when the British gained the ascendency. He did not take up arms, took no active part in public affairs, and was content to shelter his person and possessions under a cautious insignificance. About eighteen months before, Marion had met the petitioner at a gathering of the people.

The latter approached and offered our partisan his hand. But the juncture was in which it behooveth patriotism to speak out at all hazards. The struggle was for life and death, on the part equally of Whig and Tory. Marion knew the character of the person, and disdained it. To the surprise of all, who knew how scrupulous of insult he was—how indulgent and forbearing—he turned away from the trimmer and the sycophant without recognition. This treatment was greatly censured at the time, and when Marion rose in the Senate, to speak on the subject of the petition of the man whom he had so openly scorned, it was taken for granted that he would again give utterance to feelings of the sort which moved him then. The miserable offender, who was himself present, grew pale, trembled, and gave up his cause as lost. What was his surprise and delight to hear the venerable patriot advocate his application! He was successful in obtaining for the suppliant the mercy which he implored. The opponents of the petitioner, some of whom were of that class of patriots who hunger for the division of the spoils, were aghast, and having counted on Marion's support, now loudly proclaimed his inconsistency. But to these his answer was equally prompt and satisfactory. His reasons were true to his principles. He had been governed in his previous views by the necessity of the case. With the disappearance of that necessity he recognized other laws and influences. "Then," said he, "it was war. It is peace now. God has given us the victory; let us show our gratitude to heaven, which we shall not do by cruelty to man."

The expediency of humanity was always the uppermost sentiment with Marion. A nobler expression of it never fell from the lips of mortal.

The next anecdote of the legislative career of Marion is one which directly related to himself. At an early period in the action of the Assembly, after the war, it was deemed advisable to introduce a bill by which to exempt from legal investigation the conduct of the militia while the war had lasted. It was thought, justly enough, that, from the nature of the services in which they were engaged, and necessities which coerced them, they might need, in numerous instances, to be sheltered from legal persecution. They had been compelled to war with a heavy hand, to seize frequently upon private property, and subject the possessions of the citizen to the exigencies of the community. The necessities of the service being recognized, the Legislature were ready to justify them; and the Act which was prepared for the purpose, included amongst others, thus specially exempted, the name of Marion. But, scarcely had it been announced from the paper, when the venerable man arose, and with flushed cheeks and emphatic brevity, demanded that his name should be expunged from the catalogue. He declared himself friendly to the Bill—he believed it to be equally just and necessary; but for own part, as he was not conscious of any wrong of which he had been guilty, he was not anxious for any immunity. "If," said he, "I have given any occasion for complaint, I am ready to answer in property and person. If I have wronged any man I am willing to make him restitution. If, in a single instance, in the course of my command, I have done that which I cannot fully justify, justice requires that I should suffer for it."

So proud was his integrity, so pure and transparent was his happy consciousness of a mind fixed only on good, and regulated by the sternest rules of virtue, and the nicest instincts of gentleness and love! The Bill passed into a law, but the name of Marion, omitted at his requisition, is nowhere present, as showing that he needed other security than that which is afforded to the meanest citizen under the keenest scrutiny of justice.

Marion did not confine his objections to the continued operation of the Confiscation Act, to the single instance which we have given. We have reason to believe that his labors to remedy its hardships, and restrain its severities, were uniform and unremitting. There is no doubt that he favored the original bill. He considered it a war measure, and necessary to the prosecution of the war. The propriety of the distinction which he made just after the war was over, obvious enough to us now, was not so evident at a season when the victors were looking after the division of the spoils. The subject became one of considerable excitement, and we may say in this place, that, after time had mollified the popular feeling in some degree, the State admitted the greater number of the offenders to mercy and restored their estates. But there is reason to believe that the humane sentiments which Marion taught, were not universal, and met with most violent opposition. His feelings on the subject were not only declared with frankness, but with warmth and energy. Dining at the table of Governor Matthews, while the strife was highest, he was called upon by his Excellency for a toast. Lifting his glass, with a smile, he promptly gave the following—"Gentlemen, here's damnation to the Confiscation Act."

Though, in the language of Moultrie, "born a soldier," and yielding so many of his youthful and mature years to the habits of the camp and field, there was nothing of a harsh or imperious nature in his temper or his manner. The deportment of the mere soldier seems to have been his aversion. He preferred the modest and forbearing carriage which is supposed to belong more distinctly to civil than to military life. No novelty of situation, no provocation of circumstance, nothing in the shape of annoyance or disaster, was suffered so to ruffle his mood as to make him heedless or indifferent to the claims or sensibilities of others. He never conceived that any of his virtues gave him a right to trespass upon the proprieties of social or public life. An anecdote is related of him

which illustrates the veneration which he entertained for the regulations
of society and law. It appears that, when the war was over, one of his
closest intimates and nearest friends—one whom he had trusted long,
and who had shared with him in all his campaigns, stood within the
perils of the law for some offence of which the facts have not been
preserved. Presuming upon his well—known services, and the favor in
which he was held by the public, he refused to submit to the ordinary
legal process, and bade defiance to the sheriff. While maintaining this
position, Marion sought him out. He used no argument to convince the
offender of his error, for that, he felt assured, the other sufficiently knew.
But he addressed him in a style, and with words, which conveyed much
more than any ordinary argument. "Deliver yourself," said he, "into the
hands of justice—submit to the process of the sheriff, and my heart and
hand are yours as before—resist—refuse—and we are separated forever."
It need not be said that under such an exhortation the refractory spirit
was subdued. How much to be regretted it is that so few anecdotes have
been preserved of his character, illustrating a life which, according to all
testimony, was consistent throughout in a just appreciation of all that was
pure, virtuous and becoming, in the character of the individual man.

Early in the year 1783, the following resolutions passed the Senate of
South Carolina, Marion, who was a member, not being present at the time:

Senate, South Carolina,
February 26, 1783.
"RESOLVED, nem.con., That the thanks of this House be given
to Brigadier General Marion, in his place, as a member of this House,
for his eminent and conspicuous services to his country.
"RESOLVED, nem.con., That a gold medal be given to Brigadier
General Marion, as a mark of public approbation for his great, glorious,
and meritorious conduct."

Two days after, Marion being in his place in the Senate, the President
took occasion to convey to him the sense of these resolutions, in a neat
and highly laudatory speech. He said, among other things—

"When I consider the occasion which calls me to address you, I am
filled with inexpressible pleasure; but when I reflect on the difficulty of
doing justice to your distinguished merit, I feel my own inefficiency. What
sentiments or words shall I make use of equal to the task! I scarce dare
trust my own, especially after what has been said by several honorable

persons on this floor, respecting your great, your glorious, and meritorious conduct; and I most earnestly wish, for my own sake, for yours, Sir, and for the honor of this House, that I could avail myself of their eloquence… Your conduct merits the applause of your countrymen—your courage, your vigilance, and your abilities have exceeded their most sanguine expectations; and have answered all their hopes. Whilst the virtue of gratitude shall form a part of our national character, your important services to this country can never be forgotten," &c.

To this Marion replied with simple brevity:

"Mr. President: The approbation which this House have given of my conduct, in the execution of my duty, gives me very pleasing and heartfelt satisfaction. The honor which they have conferred on me this day, by their thanks, will be remembered with gratitude. I shall always be ready to exert my abilities for the good of the state and the liberties of her inhabitants. I thank you, Sir, for the polite manner in which you have conveyed to me the thanks of the Senate."

Whether the medal was really given, or only voted, is a fact that we have no means of ascertaining. It is to be feared that the action of the Senate went no farther than the resolution and the speech. It probably remains a reproach against the republic, in this, as in numerous other instances, that, knowing what gratitude required, we would yet forego the satisfaction of the debt. Cheaply, at best, was our debt to Marion satisfied, with a gold medal, or the vote of one, while Greene received ten thousand guineas and a plantation. We quarrel not with the appropriation to Greene, but did Marion deserve less from Carolina? Every page of her history answers "No!"

By the Legislative session of 1784, Fort Johnson, in the harbor of Charleston, was fitted up and garrisoned by the State. In the unstable condition of things, so immediately after the war, some such fortress might well be deemed essential to the security of the port. Marion was appointed Commandant of the Fort, with an annual salary of £500. The office was in all probability made for him. His necessities were known, and its salary was intended to compensate him for his losses during the war. But the duties of the office were nominal. Even its possible uses soon ceased to be apparent; and, with a daily increasing sense of security, the people murmured at an appropriation which they considered unnecessarily burdensome. The common mind could not well perceive that the salary was not so much yielded for what was expected of the office, as for what had already been performed. It was not given for present, but for past services. It was the payment of a debt incurred, not a simple appropriation for the liquidation of one growing out of current performances. Legislative reformers waged constant war against it, and it was finally cut down to five hundred dollars. A smile of fortune,—one of the fairest perhaps, that had ever shone on our hero,—just then relieved him from the mortifying necessity of holding a sinecure which his fellow citizens pronounced an incumbrance. It had been observed by his friends that there was a lady of good family and considerable wealth, who appeared to take a more than ordinary interest in hearing of his exploits. Modest and reserved himself, Marion was not conscious of the favorable impression which he had made upon this lady. It was left for others to discover the state of her affections. They remarked the delight with which, like

The gentle lady wedded to the Moor,

she listened to the tale of his achievements, his

Hair—breadth 'scapes in th' imminent deadly breach,
Of being taken by the insolent foe.—

and they augured favorably of the success of any desire which he might express to make her the sharer in his future fortunes. On this hint he spake. Miss Mary Videau, like himself, came of the good old Huguenot stock, the virtues of which formed our theme in the opening chapter of this narrative. He proposed to her and was accepted. Neither of them was young. It was not in the heyday of passion that they loved. The tie that bound them sprang from an affection growing out of a just appreciation of their mutual merits. She is reported to have somewhat resembled him as well in countenance as character. She certainly shared warmly in his interests and feelings. She readily conformed to his habits no less than his wishes—partook of his amusements, shared his journeys—which were frequent—and still, in his absence, could listen with as keen a zest to his praises, as before their marriage. During the summer months, it was his almost yearly custom to retire to the mountains of the interior. She was always his companion. On such occasions, he was guilty of a piece of military ostentation of which nobody could have accused him while a military man. He had preserved carefully, as memorials of an eventful history, his marquee, camp bed, and cooking utensils, just as he had done while in the Brigade, during the last twelve months of his military life.

These were carefully taken with him; and, with his faithful servant Oscar, and his two sumpter mules, were still the companions of his wanderings. They were coupled no doubt with many associations as interesting to his heart as they were trying to his experience. They were, perhaps, doubly precious, as they constituted the sum total of all that he had gathered— besides an honorable fame—from his various campaignings.

The marriage of Marion, like that of Washington, was without fruits. This may have baffled some hopes, and in some degree qualified his happiness, but did not impair his virtues. He adopted the son of a relative, to whom he gave his own name, in the hope of perpetuating it in the family, but even this desire has been defeated, since the heir thus chosen, though blessed with numerous children, was never so fortunate as to own a son.

In the decline of life, in the modest condition of the farmer, Marion seems to have lived among his neighbors, very much as the ancient patriarch, surrounded by his flock. He was honored and beloved by all. His dwelling was the abode of content and cheerful hospitality. Its doors were always open; and the chronicler records that it had many chambers. Here the stranger found a ready welcome, and his neighbors a friendly counsellor, to the last. His active habits were scarcely lessened in the latter years of life. His agricultural interests were managed judiciously, and his property underwent annual increase. Nor did his domestic interests and declining years prevent him from serving the public still. He still held a commission in the militia, and continued to represent the parish of St. John's, in the Senate of the State. In May, 1790, we find him sitting as a member of the Convention for forming the State Constitution; but from this period he withdrew from public life, and, in 1794, after the reorganization of the State militia, he resigned his commission in that service to which he had done so much honor. On this occasion he was addressed by an assembly of the citizens of Georgetown, through a special committee of four, in the following language.[76]

"CITIZEN GENERAL—At the present juncture, when the necessity of public affairs requires the military of this State to be organized anew, to repel the attacks of an enemy from whatever quarter they may be forced upon us; we, the citizens of the district of Georgetown, finding you no longer at our head, have agreed to convey to you our grateful sentiments for your former numerous services. In the decline of life, when the merits of the veteran are too often forgotten, we wish to remind you that yours are still fresh in the remembrance of your fellow citizens. Could it be possible for men who have served and fought under you, to be now forgetful of that General, by whose prudent conduct their lives have been saved and their families preserved from being plundered by a rapacious enemy? We mean not to flatter you. At this time it is impossible to suspect it. Our present language is the language of freemen, expressing only sentiments of gratitude. Your achievements may not have sufficiently swelled the historic page. They were performed by those who could better wield the sword than the pen—by men whose constant dangers precluded them from the leisure, and whose necessities deprived them of the common implements of writing. But this is of little moment. They remain recorded in such indelible characters upon our minds, that neither change of circumstances, nor length of time, can efface them. Taught by us, our children shall hereafter point out the places, and say, 'here, General Marion, posted to advantage, made a glorious stand in defence of the liberties of his country—there, on disadvantageous ground, retreated to save the lives of his fellow citizens.' What could be more glorious for the General, commanding freemen, than thus to fight, and thus to save the lives of his fellow soldiers? Continue, General, in peace, to till those acres which you once wrested from the hands of an enemy. Continue to enjoy dignity accompanied with ease, and to lengthen out your days blessed with the consciousness of conduct unaccused of rapine or oppression, and of actions ever directed by the purest patriotism."

The artless language of this address was grateful to the venerable patriot. In its truth and simplicity lay its force and eloquence. It had truly embodied in a single sentence the noble points of his career and character. He lived in the delightful consciousness of a pure mind, free from accusation—and no higher eulogy could be conferred upon the captain of citizen soldiers, than to say, he never wantonly exposed their lives, but was always solicitous of their safety. To this address his answer was verbal. He no longer used the pen. The feebleness of nature was making itself understood. That he felt himself failing may be inferred from his withdrawal from all public affairs. But his mind was cheerful and active to the last. He still saw his friends and neighbors, and welcomed their coming—could still mount his horse and cast his 'eye over his acres.' The progress of decline, in his case, was not of that humiliating kind, by which the faculties of the intellect are clouded, and the muscles of the body made feeble and incompetent. He spoke thoughtfully of the great concerns of life, of death, and of the future; declared himself a Christian, an humble believer in all the vital truths of religion. As of the future he entertained no doubt, so of the awful transition through the valley and shadow of death, he had no fear. "Death may be to others," said he, "a leap in the dark, but I rather consider it a resting—place where old age may throw off its burdens." He died, peaceful and assured, with no apparent pain, and without regret, at his residence in St. John's parish, on the 27th day of February, 1795, having reached the mature and mellow term of sixty—three years. His last words declared his superiority to all fears of death; "for, thank God," said he, "I can lay my hand on my heart and say that, since I came to man's estate, I have never intentionally done wrong to any."

Thus died Francis Marion, one of the noblest models of the citizen soldier that the world has ever produced. Brave without rashness, prudent without timidity, firm without arrogance, resolved without rudeness, good without cant, and virtuous without presumption. His mortal remains are preserved at Belle—Isle, in St. John's parish. The marble slab which covers them bears the following inscription:—"Sacred to the memory of Brigadier—General Francis Marion, who departed this life on the 29th of Feb., 1795, in the sixty-third year of his age, deeply regretted by all his fellow citizens. History will record his worth, and rising generations embalm his memory, as one of the most distinguished patriots and heroes of the American Revolution; which elevated his native country to honor and Independence, and secured to her the blessings of liberty and peace. This tribute of veneration and gratitude is erected in commemoration of the noble and disinterested virtues of the citizen, and the gallant exploits of the soldier, who lived without fear, and died without reproach."

This inscription was the tribute of an individual, not of the country. The State of South Carolina has conferred his name upon one of its district divisions. But a proper gratitude, not to speak of policy, would seem to require more.

If it be we love
His fame and virtues, it were well, methinks,
To link them with his name i' the public eye,
That men, who in the paths of gainful trade,
Do still forget the venerable and good,
May have such noble monitor still nigh,
And, musing at his monument, recal,
Those precious memories of the deeds of one
Whose life were the best model for their sons.

END

NOTES

Chapter I

1. Mémoires et Observations faites par un Voyageur en Angleerre, 12mo. La Haye, 1698, p. 362. Quoted by Browning in his History of the Huguenots.

2. Browning: History of the Huguenots. London: Whittarer and Co. 1840. p. 256. Of the Refugees from France, Hume says, "near fifty thousand passed over into England;" and Voltaire writes that "one of the suburbs of London was entirely peopled with French workers of silk."

3. Dalcho, in his Church History says, "upwards of one hundred families."

4. The narrative of Mrs. Judith Manigault, wife of Peter Manigault, as quoted by Ramsay.—Hist S. C. Vol. I. p. 4. For a graphic detail of the usual difficulties and dangers attending the escape of the Huguenots from France, at the period of migration, see the first portion of this letter.

5. Lawson's "Journal of a Thousand Miles' Travel among the Indians, from South to North Carolina," is a work equally rare and interesting. This unfortunate man fell a victim to his official duties. He was confounded, by the savages, with the government which he represented, and sacrificed to their fury, under the charge of depriving them, by his surveys, of their land. He was made captive with the Baron de Graffenreid. The latter escaped, but Lawson was subjected to the fire-torture.

6. "The inhabitants [of St. James, otherwise French Santee] petitioned the Assembly, in 1706, to have their settlement made a parish; and, at the same time, expressed their desire of being united to the Church of England, whose doctrines and discipline they professed highly to esteem. The Assembly passed an act, April 9, 1706, to erect the French settlement of Santee into a parish."—*Dalcho's Historisal Account*, ch. ix., p. 295.

7. See "A new Voyage to Carolina, containing the exact description and natural history of that country, &c.; and a journey of a thousand miles, travelled through several nations of Indians. By John Lawson, Gent., Surveyor-General of North Carolina. London, 1709."

8. It is one of the qualifications of the delight which an historian feels while engaged in the details of those grateful episodes which frequently reward his progress through musty chronicles, to find himself suddenly arrested in his narrative by some of those rude interruptions by which violence and injustice disfigure so frequently, in the march of history, the beauty of its portraits. One of these occurs to us in this connection. Our Huguenot settlers on the Santee were not long suffered to

pursue a career of unbroken prosperity. The very fact that they prospered—that, in the language of Mr. Lawson, "they outstript our English," when placed in like circumstances—that they were no longer desolate and dependent, and had grown vigorous, and perhaps wanton, in the smiles of fortune—was quite enough to re-awaken in the bosoms of "our English" the ancient national grudge upon which they had so often fed before. The prejudices and hostilities which had prevailed for centuries between their respective nations, constituted no small part of the moral stock which the latter had brought with them into the wilderness. This feeling was farther heightened, at least maintained, by the fact that France and England had contrived to continue their old warfare in the New World; and, while French emissaries were busy in the back parts of the colony, stimulating the Creeks and Cherokees to hostility, it was perhaps natural enough that the English, whose frontiers were continually ravaged in consequence, should find it easy to confound the "*parley-vows*," their enemies, with those, their neighbors, who spoke the same unpopular language. It is not improbable, on the other hand, that the Huguenot settlers were a little too exclusive, a little too tenacious of their peculiar habits, manners, and language. They did not suffer themselves to assimilate with their neighbors; but, maintaining the policy by which they had colonized in a body, had been a little too anxious to preserve themselves as a singular and separate people. In this respect they were not unlike the English puritans, in whom and their descendants, this passion for homogeneousness has always been thought a sort of merit, appealing very much to their self-esteem and pride. In the case of the French colonists, whether the fault was theirs or not, the evil results of being, or making themselves, a separate people, were soon perceptible. They were subjected to various political and social disabilities, and so odious had they become to their British neighbors, that John Archdale, one of the proprietors, a man like Wm. Penn (and by Grahame, the historian, pronounced very far his superior), equally beloved by all parties, as a man just and fearless, was, when Governor of the colony, compelled to deny them representation in the colonial Assembly, under penalty of making invalid all his attempts at proper government. Under this humiliating disability the Huguenots lived and labored for a considerable period, until the propriety of their lives, the purity of their virtues, and their frequently-tried fidelity in the cause of the country, forced the majority to be just. Au act, passed in 1696, making all aliens, *then* inhabitants, free—enabling them to hold lands and to claim the same as heirs—according liberty of conscience to all Christians (except Papists), &c.—placed our refugees on a footing of equality with the rest of the inhabitants, and put an end to the old hostilities between them.

CHAPTER II

9. Weems speaks of six children only, naming all the sons and one of the daughters. Of her, he frankly says, "I have never heard what became; but for his four brothers, I am happy to state, that though not formidable as soldiers, they were very amiable as citizens." James tells us of two daughters, not naming either, but describing them as "grandmothers of the families of the Mitchells, of Georgetown, and of the Dwights, formerly of the same place, but now of St. Stephen's parish." Such particularity might be presumed to settle the question.

10. Weems represents the captain and mate, as throwing themselves overboard in a state of frenzy, and there is nothing improbable or unnatural in the statement. Privation of food, the use of salt water, and exposure in an open boat to a burning sun, might very well produce such an effect. The only difficulty, however, consists in the simple fact that we have no other authority for the statement. James is silent on the point, and contents himself with simply stating the death of two of the crew. Weems, however, adds that of two others, whose end receives, as usual, quite a dramatic finish at his hands. He suffers none to live but "little Marion," and, in the exuberance of his imagination, actually goes so far as to describe the particular food, "chocolate and turtle broth," by which the youthful hero is recruited and recovered. By this he designs to show, more emphatically, the immediate interposition, in his behalf, of an especial providence. The truth is, that any attempt at details where so little is known to have been preserved, must necessarily, of itself, subject to doubt any narrative not fortified by the most conclusive evidence. Unfortunately for the reverend historian, his known eccentricities as a writer, and fondness for hyperbole, must always deprive his books—though remarkably useful and interesting to the young—of any authority which might be claimed for them as histories. As fictions from history, lively and romantic, they are certainly very astonishing performances; have amused and benefited thousands, and entitle the writer to a rank, in a peculiar walk of letters, which has not yet been assigned him.

CHAPTER III

11. Judge James' Life of Marion, p. 17.
12. Hewatt's Hist. S. C.

CHAPTER IV

13. Moultrie in his Memoirs, vol. 2, p. 223, would seem to set settle the question in the negative, whether Marion was or was not in the preceding campaign. He says, "General Marion and *himself entered the field of Mars together*, in an expedition against the Cherokee Indians, under the command of Colonel James Grant, in 1761, when I had the honor to command a light infantry company in a provincial regiment; he was my first lieutenant. He was an active, brave and hardy soldier, and an excellent partisan officer." This is very far however from being conclusive, inasmuch as we have seen that Marion *entered the field of Mars* two years before, under the command of his brother, in the first campaign of Lyttleton against the Indians. This latter fact is settled beyond all question.
14. Weems, pp. 21. Horry's MS. Memoir, pp. 58.
15. In a letter quoted by Weems.

CHAPTER V

16. "For St. John's, Berkeley County—James Ravenel, Daniel Ravenel, *Job Marion*, John Frierson, Esqes., Mr. Gabriel Gignilliat, *Mr. Francis Marion*." Journals of the Provincial Congress of South Carolina.
17. It is not so generally known that South Carolina did her part, as well as Massachusetts, in destroying teas and stamped paper.

18. A letter from *Isaac Marion*, one of the brothers of our subject, who dwelt at Little River, the Northern boundary of the province, is worthy of quotation, as serving to show that he was animated with the same public spirit that possessed his more distinguished kinsman. It was written to accompany the express, which brought the news of the battle of Lexington. A letter to him, from R. Howe, of N. C., forwarding the express, remarking, "I know you stand in no need of being prompted when your country requires your service"—would seem to show that he too had shared in the reputation of his brother. The following is the letter of Isaac Marion, addressed to the Committee of Safety of Little River.

> *BOUNDARY, May 9, 1775, Little River.*
> *Gentlemen of the Committee;—I have just now received an express, from the Committee of the Northern Provinces, desiring I would forward the enclosed packet to the Southern Committees. As yours is the nearest, I request for the good of your country, and the welfare of our lives, liberties, and fortunes, you'll not lose a moment's time, but dispatch the same to the Committee of Georgetown, to be forwarded to Charleston. In meantime, am, gentlemen,*
> *Your obliged humble servant, &c.*
> *ISAAC MARION.*

To Danness, Hawkins and others.

19. Drayton's Memoirs, Vol. i, p. 28.

20. Drayton's Memoirs, vol. i., p. 265. *Note.*

21. Letter of General Greene. See Johnson Greene

22. Weems, in his Life of Marion, represents the cannon as made up principally of *twenty-four* and *thirty-six* pounders; but the official accounts are as I have given them. See Drayton's Memoirs, vol. ii., p. 290–1.

23. Two ships of fifty guns; five of twenty-eight; 1 of twenty-six and a bomb-vessel. Moultrie, vol. i. p. 174–5.

24. Weems says 100.

25. British account.

26. Moultrie, Memoirs, Vol. i., note, p. 177.

27. MS. Life of Brig.-Gen. Peter Horry, p. 21.

28. Gen. Horry (then a captain) thus relates the incident: "I commanded an eighteen pounder in the left wing of the fort. Above my gun on the rampart, was a large American flag hung on a very high mast, formerly of a ship the men of war directing their fire thereat, it was, from their shot, so wounded, as to fall, with the colors, over the fort. Sergeant Jasper of the Grenadiers leapt over the ramparts, and deliberately walked the whole length of the fort, until he came to the colors on the extremity of the left, when he cut off the same from the mast, and called to me for a sponge staff, and with a thick cord tied on the colors and stuck the staff on the rampart in the sand. The Sergeant fortunately received no hurt, though exposed for a considerable time, to the enemy's fire. Governor Rutledge [after the battle], as a reward, took his small sword from his side, and in presence of many officers, presented it to Sergeant Jasper, telling him to wear it in remembrance of the 28th June, and in remembrance of him. He also offered Jasper a Lieutenant's

commission, but as he could neither read nor write, he modestly refused to accept it, saying, 'he was not fit to keep officers' company, being only bred a Sergeant.'"
—MS. Life of Brig.-Gen. Peter Horry, pp.19–20.

CHAPTER VI

29. Drayton's Memoirs, vol. ii., p. 336.

30. When the British under Prevost, were in possession of the neighboring islands, Moultrie writes, "we were apprehensive the enemy would attempt to surprise Fort Moultrie; we, therefore, always kept a strong garrison there under General Marion."

31. "He was a perfect Proteus, in ability to alter his appearance; perpetually entering the camp of the enemy, without detection, and invariably returning to his own with soldiers he had seduced, or prisoners he had captured."

32. Moultrie's Mem. vol. ii., p. 24.

33. Major-General T. Pinckney's account of siege or Savannah, quoted by Garden.

34. Major-General Thomas Pinckney, in a letter quoted by Garden.

35. Major-General Thomas Pinckney. See Garden.

36. Major General T. Pinckney.

CHAPTER VII

37. MS. Memoir of Gen. Horry, p. 55.

38. Moultrie's Memoirs, Vol. ii., *Correspondence.*

39. There were two Horrys, brothers, both of whom were very brave and distinguished adherents of our partisan. Peter Horry held a captain's commission in the same regiment with Marion, at the battle of Fort Moultrie. Hugh Horry was the particular favorite of his General. A life of Marion, purporting to be in part by the former, but really composed entirely by the Rev. M. L. Weems, from facts furnished by Horry, is already well known to be public. A MS. life of Peter Horry is now before me, and has furnished me with several illustrations of the war, during this narrative. Both of these brothers served under Marion to the close of the war, with equal courage and fidelity.

40. Narrative of the Campaign of 1780, by Col. Otho Williams.

CHAPTER VIII

41. The British officers betrayed a singular reluctance to accord to the Americans their military titles. The reader will recollect the letter of General Gage to *Mr.* Washington, which the latter very properly refused to receive. The very attempt here made to sneer away the official, adds to the personal importance of the individual; and we yield to plain Mr. Marion, with his ragged followers, who, untitled, could give such annoyance to His Majesty's officers, a degree of respect which his title might not otherwise have commanded.

42. Tarleton's Campaigns, 4th ed. pp. 171.

CHAPTER IX

43. See ante, p. 50–52.

44. Moultrie's Memoirs.

45. Memoirs, vat. ii. p. 174.
46. Moultrie, vol. ii. p. 236.
47. MS. Memoirs of General Horry.
48. James' Memoir, p. 122

Chapter X
49. Johnson's Greene, vol. i.
50. MS. Life of Horry by himself, pp. 84–87.
51. MS. of Horry, p. 89.
52. Weems, speaking for Horry, tells us that he met with Captain Merritt after the war in New York, who recognized him, and told him that he had never had such a fright in all his life as upon that occasion. "Will you believe me, sir," said he, "when I assure you that I went out that morning with my locks of as bright an auburn as ever curled upon the forehead of youth, and by the time I had crawled out of the swamp into Georgetown that night, they were as grey as a badger!"
53. MS. of Horry.
54. December 30, 1780.
55. Correspondence of Marion, quoted by James.

Chapter XI
56. History of Greene, p. 225, vol. ii.
57. Judge James' Sketch of Marion.
58. MS. Memoir, p. 51.
59. Anecdotes, first series, p. 30.
60. General Marion, in his swamp encampment, inviting the British officer to dinner. Painted by J. B. White; engraved by Sartain; published by the Apollo Association.
61. Henry Lee's Memoirs. He adds: "His visage was not pleasing, and his manners not captivating. He was reserved and silent, entering into conversation only when necessary, and then with modesty and good sense. He possessed a strong mind, improved by its own reflections and observations, not by books or travel. His dress was like his address—plain, regarding comfort and decency only. In his meals he was abstemious, eating generally of one dish, and drinking water mostly. He was sedulous and constant in his attention to the duties of his station, to which every other consideration yielded. Even the charms of the fair, like the luxuries of the table and the allurements of wealth, seemed to be lost upon him. The procurement of subsistence for his men, and the continuance of annoyance for his enemy, engrossed his entire mind. He was virtuous all over never, even in manner, much less in reality, did he trench upon right. Beloved by his friends, and respected by his enemies, he exhibited a luminous example of the beneficial effects to be produced by an individual who, with only small means at his command, possesses a virtuous heart, a strong head, and a mind directed to the common good."—Appendix to *Memoirs*, vol. i. pp. 396.
62. The dislike or indifference of Marion, to anything like mere military display, was a matter of occasional comment, and some jest, among his followers. Among other proofs which are given of this indifference, we are told, that, on one occasion, attempting to draw his sword from the scabbard, he failed to do so in consequence

of the rust, the result of his infrequent employment of the weapon. Certainly, a rich event in the life of a military man. The fact is, that Marion seldom used his sword except in battle, or on occasions when its employment was inseparable from his duties. Long swords were then in fashion, but he continued to wear the small cut and thrust of the second regiment. Such a weapon better suited his inferior physique, and necessarily lessened the motives to personal adventure.

63. Garden—Anecdotes—First Series, pp. 22.

64. The brigade of Marion was for a long period without medical attendance or a surgeon to dress his wounded. If a wound reached an artery the patient bled to death. To illustrate the fierce hostility of Whigs and Tories, a single anecdote will suffice. On one occasion, Horry had three men wounded near Georgetown. A surgeon of the Tories was then a prisoner in his ranks, yet he positively refused to dress the wounds, and suffered a fine youth named Kolb, to bleed to death before his eyes, from a slight injury upon the wrist.

65. Horrys MS., from which the several extracts preceding have been made.—pp. 100–103.

66. He set up on trees and houses, in public places, proclamations in substance thus, that Major —— and Capt. —— did not belong to his brigade, that they were banditti, robbers and thieves,—were hereby deemed out of the laws, and might be killed wherever found.—Horry's MS. pp. l04, 105.

67. MS. pp. 55.

CHAPTER XII

68. Lee's Memoirs, vol. i. pp. 164.

69. Lee, vol. i. p. 249

CHAPTER XIII

70. Horry's MS

71. Horry's MS., pp. 59, 60

CHAPTER XIV

72. Horry's MS. Narrative, pp 74-5.   Ibid, p. 75.

CHAPTER XV

73. See a biographical sketch of Tarlton Brown, of Barnwell, S.C., a soldier in the revolutionary army. Charleston, 1844, p. 8.

74. Johnson's Greene, vol. ii., p. 146.

CHAPTER XVIII

75. Johnson's Life of Greene, Vol. ii., p. 319.

CHAPTER XXI

76. The committee consisted of Messrs. William D. James, Robert Brownfield, Thomas Mitchel, and Joseph Blythe.

Visit us at
www.historypress.net